The Economics of Competitive Sports

NEW HORIZONS IN THE ECONOMICS OF SPORT

Series Editors: Wladimir Andreff, *Department of Economics, University of Paris 1 Panthéon Sorbonne, France* and Marc Lavoie, *Department of Economics, University of Ottawa, Canada*

For decades, the economics of sport was regarded as a hobby for a handful of professional economists who were primarily involved in other areas of research. In recent years, however, the significance of the sports economy as a percentage of GDP has expanded dramatically. This has coincided with an equivalent rise in the volume of economic literature devoted to the study of sport.

This series provides a vehicle for deeper analyses of the demand for sport, cost–benefit analysis of sport, sporting governance, the economics of professional sports and leagues, individual sports, trade in the sporting goods industry, media coverage, sponsoring and numerous related issues. It contributes to the further development of sports economics by welcoming new approaches and highlighting original research in both established and newly emerging sporting activities. The series publishes the best theoretical and empirical work from well-established researchers and academics, as well as from talented newcomers in the field.

Titles in the series include:

The Economics of Competitive Sports

Edited by

Plácido Rodríguez

University of Oviedo, Spain

Stefan Késenne

University of Antwerp and KU Leuven, Belgium

Ruud Koning

University of Groningen, the Netherlands

NEW HORIZONS IN THE ECONOMICS OF SPORT

Cheltenham, UK • Northampton, MA, USA

Published by
Edward Elgar Publishing Limited
The Lypiatts
15 Lansdown Road
Cheltenham
Glos GL50 2JA
UK

Edward Elgar Publishing, Inc.
William Pratt House
9 Dewey Court
Northampton
Massachusetts 01060
USA

A catalogue record for this book
is available from the British Library

Library of Congress Control Number: 2014959467

This book is available electronically in the **Elgar**online
Economics subject collection
DOI 10.4337/9781783474769

ISBN 978 1 78347 475 2 (cased)
ISBN 978 1 78347 476 9 (eBook)

Typeset by Servis Filmsetting Ltd, Stockport, Cheshire
Printed and bound in Great Britain by T.J. International Ltd, Padstow

Contents

Contributors

 Jeroen Achterhof, Master's student in Econometrics, Operations Research and Actuarial Studies at the University of Groningen. His research interests include actuarial science and sports economics.

 Madeleine Andreff, former Senior Lecturer in Econometrics and Statistics at the University Paris Est, Marne-la-Vallée. Author of several articles in sports economics.

 Wladimir Andreff, Professor Emeritus at the University of Paris 1 Panthéon-Sorbonne; Honorary President of the International Association of Sports Economists and the European Sports Economics Association; author and editor of books: *Handbook on the Economics of Sport* with Stefan Szymanski, *Recent Development in Sports Economics* and *Contemporary Issues in Sports Economics*; and author of over 100 articles in sports economics.

 Xiao Gang Che, Lecturer (Assistant Professor) at Durham University Business School (UK). His research interests are applied microeconomic theory, applied game theory, auctions, and contest. He has published in several scientific journals such as *Mathematical Social Sciences* and *Economics Letters*.

 Julio del Corral, Associate Professor at the University of Castilla-La Mancha, Campus of Ciudad Real in the Department of Economic Analysis and Finance. His research interests are efficiency and productivity analysis, sports economics and applied econometrics. He has published in several scientific journals such as *Journal of Sports Economics*, *International Journal of Forecasting* and *Food Policy*.

 David Forrest, Honorary Professor in Economics in the University of Liverpool (UK) and Honorary Professor at Macau Polytechnic Institute. He specializes in analysis of the sports and gambling industries. He is experienced in working with the gambling sector, including research and advisory activities for the Responsible Gambling Trust and the UK Gambling Commission. He contributes substantially to literature on sport and gambling markets. Outlets include such as *Economic Inquiry*, *Southern Economic Journal*, *Scottish Journal of Political Economy*, *International Journal of Forecasting* and *European Journal of Operational Research*.

Bernd Frick, Professor of Organizational, Media, and Sports Economics in the Department of Management and Vice-President of the University of Paderborn, Germany. He has published more than 60 refereed papers in peer-reviewed journals and is currently working on a monograph entitled 'Conquering the pitch: the economics of the world's greatest team sport'.

Pedro Garcia-del-Barrio, Associate Professor of Economics and Vice-Dean in the School of Economics and Social Sciences at the Universitat Internacional de Catalunya (UIC). He has collaborated in developing a methodology for evaluating media value in sports and is currently the academic director of MERIT Social Value. His research interests include labour and sports economics. Recent publications include papers in journals such as *Economic Modelling*, *Managerial and Decision Economics*, *Journal of Sports Economics*, *Journal of Productivity Analysis*, *Review of Industrial Organization* and *Journal of Economics*.

Colin Green, Professor of Economics at the Lancaster University Management School. His research interests cover labour, education, personnel and health. He is currently Co-editor of *Education Economics*, Associate Editor of *Journal of Economic Behavior and Organization* and organizes the annual International Workshop on Applied Economics of Education. He has published a range of articles in journals such as *Journal of Health Economics*, *Oxford Economic Papers*, *British Journal of Industrial Relations*, *Economica*, *Labour Economics* and *Economic Inquiry*.

Brad R. Humphreys is on the faculty in the Department of Economics, College of Business and Economics, at West Virginia University. He has published more than 80 articles on sports economics, sport finance, and other topics in peer-reviewed journals in economics and public policy. He is on the editorial board of the *Journal of Sports Economics* and serves as Editor-in-chief of *Contemporary Economic Policy*. He is a past president of the North American Association of Sports Economists.

Stefan Késenne, Emeritus Professor of Economics at the University of Antwerp and KU Leuven, Belgium. He has published in numerous specialized journals such as the *European Economic Review, Journal of Industrial Economics, Scottish Journal of Political Economy, Journal of Sports Economics* and the *European Sports Management Quarterly*. He is also the author of the book *The Economic Theory of Professional Team Sport: An Analytical Treatment*.

Ruud Koning, Professor of Sport Economics at the University of Groningen. He is on the editorial boards of *International Journal of Sports Finance* and *Journal of Quantitative Analysis of Sports*. His research interests are sports economics and (applied) econometrics.

Ian G. McHale, Reader in Statistics at the University of Manchester, UK. Ian was creator of the official player ratings system of the English Premier League, the EA SPORTS Player Performance Index. He is Chair of the Statistics in Sport Section of the Royal Statistical Society. His research interests include statistics in sport and the analysis of gambling markets and various gambling issues. He has published in a wide range of journals including: the *Journal of the Royal Statistical Society (Series A)*, the *International Journal of Forecasting, Economics Letters* and the *European Journal of Operational Research* and serves on the editorial board of the *Journal of Quantitative Analysis of Sports*.

Juan Prieto-Rodríguez, Professor of Economics at the University of Oviedo. His main fields of research focus on sports economics, cultural economics, labour economics and public economics. He has published in numerous scientific journals such as *Journal of Sports Economics, Journal of Cultural Economics, International Journal of Public Policy* and *Applied Economics*. He is also the current Executive Secretary-Treasurer of the Association for Cultural Economics International.

Francesc Pujol, Degree in Economics from the University of Fribourg (Switzerland) and the University of Barcelona, and a PhD in Economics from the University of Geneva. For his thesis he received the 'Edouard Folliet 2001' Award. A specialist in public deficit, budgetary discipline and fiscal determinants of ethics, in recent years he has been involved in the development of the Group for Research in Economics, Sport and Intangibles (ESIrg), which determines, among other things, the media value and price of athletes.

Plácido Rodríguez, Professor EU of Economics, Department of Economics, University of Oviedo. Co-editor of the books *Sports Economics after Fifty Years: Essays in Honour of Simon Rottenberg*, *The Economics of Sport, Health and Happiness* and *The Econometrics of Sport*. He was president of Real Sporting de Gijón Football Club and the current Director of the Sports Economics Observatory Foundation.

Ismael Sanz, Associate Professor, Department of Applied Economics, Faculty of Social Sciences and Law, University Rey Juan Carlos. He has made several research stays at the University of California Santa Barbara, the Australian National University, Real Colegio Complutense at Harvard University and the University of Nottingham. He has published papers in national and international journals and reports for the World Bank and the Department of Treasury of New Zealand.

Friedrich Scheel, PhD student, Department of Organization, Media and Sport Economy, Faculty of Economics, University of Paderborn, Germany. He is a lecturer and is responsible for several courses and seminars. He studies gender differences in competitive sports settings.

Robert Simmons, Professor of Economics at the Lancaster University Management School (UK). He is an expert in the economics of the game, sports and labor economics. He has advised the International Labour Organization. He is a member of the editorial board of the *Journal of Sports Economics* and editor of the *International Journal of Sport Finance*. He has published several papers in journals such as *Contemporary Economic Policy*, *Applied Economics* and *Review of Economics and Statistics*.

Stefan Szymanski, Stephen J. Galetti Collegiate Professor of Sport Management and Co-Director, Michigan Center for Sport Management at the University of Michigan. He has published several books and many papers on the business of sport. His areas of interest are: sports management and economics; sport history, culture and society; European sport and the internationalization of sport; international sports federations and the governance of sport.

J.D. Tena (PhD, Economics, University of Newcastle-upon-Tyne) is a visiting professor at Universidad Carlos III, Spain, and researcher at Università di Sassari, Italy. He also serves as a forecasting consultant for Instituto Flores de Lemus, Spain. His research focus is applied econometrics, with an emphasis on sport economics, labour economics and forecasting. His articles have appeared in journals such as *European Economic Review*, *International Journal of Forecasting*, *European Journal of Operational Research*, *Empirical Economics*, *International Regional Science Review* and *Economic Modelling*.

Fernando Tenreiro, Professor of Economics of Sport and Sport Development Policies, Universidade Lusíada de Lisboa (Portugal). His research interests are in the economic importance of sport and economics of sport federations.

Carlos Varela-Quintana, former Adjunct Professor at the University of Oviedo. Presently he is a marketing consultant for InvesMark SL and a PhD student at the University of Oviedo. His fields of specialization are market research, labour economics and sports economics.

Introduction

Plácido Rodríguez, Stefan Késenne and Ruud Koning

The essence of any sports contest is competition. The very unpredictability of the outcome of a contest distinguishes it from, say, an opera performance. An opera aficionado will know how Götterdämmerung ends; a sports fan is unable to tell the exact outcome of a contest until after the contest has finished. Of course, sports contests are organized in a broader context of competition: not only do the participants produce competition, they also compete for scarce resources. In the end, the amount of top talent is limited, and teams and organizers compete for this scarce talent.

This volume presents a state-of-the-art overview of the economics of competitive sport. It does so along two main lines: the first five chapters discuss the organization of sports and competition. How do leagues operate? The last six chapters deal with competition, rewards and outcome of the actual contests that are being organized. In the remainder of this introduction we provide a short overview of the chapters.

The first chapter by Che and Humphreys concerns competition between rival sports leagues; competition between competition. History has shown that successful incumbent leagues may attract rivals. This is one of the first contributions to study the strategic interaction between incumbent and rival leagues. In the context of sports markets, different outcomes are shown to be equilibrium outcomes: the incumbent deters a rival league; the incumbent eventually merges with the rival league, and the incumbent competes with that league.

In the second chapter, Tenreiro focuses on a very specific European phenomenon: the pyramid model of sport federations. How do federations fit in such a sports pyramid, and more importantly, what is their economic function? Tenreiro argues that private regulation of sport production by federation maximizes production and internalizes external benefits. The model of voluntary association of sports is efficient after all.

Anyone who has visited a soccer game in the 1970s and 1980s in England must have wondered about safety. Hooliganism is a major threat to any professional sport, and soccer has had its share of this type of problem. Green and Simmons show, in Chapter 3, how arrest rates around Premier

League matches have declined over time. However, football hooliganism has not been entirely eradicated. Moreover, the authors present some evidence that it has been displaced towards the lower divisions of professional soccer in England.

One prevalent finding in sports economics is home advantage. For example, in soccer, home teams tend to win slightly less than half of their games, and away teams only a quarter. Considering the importance of home advantage, the order of games during the knockout phase of the Champions League could matter: the team that plays the second leg at home will enjoy home advantage longer if the match goes into overtime. For that reason, the Union of European Football Associations (UEFA) lets the best qualified team play at home in the second leg, so potentially longer home advantage can be earned by performing well in the group stage. Varela-Quintana, del Corral and Prieto-Rodríguez analyse this effect in Chapter 4. Where should one play first in a best of two (matches) contest, home or away?

In Chapter 5, Szymanski studies a very important issue: insolvency of English soccer teams. Despite the loyalty of fans and other stakeholders (usually local governments), some teams do face insolvency. In the end, fans tend to care more about success on the field, than financial stability of their team. Between 1982 and 2010, there were 67 insolvency events involving teams who participated in one of the four professional leagues in England. Clearly, insolvencies are not frequent, but they do occur. Szymanski discusses the pattern of insolvencies since 1945, and examines some of the causes for insolvencies. Clearly, this chapter is particularly relevant in the context of the UEFA's Financial Fair Play initiative, which aims to prevent insolvencies.

These first five chapters concern the organization of sport and competition. The remaining six chapters concern competition as usually analysed by sports economists: they study competitive balance, demand, rewards and the determinants of outcomes of sporting contests.

What is the optimal competitive balance in a sports league? Késenne answers this question in Chapter 6, taking both preferences of supporters and spectators into account. He argues that it is very hard to justify a very unbalanced competition. In particular, the growing importance of more neutral television viewers warrants a more balanced competition.

Live soccer demand (that is, demand by supporters actually visiting the game in the stadium) is examined in Chapter 7. Koning and Achterhof look at the two professional leagues in the Netherlands, and examine whether the same covariates determine attendance at both levels. They conclude that team fixed effects (local drawing potential) are important, and so are form of the home and away team. Weather conditions do matter for attendance of games in the lower league, but not for the attendance of games in the highest league.

Garcia-del-Barrio and Pujol take on a controversial topic in Chapter 8: they analyze the effects of identical money prizes for male and female tennis players. They argue that female players contribute less to the spectacle than men, and that economic efficiency and rationality are not the reasons for equality of payments to male and female tennis players.

Athletes tend to invest in their sport-specific human capital for a long time. This makes the question of career duration especially relevant. That is the topic of Chapter 9, where Frick, Humphreys and Scheel analyze determinants of career duration in three different sports: ski jumping, golf and auto racing. All these sports can be considered to be capital-intensive sports as they require specialized equipment, and facilities (jumping slopes, golf courses and race tracks) that are expensive to maintain. They conclude that these extensive, specialized capital requirements may reduce career lengths.

The last two chapters concern the determinants of success at international, major tournaments. Forrest, McHale, Sanz and Tena look at the determinants of medal totals at the summer Olympic Games. A unique feature of their discussion is their focus on the sport-by-sport table rather than the aggregate medals table. In earlier literature, medals success has been shown to depend on gross domestic product (GDP) and population size, here it is shown that the magnitude of these effects differ by sport.

In the final chapter, Andreff and Andreff come back to the unpredictability of sporting outcomes. They examine predictions of sport performances from the 2008 summer Olympic Games to the 2010 Fédération Internationale de Football Association (FIFA) World Cup, and show that economic predictions of sporting performances should be taken with a pinch of salt.

The editors express their thanks to the sponsors and stakeholders who made this book possible: Fundación del Fútbol Profesional, CajAstur, Universidad de Oviedo, Consejo Superior de Deportes, Ayuntamiento de Gijón (Sociedad Mixta de Turismo), PCTI Asturias, Fundación Observatorio Económico del Deporte (FOED), Facultad de Comercio, Turismo y Ciencias Sociales Jovellanos and Departamento de Economía de la Universidad de Oviedo.

PART I

Organization of Sports and Competition

1. Rival sports league formation and competition

Xiao Gang Che and Brad R. Humphreys

1 INTRODUCTION

Relatively little past research modeled rival league formation in professional sports markets. Competition in sport takes several forms: competition between individual athletes, competition between teams in leagues, competition between national teams in international contests, competition for incoming and existing players, and so on. One of the least analyzed forms of competition is competition between leagues in the same sport. In this chapter, we develop a model of competition between sports leagues.

The only previous paper to examine league formation in sports was Quirk and Fort (1997), who developed a model of the profits earned by incumbent and rival leagues, and the interaction between them; this model featured heterogeneous cities; some cities can support two teams while other cities can support only one. The model by Quirk and Fort (1997) features competition between leagues in the form of a 'war' that reduces the profits earned by teams in both leagues due to competition for fans and players. In this model rival league formation is deterred only through the presence of side payments from the incumbent league to owners of teams in a rival league. In this sense, the model cannot explain why no rival league has emerged in any of the professional sports leagues in North America in past decades.

Here, we develop a model of competition and strategic interaction between professional sports leagues providing games in the same sport in a single market.[1] Our model first focuses on the economic decisions made by an existing incumbent league and then introduces a rival league. The model assumes that a certain number of homogenous cities exist, and that the incumbent league places teams in a subset of these cities. We do not model the formation of incumbent leagues.

The question we focus on in the model is based on a common outcome in professional sports leagues: we often observe the outcome of a single dominant monopoly league a specific sport in a market and also observe the periodic formation of rival leagues. Despite significant increases in population and real income over time, we do not observe competing dominant leagues in any professional team sport in North America.

The question we identify above has received almost no attention from economists. We see no previously proposed explanation for why a single monopoly league in each professional team sport per market should naturally emerge as a stable equilibrium outcome. North America should be able to support multiple competing leagues in the same sport. The population of the United States and Canada exceeds 340 million, which seems large enough to support multiple top-level leagues. The population of the US and Canada in 1901 was more than 80 million; in that year, two professional baseball leagues existed at the highest level. Nearly all of the teams playing in those two leagues are still playing baseball today at the top level, despite vicious head-to-head competition between those two leagues for players and fans over the period 1901–03. In addition, the sole source of revenue in 1901 was game-day revenues, which was limited by the number of people who lived near stadiums, since travel was slower and more difficult. If a market with more than 80 million potential fans can support two baseball leagues playing at the top level, an integrated market with almost 350 million potential fans that can generate ticket, broadcast and sponsorship revenues from many more residents might be expected to support four leagues playing at the top level and competing with each other for fans and players. Note that total attendance in the National League and American League in 1901 was 3.6 million and the combined population of the US and Canada was 82.8 million, or 43 attendees per 1000 population. Total attendance in the Major League Baseball in 2010 was 76 million and the combined population of the US and Canada was 343 million, or 21 attendees per 1000 population. The total population has increased by a factor of five over this period and the simple fraction of the population attending a game has increased by a factor of five, yet the two leagues have merged, so the unified leagues playing baseball at the highest level has decreased from two to one. The number of teams has only increased from 16 to 30; in 1901 there was one top-level baseball team for every 5.1 million North Americans; in 2010 there was one top level baseball team for every 11.4 million.

There has been no shortage of potential new competitors for Major League Baseball, and other professional team sports, in North America over the past century. Yet a single top-level league currently exists in professional football, basketball, baseball and hockey in North America. Much of the rival league formation in North America took place over the period 1880–1980.[2] The lack of rival league formation in the past 30 years suggests that deterrence is an important factor in rival league formation.

Population and income has increased significantly over this period, and new media such as satellite and cable television and the Internet significantly increased the revenues earned by professional sports leagues. Since no rival leagues have formed in this seemingly lucrative environment, incumbent leagues may effectively deter entry by rivals.[3]

We develop a game-theoretic model of entry and deterrence of rival professional sports leagues. The model contains strategic interaction between leagues, monopsony power in the presence of a single league, expansion by the incumbent league, uncertain success by a rival, competition between leagues for players when rival leagues form, and the potential for a merger between the incumbent and rival league. The model predicts that the only observable outcomes will be expansion by the incumbent to deter the formation of a rival league, or a merger between the incumbent league and a successful rival. Competing rival leagues do not emerge as an equilibrium outcome in this model, consistent with observed outcomes in professional sports leagues.

One paper with a similar model to ours is Che and Humphreys (2015). Although some of their results are similar to the results derived here, this model is based on a different set of assumptions and examines different questions. The main focus here is to analyze the entry or formation decision of the rival league, and unlike this model, Che and Humphreys (2015)'s analysis only focuses on North American sports markets. Here we focus on the optimal strategies for the incumbent league, in particular, whether or not the incumbent league should merge with the new entrant league after the entry of a rival league. Modeling this league-level behavior provides additional insights into economic behavior in these markets.

2   A MODEL OF LEAGUE BEHAVIOR AND INTERACTION

Consider the case where an incumbent dominant professional sports league exists in a certain market. This league operates as a monopolist, the sole provider of events in a professional sport in this market. The market contains N cities large enough to support a professional sports team. To simplify the model, we assume that the N cities in this market are homogenous, in terms of their size, population, and revenue generating potential. The league only needs to determine the number of teams in the league, not the allocation of teams to cities. Let $2 \leq n \leq N$ be the number of the teams in the league. Each team operates as a monopolist in each city and faces a downward sloping demand curve for the service provided by the team, which can be interpreted as games. This leads to a downward sloping market demand curve for the professional sport. The number of teams in the league (n) determines the total revenue $R(n)$ generated by the league. Given a downward sloping market demand curve, $R'(n) > 0$ and $R''(n) < 0$. We assume that the league operates as a syndicate, in that all revenues generated are shared equally by the teams in the leagues.[4]

Assume that labor inputs consist entirely of players, rosters are fixed, and labor inputs are homogenous; under these assumptions the total wage bill for each team is w_o and the total wage bill for the league is $w_o n$. The initial profit earned by the dominant league is given by:

$$R(n) - w_o \cdot n > 0 \qquad (1.1)$$

The league chooses $2 \leq n^* < N$ to maximize total league profits in this market, where n* satisfies:

$$R'(n^*) = w_{c0}. \qquad (1.2)$$

We assume that $n^* < N$, so the profit maximizing league size leaves some cities without a team. Kahn (2007) shows that this assumption is consistent with the presence of a fixed pool of talent spread over a potentially expanding monopoly league generating a negative externality on fans in the form of lower team quality. If $n^* = N$ then the optimum league size features a team in every city in the market. In part, this assumption is needed to make the study of rival leagues a non-trivial exercise. When $n^* = N$, the incentive for a rival league to form is significantly reduced. However, this assumption has empirical support in North America; every city large enough to support a professional sports franchise does not have one. For example, Los Angeles, the second largest metropolitan area in North America, has not had a professional football team since 1994. Based on the 2010 Census, 8 of the 50 largest Metropolitan Statistical Areas (MSAs) in the United States did not have a professional sports team (Riverside California, 4.3 million, Las Vegas, Nevada, 1.9 million, Austin, Texas, 1.7 million, Virginia Beach, Virginia, 1.7 million, Providence, Rhode Island, 1.6 million, Louisville, Kentucky, 1.3 million, Hartford, Connecticut, 1.2 million, and Birmingham, Alabama, 1.1 million). Birmingham has about 2000 fewer people than Buffalo, New York, the fiftieth largest MSA in the US, which is home to two professional sports teams.[5] $n^* < N$ appears to be a reasonable assumption based on the current distribution of teams across cities in North American professional sports leagues.

The incumbent league faces the following scenario: the $(N - n^*)$ cities without teams in the market represent a potentially profitable environment for a rival league to form and operate in. Assuming that adequate facilities exist in these cities, a rival league could form and place teams in these $(N - n^*)$ cities without teams in the incumbent league. To simplify the analysis, we also assume that there is no overlap in cities between the two leagues, which ensures that each league is a monopolist in a specific region. This assumption implies no interaction between the two leagues in terms of demand by sports fans. In other words, the two leagues are not substitutes in consumption for fans.

We also assume that the supply of talent, in terms of players, is fixed. This assumption is consistent with the standard model of sports leagues (Fort and Quirk, 1995), and is referred to as the Walrasian fixed-supply conjecture in the literature. We note that this assumption is controversial. Szymanski (2004) shows that an alternative assumption based on a contest-Nash conjecture consistent with a variable supply of talent generates different predictions about league outcomes. We plan to relax this fixed talent assumption in future research. The assumption of fixed talent appears to be reasonable in the short run, as it takes time to acquire the skills to play a sport at the highest level.

The primary implication of a fixed pool of talent is that a rival league must hire players from the incumbent league. North American professional sports leagues have significant monopsony power (Kahn, 2000), so the salary paid to players can be well below players' marginal revenue product. This monopsony power comes from entry drafts, salary caps, and limited free agency. The presence of a rival league will reduce the monopsony power of the incumbent league, as teams in the rival league will bid players away from teams in the incumbent league. This will increase salaries of players in both leagues, as players will have an outside option when bargaining with team owners over salaries.

Under this scenario, the incumbent league faces two choices: either expand into cities with no team to deter a rival league from forming or not expand and let a rival league form. Vrooman (1997) develops a model of league expansion, although this model does not consider expansion in the context of rival league formation. We assume that any rival league that forms will succeed with a positive probability $q(e)$, where e is the effort level the entrant invests into the rival league. Not all rival leagues succeed; in some cases, a rival league lacks sufficient organizational ability, coordination, marketing or quality to attract fans. Quirk and Fort (1997) discuss the features of rival leagues formed in North America over the past 150 years in detail. We assume that the effort variable, e reflects all of these factors.

If the incumbent league chooses to expand into the $(N - n^*)$ cities without teams, the total league wage bill increases to $w_e \cdot N > w_o \cdot n^*$. The wage bill of each team also increases ($w_o < w_e$) as additional teams implies increased competition for a fixed pool of talent. After expansion, total league profits are $R(N) - w_e \cdot N$.

If the incumbent league chooses to allow a rival league to form, then the rival league places teams in the $N - n^*$ cities with no teams in the incumbent league. The rival league can affect the probability that it succeeds and becomes an established league by choosing an investment level e. This e captures resources put toward marketing, promoting and publicizing the new league, as well as resources devoted to other joint-venture activities that would help to promote successful establishment of a new sports league.

If the league is unsuccessful, which happens with probability $1 - q(e)$, then the incumbent league still obtains the profit characterized by equation (1.1) with n^* teams in the incumbent league. If the rival league is successful, both leagues will exist concurrently in the market; the incumbent and the entrant will earn $R(n^*)$ and $R(N - n^*)$, revenues respectively. However, the successful formation of the rival league creates an outside option for talent moving between the leagues, which will drive up salaries, and the wage bill for each team in the league to a higher level w_r, because of the fixed supply of talent.

To improve their bargaining position with players and reduce salaries, the incumbent and successful rival league can merge and form a single united league. The merged league would contain some or all of the teams from the rival league. This merger will benefit both leagues by reducing the bargaining power of the players and increasing the monopsony power of the merged leagues. The merger will result in a lower team wage bill (w_m) than under the outcome with two competing leagues $(w_m < w_r)$. However, in this merged league, the incumbent has to divide total revenue with teams in the rival league. We assume that the incumbent league offers a 'take-it-or-leave-it' revenue sharing offer with proportions δ and $1 - \delta$ between the incumbent and the rival, respectively, where $0 \leq \delta \leq 1$. The profits for the incumbent and rival are $\delta R(N) - w_m n^*$ and $(1 - \delta)R(N) - w_m(N - n^*)$, respectively.

The actual details from mergers that took place between incumbent and rival leagues contain significant heterogeneity. In a few cases, all teams in the rival league were merged into the incumbent league, but in most cases only a subset of the teams in the rival league successfully merged. In some cases, the owners of rival league teams that did not merge were compensated with cash payments. The mergers frequently involve lump-sum payments from merging rival teams to existing incumbent teams, in the form of side payments for reduction of monopoly power in certain cities, expansion fees, player transfer and other arrangements. Mergers also contain agreements about limited sharing of revenues generated by national broadcast rights, licensed merchandize and other commonly shared revenue streams in North American professional sports leagues for some specified period. We assume that the 'take-it-or-leave-it' revenue sharing offer of δ and $1 - \delta$ captures all of these myriad details in a single parameter.

We now have enough analytic framework to specify a sequential game-theoretic model of rival league formation that captures the strategic inter-action between the incumbent league and a potential rival summarized above. Solving the model requires some additional assumptions. Without loss of generality, we assume that:

Assumption 1: $R(n^*) - w_o n^* > R(N) - w_e N > 0$. This assumption implies that given w_o, the incumbent does not have an incentive to expand the current league to other cities in the market. This is equivalent to assuming $n^* < N$.

Assumption 2: $q(e)R(N - n^*) - w_r (N - n^*) \geq 0$ and $R(x) - w_r(x) \leq R(N) - w_m N$, where $2 \leq x \leq N$. The first inequality implies that, given that there are n^* teams in the incumbent league, the new entrant has an incentive to form a rival league, although the salaries and team's wage bills become higher after the rival league has formed. The second inequality reflects the fact that when either the incumbent league chooses to expand or the two leagues choose to merge, the increase in the league's bargaining power with players will produce higher expected profits, even though there are more teams in the merged league.

Assumption 3: $q(e)$ is increasing and concave in e, and $q(e) = 0$. This assumption reflects how the effort level the rival invests will affect the probability of a rival league succeeding.

These assumptions allow us to model the interaction between an incumbent league and a potential rival league as a sequential multi-stage game that reflects the important roles of expectations and deterrence in rival league formation. The timing of the game played by the incumbent and rival league can be characterized by the following three stages:

Stage One: The incumbent decides to either expand the current league or not expand and let a rival league form.
Stage Two: After observing the incumbent's decision, the entrant is deterred if the incumbent chooses to expand to include teams in new cities; the rival chooses to form a new league, enter the market, and invest effort e if the incumbent league chooses not to expand.

Stage Three: If the new league is not successful, the entrant leaves the market and the incumbent league maintains its monopoly position in the market. If the new league is successful, both leagues exist concurrently and can choose to merge, reducing salaries and team payrolls by increasing their monopsony power and reducing the bargaining power of players. However, the incumbent league has to offer a revenue sharing rule, δ, to the entrant, splitting the total profits earned in the market.

2.1   The Rival League Formation Game

In this section, we solve the three-stage game by backward induction. We first characterize the conditions under which a rival league will merge with the incumbent league in Stage Three. Next, we derive an expression for the optimal strategy, characterized by an effort level e, chosen by the rival league after entry in Stage Two. If the new league is not successful, the rival league earns zero profits and the incumbent league's profits are $R(n^*) - w_o n^*$. Thus, we restrict our attention on the case where the rival league succeeds. In this case, the incumbent offers a 'take-it-or-leave-it' revenue sharing arrangement where the rival league gets $1 - \delta$ of the profits and the incumbent league keeps δ. Under these conditions, the payoffs of the entrant are such that, if the rival league does not accept the offer revenue sharing offer, rival league profits are $R(N - n^*) - w_r(N - n^*)$; if the offer is accepted, the profits earned by teams in the (former) rival league are $(1 - \delta)R(N) - w_m(N - n^*)$ and profits earned by teams in the incumbent league are $(\delta)R(N) - w_m(n^*)$. The key factor in this stage is the size of the revenue sharing rule offered by the incumbent league to the rival league if they merge.

The decisions made by the rival and incumbent leagues in Stage Three of the game can be summarized by the following lemma, which describes the optimal revenue sharing offer made by the rival league.

Lemma 1
There exists a 'take-it-or-leave-it' revenue sharing offer δ^* such that if the incumbent league offers δ in the interval $[\delta^*, 1]$, the two leagues will exist concurrently in a same market; otherwise, the rival and incumbent league will choose to merge. The 'take-it- or-leave-it' revenue sharing offer is:

$$\delta = 1 - R(N - n^*) - (w_r - w_m)(N - n^*) / R(N)$$

The proof is straightforward. If $R(N - n^*) - w_r (N - n^*) < (1 - \delta)R(N) - w_m(N - n^*)$, the rival league will accept the revenue sharing offer from the incumbent; otherwise, the rival league rejects. The threshold value for the 'take-it-or-leave-it' revenue sharing offer, δ^*, is consistent with $R(N - n^*) - w_r(N - n^*) = (1 - \delta)R(N) - w_m(N - n^*)$. If the incumbent league makes an offer above the threshold value, the rival league will choose not to merge, because it will not get a large enough share of the profits in the merged league. If no merger takes place, two leagues will operate concurrently in the market and salaries and team wage bills will increase as a result of the reduced bargaining power in each league because of the outside option available to players.

We next characterize the conditions under which the incumbent league is willing to merge when a rival league successfully forms. If the incumbent league chooses not to merge with the rival, the incumbent leagues' profits are $R(n^*) - w_r n^*$; if the merger takes place, the rival league's profits are $\delta R(N) - w_m n^*$. When these two payoffs are equal, there exists a threshold value δ^{**} for the incumbent league such that the incumbent league will not merge with the rival if $\delta^* < \delta^{**}$, and the incumbent league offers $1 - \delta^*$ to the entrant league; the incumbent league will merge if $\delta^* \geq \delta^{**}$.

Given the optimal strategies of the incumbent and rival league, conditional on the success of the rival league, we move backward to solve the second stage of the game. If the incumbent league expands into the $N - n^*$ cities with no teams, it is obvious that the rival league will optimally choose not to form. However, if the incumbent league chooses not to expand, from Assumption 2, it will be profitable for the rival to enter the market and form the league. Thus, we only need to focus on the effort level e chosen by the rival league.

The effort level e the rival will invest depends on whether, in equilibrium, the incumbent will make a revenue sharing merger offer above or below the cutoff value δ^*. Thus, we separately analyze two cases that define two reaction functions:

1. If the rival league expects that the incumbent league will choose to merge and offer $1 - \delta^*$, conditional on the rival league being successful, the $\delta^* \geq \delta^{**}$ and the expected profits of the rival league are:

$$q(e)(1 - \delta^*)R(N) - w_m(N - n^*). \qquad (1.3)$$

Differentiating equation (1.3) with respect to e yields:

$$q'(e^*)(1 - \delta^*)R(N) = 1 \qquad (1.4)$$

where e^* is the *ex-ante* effort level the rival league invests, if a merger will be offered conditional on the new league being successful.

2. If the entrant expects that the incumbent will choose not to merge, then $\delta^* < \delta^{**}$ and the expected profits of the rival league are:

$$q(e^{**})R(N - n^*) - w_r(N - n^*). \tag{1.5}$$

Differentiating equation (1.5) with respect to e yields:

$$q'(e^{**})R(N - n^*) = 1 \tag{1.6}$$

where e^{**} is the *ex-ante* effort level the rival league invests, if merger will not be offered conditional on the new league being successful.

Based on the two reaction functions for the rival league in the two cases above, the rival league's optimal strategy can be characterized by the following lemma:

Lemma 2
Suppose that Assumptions 1–3 hold.

I.   If $\delta^* \geq \delta^{**}$, then the rival league invests e^* in forming the new league; conditional on being successful, the incumbent league offers $(1 - \delta^*)$ to the rival.
II. If $\delta^* < \delta^{**}$, then the rival league invests e^{**} in forming the new league; the incumbent league will never choose to merge with the entrant.

The proof for Lemma 2 is straightforward. Lemma 2 shows an important implication that when an entrant decides to enter the market and form a new league, his effort on the formation depends on whether or not the incumbent has an incentive to merge conditional on the new league being successful. Furthermore, given that $R(N - n^*) > (1 - \delta^*)R(N)$, we have that $e^* < e^{**}$, which indicates that the opportunity of merger with the incumbent benefits the entrant, as he can lower his investment in the new league formation.

2.2   The Incumbent League's Optimal Strategy

In this section we move backward to the first stage of the game and, given the rival league's strategy identified for Stage Two, characterize how the incumbent league decides whether to expand to deter new league formation or allow a new league to form and potentially merge with this new league, conditional its success.

From the previous analysis of the rival league's optimal response to a potential merger offer, the incumbent's strategy in the first stage depends on three possible outcomes:

Outcome 1: If the incumbent league chooses to expand, total profits are

$$R(N) - w_e N. \tag{1.7}$$

Outcome 2: If the incumbent league allows a rival league to form and then merges with the rival league, and if the new league is successful, the incumbent league's expected profits are

$$q(e^*)[\delta^* R(N) - w_m n^*] + (1 - q(e^*))[R(n^*) - w_o n^*]. \tag{1.8}$$

Outcome 3: If the incumbent league allows a rival league to form and does not merge with the rival league, and if the new league is successful, the incumbent league's expected profits are

$$q(e^{**})[R(n^*) - w_r n^*] + (1 - q(e^{**}))[R(n^*) - w_o n^*]. \tag{1.9}$$

Given the profits earned by the incumbent league in these three outcomes, if $\delta^* \geq \delta^{**}$, it is straightforward to see that, from Assumption 1, the profits earned by the incumbent league in Outcome 2 is strictly greater than the profits earned in Outcome 3; in other words, Outcome 3 is dominated by Outcome 2. Thus, our analysis needs only to focus on comparing Outcomes 1 and 2. It is obvious that if the profits earned by the incumbent league under Outcome 1 are greater than the profits earned by the incumbent league under Outcome 2, the incumbent league will choose to expand to deter rival league formation; otherwise, the incumbent league will allow a rival league to form and then merge with that rival if and only if the new league is successful.

Thus, given the response of the incumbent, the effort chosen by the rival league, e^*, and the revenue sharing offer made by the incumbent league, δ^*, we can characterize the equilibrium in this game.

Proposition 1: Suppose that $\delta^* \geq \delta^{**}$. If $[(1 - q(e^*)\delta^* R(N) - (N - n^* q(e^*)) w_m]/(1 - q(e^*)) \leq R(n^*) - n^* w_o$, there exists a subgame perfect equilibrium where the incumbent allows a rival league to form; the rival league invests e^* in forming the new league; conditional on being successful, the incumbent league offers $(1 - \delta^*)$ to the entrant and the two leagues merge. Otherwise, the incumbent chooses to expand the current league to deter rival league formation.

Proof. Given that $\delta^* \geq \delta^{**}$, if the profits earned by the incumbent league in Outcome 1 are less than the profits earned in Outcome 2, then $[(1 - q(e^*)\delta^* R(N) - (N - n^* q(e^*))w_m] / (1 - q(e^*)) \leq R(n^*) - n^* w_o$. This expression shows that it is optimal for the incumbent league to expand to deter a rival league from forming. Given that expansion is chosen by the incumbent league, the entrant invests e^* in the $N - n^*$ cities to form a new league with a probability of success $q(e^*)$. Then, as shown in Lemma (1) and part I of Lemma 2, if the rival league is successful, then the incumbent league offers $(1 - \delta^*)$ to the rival league in the subgame perfect equilibrium; the two leagues will merge. However, if the new league is unsuccessful, the current league still operates with teams in n^* cities in the market.

If the profits earned by the incumbent league are greater under Outcome 1 than under Outcome 2, then it will be optimal for the incumbent league to expand into the other $N - n^*$ cities in the market. A rival league will not form under this condition, as expected profits from the rival league are negative.

We next turn to the case where $\delta^* < \delta^{**}$. From part II of Lemma 2, Outcome 3 is strictly greater than Outcome 2, which implies that it is optimal for the incumbent league to not merge with the rival, even if the rival league is successful. Thus, in the following, our analysis must only focus on the incumbent's decision to expand or not expand. We state the result as follows

Proposition 2: Suppose that $\delta^* < \delta^{**}$. There exists a rival league investment level e such that if $e^{**} < e$, the incumbent allows a rival league to form; in this case, the rival league invests e^{**} in the new league with a success probability (e^{**}). Otherwise, the incumbent chooses to expand.

Proof. If $\delta^* < \delta^{**}$, the incumbent league will not choose to merge even if the rival league is successful. Thus, we restrict our attention to the incumbent league's choice in stage one. Given Assumptions 1 and 2, we know that $R(n^*) - w_r n^* < R(N) - w_m N < R(n^*) - w_o n^*$ and thus there should exist an optimal rival league investment choice e to ensure that equation (1.6.) equals equation (1.8). As a result, there exists a subgame perfect equilibrium in which the incumbent league expands to deter new league formation if $e^{**} \geq e$ and allows a new league to form if $e^{**} < e$.

Propositions 1 and 2 characterize observed outcomes in terms of rival league formation in markets for professional sports since the formation of the first professional team sports league in the late nineteenth century. Sports leagues operate as monopolists in the North American market. Even though rival leagues occasionally form, in the long run these rival leagues either merge with the incumbent league or fail. This demonstrates that it is very likely that $\delta^* < \delta^{**}$.

The main reason why the incumbent leagues are willing to merge may be because of the fixed supply of talent and the existing monopsony power of sports leagues. A merged league will have a lower salary level and team wage bill than two competing dominant leagues. In our model, this implies that the benefit from low wages outweighs the costs of the merger, through revenue sharing with new teams. If the incumbent league and a successful rival do not choose to merge, both will be worse off as it drives up salaries and team payrolls because of the outside option provided to players.

3 CONCLUSIONS

We develop a game-theoretic model of strategic interaction between competing professional leagues to explain observed patterns in rival league formation. Relatively little research has focused on explaining a key puzzle in rival league formation: why do we observe only a single, dominant monopoly league in all North American professional team sports? This market appears to be large enough to support more than one league playing at the highest level in each sport, both in terms of the number of consumers and the number of athletes. The model predicts that this is a subgame perfect equilibrium outcome. Based on expected outcomes related to revenue sharing, bargaining over players, and the probability of a rival league succeeding, no other outcome would be observed even though competing professional leagues can potentially exist. The model is also sufficiently general to include the possibility of a merger between the incumbent and rival league, another commonly observed outcome.

The model also explains the high salaries paid to professional athletes in team sports. One common explanation for the high salaries earned by professional athletes is that they possess relatively scarce abilities and their employers earn high revenues, suggesting a very high marginal revenue product for professional athletes. The model developed here predicts that an incumbent league will pay high salaries to existing players to deter rival league formation. A potential rival league will realize that attracting high-quality players from the incumbent league will be very expensive, and will choose not to form because of the negative expected profits generated by high wage bills. This prediction is broadly consistent with outcomes observed in professional sports markets.

This model can be extended in several directions. While this is an initial effort at modeling rival league formation, several important assumptions could be relaxed to make the model sufficiently general to explain the rich variety of economic behavior observed in sports leagues. First, rather than assume that salaries and total wage bills increase when two dominant leagues compete, bargaining between teams and players under a single incumbent league and two competing leagues could be added to the model. This would relax a key assumption made here. Second, the assumption of a fixed number of homogenous cities capable of supporting a professional sports team could be relaxed. Heterogeneity clearly exists among cities in terms of their ability to generate revenues and support professional sports teams. New York, Chicago and Los Angeles currently support more than one team in Major League Baseball, the National Basketball Association, the National Football League and the National Hockey League. Heterogeneity in the ability to support teams might generate different predictions, and help explain why rival leagues sometimes place teams in the same city as incumbent leagues. In a related point, population growth continually produces new cities capable of supporting a professional team. If incumbent monopoly leagues will not expand into these cities, this generates a significant incentive for a rival league to form. The current model includes only competition for a fixed number of heterogeneous cities with a single team. Increases in the number of potential host cities could generate different predictions about optimal strategies for incumbent and rival leagues.

Finally, this analysis does not examine the welfare implications of rival league expansion. Fans represent only a source of revenue in this model. However, the limited supply of teams provided by existing monopoly leagues leads to welfare losses for residents of cities without teams. The formation of a rival league will generate welfare gains for these consumers, based on increased access to teams and greater variety in entertainment options in cities that did not have a team when only a single dominant league existed. An extended model including consumer preferences and budget constraints can shed additional light on the key issue of the welfare implications of dominant monopoly sports leagues that successfully deter entry by rival leagues.

NOTES

1. Cyrenne (2009) develops a similar model to explain strategic interaction among teams in an existing professional sports league. Dietl et al. (2008) and Madden (2011) develop similar models of within-league strategic interaction.
2. Che and Humphreys (2015) provide details about rival league formation in North America over this period.
3. Szymanski and Ross (2007) discuss the effect of horizontal anti-trust restraints on rival league formation, which may provide an alternative explanation.

4. While this does not reflect the complexity of actual revenue sharing arrangements in professional sports leagues, it simplifies the analysis considerably. Quirk and Fort (1997) and Vrooman (1997) make a similar assumption.
5. The only exception in North America is Green Bay, Wisconsin, population 309 000, ranked 152nd largest MSA in the US and home to the Green Bay Packers.

REFERENCES

Che, X. and Humphreys, B. (2015), 'Competition between sports leagues: theory and evidence on rival league formation in North America', *Review of Industrial Organization*, **46** (2), 127–43.

Cyrenne, P. (2009), 'Modelling professional sports leagues: an industrial organization approach', *Review of Industrial Organization*, **34** (3), 193–215.

Dietl, H.M., Franck, E. and Lang, M. (2008), 'Overinvestment in team sports leagues: a contest theory model', *Scottish Journal of Political Economy*, **55** (3), 353–68.

Fort, R. and Quirk, J. (1995), 'Cross-subsidization, incentives, and outcomes in professional team sports league', *Journal of Economic Literature*, **33** (3), 1265–99.

Kahn, L.M. (2000), 'The sports business as a labor market laboratory', *The Journal of Economic Perspectives*, **14** (3), 75–94.

Kahn, L.M. (2007), 'Sports league expansion and consumer welfare', *Journal of Sports Economics*, **8** (2), 115–38.

Madden, P. (2011), 'Game theoretic analysis of basic team sports leagues', *Journal of Sports Economics*, **12** (4), 407–31.

Quirk, J.P. and Fort, R.D. (1997), *Pay Dirt: The Business of Professional Team Sports*, Princeton, NJ: Princeton University Press.

Szymanski, S. (2004), 'Professional team sports are only a game: the Walrasian fixed-supply conjecture model, contest-Nash equilibrium, and the invariance principle', *Journal of Sports Economics*, **5** (2), 111–26.

Szymanski, S. and Ross, S.F. (2007), 'Governance and vertical integration in team sports', *Contemporary Economic Policy*, **25** (4), 616–26.

Vrooman, J. (1997), 'Franchise free agency in professional sports leagues', *Southern Economic Journal*, **64** (1), 191–219.

2. The pyramid market of the European Sports Model: the economics of federations

Fernando Tenreiro

1 INTRODUCTION

Among other decisions taken by the European Union, the Bosman Case (1995)[1] and the determination that sports activities should be considered within the context of the EU policy on competition (see the Meca-Medina Case, 2006)[2] represented the recognition of the economic substance at continental level of a market that hitherto had assumed no more than national relevance. The policy on competition is related to a market of perfect competition, while over the past 20 years, economic inefficiencies have appeared in the European sports economy, calling into question the achievements made by European sport in the twentieth century.

Specifically, the following transformations have taken place: Andreff and Staudohar (2002, in Barros et al., 2002) identify the transformation of non-profit clubs into predominantly profit-seeking organizations; Chappelet (2010) finds a more complex situation with regard to the sports federations and questions the issue of autonomy in European sport in the relationship between the State and the EU, in the internal structure of the federations and in the regulations of associations, in the nature of sports events or established commercial ties; the importance of network externalities is emphasized in the White Paper on Sport (European Union, 2006), in Tenreiro (2011) and confirmed in the statistical data of the Amnyos Report (Amnyos et al., 2008) and the Eurobarometer Survey (2010).

Economic failures have occurred, for example in the capture of externalities in which private for-profit agents seek to assert their power over the sport's governing bodies. The G-14 group of Europe's elite football clubs has recently threatened to organize its own Champions League, breaking away from the European administrator, the Union of European Football Associations (UEFA); Andreff (2005) refers to the muscle drain of young talents; Kirkeby (2009) suggests that a separation is taking place between the top and the base of the sporting pyramid; the most recent decisions of the European institutions establish new forms of externality capture, for example, the European Court of Justice rulings[3] in relation to the monopoly ownership of television rights of transmission of the English Premier League (EPL), the Swiss courts' deliberations on the FC Sion case[4] and the proposal of certain EPL club owners to terminate[5] the relegation and promotion system that currently applies between the EPL and the lower division. These actions damage the social capital accumulated by European sport and could threaten the continuation of the benefits gained over the past 100 years (see the White Paper on Sport; European Union, 2006).

The European Union risks losing its sporting capital owing to the nonexistence of an adequate economic rationale in its European Sports Model. The consequences of the EU institutions' actions would be unpredictable were it not for the example of Portugal. In the past 20 years, the country has witnessed the capture of the external benefits to sport by commercial, profit-seeking organizations, the economic inefficiency of sports production on the part of the associations and divergence from the European average (see Tenreiro, 2011). The European Sports Model exhibits a differentiated development, the northern countries generating a better product, with the southern countries in second place and those of eastern Europe last, according to Stefan Szymanski (2010), as the Eurostrategies (Eurobarometer, 2014) in part confirms. Portugal in particular shows difficulties in converging on the European average, suggesting the need to better understand the economic characteristics of the European Sports Model.

The present chapter considers that the federations are monopolies that maximize, with economic efficiency, the social welfare of the European Sports Model. In order to avoid repeating the mistakes that have come with European success and to work towards the convergence of the sub-models of European sports development, targeting the maximization of welfare, it is necessary, first, to consider the specificity of the sporting good and its production, which guarantees the property rights and the behaviour of the sporting monopolies. Secondly, we analyse the economic characteristics intrinsic to the behaviour of the monopolies formed by the federations in the market and examine the resolution of situations related to the failure of the monopolistic federations. Thirdly, we consider the regulation of the sports market, from the perspective of both private (Coase, 1960), and public regulation.

2   ECONOMIC FRAMEWORK

To characterize sport federations as economic monopolies, we need first
to follow the development of the economy of sport to identify the pecu-
liarities found in literature and, second, considerations of monopolistic
competition are suggested briefly to support maximization of welfare by
the sport monopolies.

As an instrument, the economics of the sports federations is a necessity
arising from two limiting factors: first, for instance, the economics applied
to professional sport does not embrace the entire market of sport; and,
second, there are limits to its application to what is a peculiar good like
sport recreation.

The development of the economics of sport is observed, first, by
taking into consideration the professional sports market, followed by the
characteristics of the sports federation market.

In the 1990s, in order to understand the sports market, the European
Union (EU) defined the European Sports Model[6] as a pyramid of sports
production comprising competitions for clubs, with promotion and relegation activated according to the number of points won and with financial
mechanisms of solidarity to assist lower-tier clubs as fundamental characteristics. This is in contrast to the US model, in which the structure of
closed competitions designed for the maximization of profit is central to
the purpose of leagues consisting of commercial, that is, profit-seeking
organizations.

The increasing complexity of economic relations has diminished the
importance of the federations, since they are non-profit organizations.
However, since the mid-1990s, the top European clubs have been transformed into commercial businesses, as Andreff and Staudohar (2001)
highlight. In football and other sports, there have been lawsuits that challenge the structure of the European Sports Model. This ever more complex
and contradictory economic situation has deepened, as the examples given
in the previous point suggest, with commercial partners seeking to acquire
the network externalities of the European federations at zero cost.

It is important to note that sport economics as a European research
field is a relatively recent phenomenon. The longer-established US model
of sport economics literature was the first to challenge European sport
with its own economic efficiency. The International Association of Sports
Economists (IASE), which was founded in 2000, holds annual conferences
that generate the publication of thematic journals (see Barros et al., 2002).
In addition, university research centres organize the conduct of specialist analyses, such as that into European football, presented at the Rimini
Conference in 2004, and another that contributed to the Independent

European Sport Review by UEFA and the EU (2006). European sport is opening up to new lines of economics research, which suggests a degree of convergence with the US model (Szymanski and Kuipers, 1999).

The pyramid structure of the sports market was analysed by Gratton and Taylor (2000), relating it to recreation and high-level performance. The authors additionally noted two other non-sport sectors: one in the upward direction[7] and the other downward,[8] as was applied sectorally in the Vilnius definition and later to the creation of the Sports Satellite Account (2006). More recently, Kesenne (2007) has identified the demand for sport in terms of recreation and high-level performance.[9] Downward and Riordan (2007) went a step further, quantifying three levels of intensity in sports participation in the UK. Downward et al. (2009) identify a third source of demand for informal activity, namely, mass participation in sports in the European Sports Model pyramid; furthermore, they identify the supply of the federations and public supply. Downward and Rasciute (2010)[10] identify the levels of community sports production, the maintenance of the population's welfare to the elite level. The EU research project on the funding of grassroots sport[11] has yielded statistical data on the base of the pyramid and the participants registered in the federations.

The importance of the vertical and horizontal structuring of the production functions described can be observed in the market failures in recreational and high-level production. Borland (2006) and Kesenne (2007), in defining the activity of professional sports clubs, consider that professional clubs have no costs in transactions with the lower leagues in either the European or the US sports markets. Borland (2006), for example, suggests that the secondary league is a cost-free labour force supplier to the professional clubs. At the same time, the secondary leagues also produce spectators, consumers and all the co-products and externalities that benefit the professional leagues. Vrooman (2007) views the US secondary leagues as training institutions[12] for the cost-free production of sporting talent for the professional leagues. This is similar in structure to the amateur championships which, in the European sports market, are found within the productive structure of every federation, testifying to the existence of an input deriving from amateur production as a zero-cost externality. The Coasean solution implies that the externalities produced in the US sports market are transacted in the market, see MacDonald (2010). The talent produced by colleges and secondary leagues is a cost-free input that the clubs and professional leagues trade in the market, particularly by means of the agreements between the primary and secondary leagues. In Europe, the financial transformation of the top clubs and the freedom of movement of young players, allowing professional clubs to acquire sporting capital from Africa and Latin America, led to the decline of domestic income in the lower leagues, thereby causing negative economic and social impacts.

According to Szymanski (2010), public regulation is intended to promote the production of human, social and cultural capital at the level of social demand. MacDonald (2010) states that in the USA, the production of externalities is stimulated by Coasean mechanisms related to the behaviour of private for-profit sports organizations.

A further peculiarity calling attention to monopolistic competition relates the competition between sport federations. MacDonald (2008) writes that in Australia four sport activities – Australian football, rugby league, rugby union and football – recently amplified their participation and attained 21 million participants more than their strong competition with other activities such as cricket, V8 super cars and horse racing. In this sense Petry et al. (2004) ask federations to co-operate with each other to fight doping and compete among themselves in the sport market.

Tenreiro (2010, 2011) follows the recommendations of economists such as Neale (1964), who affirms the need to consider sport as an economic good in order to improve the definition of sports production.

In light of the contributions referred to above, the economics of the federations, which is the subject of the present chapter, takes the form of the supply side of sports production and brings a paradigm of economic rationality to the European Sports Model that is capable of questioning the challenges that the EU has recently encountered with regard to sport. These included those mentioned earlier in relation to the monopolistic selling of television broadcasting rights for professional football, the termination of promotion to and relegation from the English Premier League and the application of federations' regulations to all of the partners incorporated into their monopolistic structure of sports production, which is related to the FC Sion/UEFA case.

The typification of the sports production pyramid into production functions possessing crossed network externalities both inside and outside the sports market serves as a basis for the national and continental benchmarking that sports science has not yet developed, but could do so in the future. However, the prospect of benchmarking and the evaluation of convergence on targeted levels of social welfare do not come within the scope of the present chapter.

3 THE PRODUCT AND THE SPORTS PRODUCTION

According to Neale (1964), the sporting good is conceptually a peculiar economic product. In this section, we analyse the characteristics of the sporting good, followed by those of its production, with the aim of understanding the economic fundamentals of the sports market, primarily in the context of its characterization as a market of perfect competition, then considering other characteristics such as the monopolistic competition.

3.1   Sport as an Economic Good

In accordance with the concept of sport, the economic characteristics of the sporting good are identified as being related to physical activity, competition and technology, the latter being the differentiating factor in the pyramidal production chain.

In this chapter, we adopt the Council of Europe's (2001) definition of sport, as stated in the European Sports Charter.[13] From the economic perspective, the Charter defines the sporting good as comprising two principal products: physical activity and competition. In addition, it generates co-products related to the creation of individual well-being by means of education, health and social relations. It can cause positive externalities, such as the participant's personal well-being, or negative externalities, such as the corruption of officials, the violent behaviour of fans, or sportsmen and sportswomen resorting to doping.

The essence of the sporting product is physical activity, while it is the participants' knowledge of how to consume sport that enables its consumers to appreciate the competition in a given event and maximize the sporting good consumed. Knowing how to consume any sporting activity is indeed crucial to its consumption; it entails instruction and training in the activity's 'rules of play'.

According to Fort (2003) and Kesenne (2007), sport is basically competition. We find this statement insufficient, in that first, competition is inherent to every sport, if we consider that even the solitary runner runs against the clock, or against himself or herself, in accordance with his or her physical capacity to improve on, or sustain, the level previously attained. Secondly, the above affirmation does not explain, for example, the relevance of sporting competition, compared with non-sporting competitions, such as contests of physical prowess that can be found in television variety shows, or in the *Guinness Book of Records*. Thirdly, the identification of sport only with competition fails to explain what attracts the interest of consumers of sporting activities, whether they are participants or spectators.

A precise definition of competition should include mention of the need for rules in order to measure the physical activity as it exists in the competitive markets.[14] Competitions measure the quality of a physical activity that is well-defined in accordance with the rules of play. According to

Neale (1964), the closer the qualitative level of participants and the more uncertain the final result, the greater the competition's appeal will be for consumers. Competitions are composed of clusters of participants with similar physical capacity, technical know-how and, consequently, a similar sporting quality. Through the competitions, the participants are ranked according to the quality of each cluster. By refining the best participants (upward movers) from the weakest (downward movers), the competitions establish a new cluster of equivalent sporting values that are in place for the next season.

The competitions in a sporting activity's pyramid are organized in a bottom-up orientation, from the simplest technology to the most complex. The productivity obtained at each technological level is increasing. Let us consider, for example in Figure 2.1, that the amount invested in each worker is the same, that is, 5000 euros. The technology of each athlete or player differentiates the productivity of the human capital at each level of the activity. In the competition in League 3, the investment in human capital generates a per-capita product on the lowest curve, equivalent to the curve of 10 000 euros. In League 2, the technology enables a higher productivity of 15 000 euros, while in League 1 the federation attains the highest productivity per worker, 25 000 euros. Each league has a competition

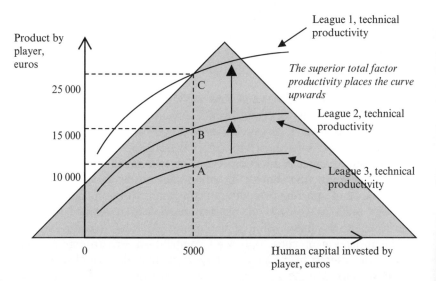

Source: Krugman and Wells (2006), adapted to sport by the author.

Figure 2.1 Technological progress and productivity in a sporting activity at various levels of its pyramid

that allows the federation to produce a determined sporting product with equivalent levels of physical and human capital and work per participant. For each level of capital invested per worker, the technology of the higher leagues generates a greater product per participant. The technology represented by the capacity to practice the given sporting activity at each level of the pyramid is fundamental if the federation is to achieve higher levels of sporting and economic output in the higher levels of competition.

The competitions are the instruments by which the technological structure of a sports federation is developed.

3.2 Co-production and Sports Externalities

The co-products and externalities in the production of sporting activities are important and their analysis is justified in order to prevent economic inefficiency. Gratton and Taylor (2000) characterize sports externalities and sport itself as a public good.

The sporting good, as a product and co-product of sport and personal and social welfare, can be traded outside the monopolistic structure of the federation in markets of perfect, or near-perfect, competition. These may be sports clubs or gymnasiums satisfying a large part of the population and ensuring socially competitive margins for the higher-income sectors of the population, which are predisposed to acquiring sporting goods from private-sector suppliers; these may take the form of associations or commercial enterprises. The externalities, in Figure 2.2, at these levels of consumption are supported either by the consumer or by the producer, generating a social optimum for the higher wealth and education segments.

At the lower levels of wealth and education, the optimum consumption of sport (see Gratton and Taylor, 2000) is affected by market failures in relation to merit goods and public goods as particular cases of externalities on the demand side and the supply of sporting goods. At these latter levels, the characteristics of the merit and public goods are more evident, suggesting redistributive policies aimed to attain the social optimum.

Similar to that noted by Baumgartner and Jost (2000) concerning the environment, the relationship of sport with co-products and externalities is not always clear, economically. The model created for the environment demonstrated that the solution for a negative externality might generate a new negative externality, owing to insufficient analysis. In concrete terms, the authors argue that a lack of information will prevent effective alternative decisions from being taken. They conclude that the complexity and degree of integration of a productive system are crucial for the choice of a cost-efficient environmental policy.

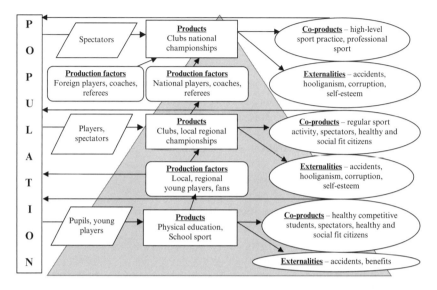

Source: The author's adaptation to sport of Baumgartner and Jost's (2000) figure on the environment.

Figure 2.2   Products, co-products and externalities of the sports production pyramid

Figure 2.2 depicts the generation of products, co-products and externalities in the vertical chain of sporting activity production.

   Among the externalities of sport, network externalities constitute a particular case. These occur from the benefits received by consumers owing to the paradigm of the sports activity. Network externalities of sports production are fundamental in all levels of the production pyramid of sports activities. According to Krugman and Wells (2006), referring to the telecommunications market, the value of the service consumed depends on the total number of consumers who consume it. There are network effects in sports production at the same level of participation and there are crossed network effects among the different levels of production and consumption. At the base of the sports production pyramid, the more people who practise a sport, the greater the benefit taken from the activity's consumption. At the top level, the better the club's quality in the championship, the greater the benefit to the other clubs competing. In a sports system, a federation will have more benefits if there are other federations with competitive behaviour in respect of the total sports production. With regard to the crossed externalities between segments in the federated production, on the one hand, an expanded production of base-level activities is observed to create benefits throughout the entire production structure, above all at the top. On the other hand, the greater the success and technical excellence obtained in top-level competition, the greater the benefits at the base level, since new participants will be attracted. As the positive externalities increase and accumulate, a critical mass effect is created, with highly proportional impacts on the entire market structure.

Various levels of sports production create network externalities within and outside of the federated structure, both the internal and external forms being vital for the success of the other levels of production. In particular, the more the informal and recreational consumption of a sport, the greater the possibilities the high-performance level will have of obtaining sponsorship from companies that sell products consumed by base-level participants. Moreover, the latter participants are the biggest consumers of high-level activities and will customarily buy merchandise associated with the sport's leading performers. The 'trickledown effect' is an efficiently conceived network effect that suggests an over-dimensioned flow of externalities, from the highest level down to the informal and recreational levels. The trickledown effect is an over-valuation of the network effect in the absence of a critical mass of sports consumption. As Collins (2010) suggests, the flow of externalities that is the determinant for sustained development of a sport is found in the externalities generated by the base-level critical mass. These consumers have the capacity to understand the objective and the technique inherent in the sporting activity and its production. These participants are thus predisposed to consume the services and goods made available to them by the top-level performers of the sport in question.

As we observed earlier, in the US model the externalities are interiorized by the professional leagues and the universities through the for-profit market, with no cross-over internalization of benefits between production levels. In the European model, the externalities are interiorized by the federations' regulation, first in accordance with the EU's White Paper on Sport and, secondly, by public regulation.

3.3   The Three Production Functions

The description of the characteristics of the sporting good suggests that sport has a production process with distinct, integrated production functions.

The analyses of Gratton and Taylor (2000), Kesenne (2007), Downward et al. (2009) and Downward and Rasciute (2010) have contributed to the identification of three sports production functions; see Figure 2.3.

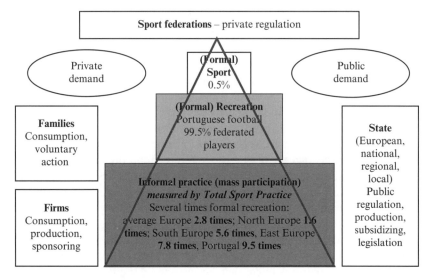

Source: Tenreiro (2011).

Figure 2.3   The economics of federations

Gratton and Taylor (2000) identify mass participation and elite perform-ance. Kesenne (2007) draws an alternative distinction of these concepts, namely, recreation and professional sport. The author further refines the definition of sports production functions, distinguishing between the rec-reational and the professional industries. Kesenne (2007, p. xiii) argues that in the professional industry, 'the consumer is the spectator', 'the producer is the club' and 'the main factor of production is the performer'. In the rec-reational sector, 'the consumer is the performer', 'performing is consump-tion' and 'the production output is the service supplied by the sports club to the participants'. This definition distinguishes between two production functions which, according to the paper's model, are interconnected and interdependent.

The model, shown in Figure 2.3, takes into consideration three funda-mental levels of sports production. The informal level corresponds to the base of the pyramid, in which the sports activities are practised without the strict discipline required in the two formal upper levels and the frequency of practice is likely to irregular. The informal level is more common on the exterior of the federated structure of production. The second level repre-sents the production of sports activities at the core of the federated pro-duction structure, corresponding to all of the activity's rules of production and of practice, in accordance with the principles and rules of the federated structure. The formal structure of production has two fundamental levels: the first recreation and amateur practice, occupying the central level of the pyramid, while the second level is high-level performance, situated at the top of the federation pyramid.

The term 'informal' (that is, mass participation) is used for motives of simplification. Nonetheless, in Figure 2.3, this level contains the total of participants in the pyramid to exemplify the pyramidal structure. In central and eastern European countries, the total sports production reaches an average of 65 per cent of the population, whereas in Portugal, the total production serves only 45 per cent.[15]

We now examine more closely the three production functions considered in the present work.

3.3.1   Production function of mass participation in sport

In Figure 2.3, the informal level corresponds to the base of the sports production pyramid. 'Informal' signifies the basic level of sporting activity, in which are found those who do not take part in regular competitions and those who have taken part in them but have ceased to compete, currently practising the activity free of the obligation to make progress or to reach the highest levels. The informal level is responsible for the broadest consumption of goods and services that are located at the upstream in sports production. These include sports equipment, food, transport and accommodation. In addition, this level accounts for the consumption of goods and services situated downstream in sports production, such as media, marketing and sponsorships. This level is vital in the consumption and production of sport, as it is at this level that any sport generates adequate benefits for the sponsors, who fund not only high-level activity, but also that of the less privileged sectors of society, for instance, youths. Informal participation is produced by public and private agents, among which some are profit-seeking companies while others are not-for-profit clubs. The most common form of production by private entities is self-production by the individual, who produces his or her own activity when, for example, he or she runs alone. Other sport-producing organizations include schools, local authorities, clubs and companies. Consumers who wish to practise a certain sport can do so in any of the producers mentioned, with no obligations as to regularity or strict obedience to the rules defined by the federation's production structure.

3.3.2   Production function of formal sport

The recreational level includes those activities that are generally practised with regularity and demand the increase of the participants' technical capacity. In more developed societies, activities correspond to levels of personal well-being at which know-how of the sporting practice is high, its consumers preferring regular practice in order to raise their competence, their consumption taking place in clubs and enterprises that compete within a federated framework. The more the amateur practises and the better its quality, the stronger will be the competitive pressure in the championship, with a higher production of sportspersons and teams of sufficient quality to reach the level required for national teams and professional sport. This level is of a greater dimension in more developed countries than in less developed countries, justifying the greater competitiveness achieved through the intense training of talented athletes and teams that have been produced by the amateur domain. Recreational production includes all participants registered in the structures of the national federations, which presumably provide for regular participation. Whereas in the central and northern European countries recreation accounts for up to 38 per cent of total participation, in southern recreational practice accounts for 15 per cent, and in eastern countries 11 per cent (see Amnyos et al., 2008; Eurobarometer, 2010). This finding suggests that one of the most significant capacities of the federation structure is to provide for the population's predisposition to practise sports. Adequate provision for all, even in terms of informal practice, would lead to higher levels of regularity, as well as the increased involvement of citizens in the clubs and enterprises that produce sports.

3.3.3 Production function of high-level performance

The highest level of sporting performance, located at the top of the pyramid, generically comprises sportspersons who compete in continental and world championships and in the Olympic Games, as well as those who are engaged in the professional domain. High-level performance production is the most sophisticated product, with the greatest intensity of sporting capital, demanding the best factors of development, which are often of international origin. With reference to football, Portugal has, in recent decades, invested strongly in the creation of a talent pool of outstanding quality, resulting in its national team located among the top ten in the Fédération international de football association (International Federation of International Football) (FIFA, 2007) rankings. At club level, FC Porto's long list of national and international successes over the past 25 years has earned it a consistently high ranking among Europe's professional football elite. In the 2010–11 season, Portugal achieved the rare distinction of having three clubs (FC Porto, Sporting de Braga and Benfica) in the semi-finals of the UEFA Europa League, followed by an all-Portuguese final. Portugal's success in football is, however, a rare exception when compared with other sports. Other European countries have sports schools specializing in a range of sports, producing world-class talent and concomitant success. Portugal's neighbour, Spain, is an excellent example. In Portugal, the percentage of high-level sportsmen and women is less than 1 per cent of the total number of participants registered in the federations, whereas the European average would be higher.[16] This means that Portugal needs to multiply several times its number of high-level performers to converge to the average level of European sport.

4 CONCLUSION

Coase (1991) observed in his Nobel Prize speech of acceptance that economists treated firms like black boxes that are independent of the functioning of the market. It seems that the attitude of economists in relation to sports federations has been similar, by not underlining their economic importance to the maximization of social welfare.

The aim of this chapter has been to understand the economic characteristics of the pyramid of sport production which is the propriety of sports federations. The definition of sport and the characteristics of its production suggest that the sports market is not one of perfect competition. Having said that the text analyses only the definition of sport and the pyramid structure of the European Model of Sport.

The study, which characterizes, in economic terms, the sporting good and its production, emphasizes the importance of sport as a good that is a complement of sporting and non-sporting co-products, and that generates externalities and network externalities. In addition, it underlines the importance of technology in the differentiation of the production of sporting goods. In particular, it appears that the production function of a sports activity consists of at least three levels, namely, informal, formal recreation and high-level performance.

Future economic analysis of the sport market should foresee if monopolistic competition, as a market instrument, rationalizes the behaviour of sport federations and contribute to the maximization of social welfare.

NOTES

1. Judgement of 15 December 1995 – Case C-415/93, available at: http://eur-lex.europa.eu/LexUriServ/LexUriServ.do?uri=CELEX:61993CJ0415:EN:PDF (accessed 18 December 2014).
2. The full text of the judgement may be found on the Court's internet site, available at: http://curia.europa.eu/juris/liste.jsf?language=en&num=C-519/04 (accessed 18 December 2014).

3. European Court of Justice (2011), Press Communiqué Nr. 3/11, 3 February 2011, on the conclusions of the Attorney General in the cases C-403/08 Football Association Premier League vs. QC Leisure & Ors and C-429/08 Football Association Premier League vs. Karen Murphy/Media Protection Services Ltd.
4. 'Uefa mulls options should Sion win Europa League case', available at: http://news.bbc.co.uk/sport2/hi/football/15323562.stm (accessed 6 November 2011).
5. 'Foreign owners want to end Premier League relegation and promotion', *Guardian*, available at: http://www.guardian.co.uk/football/2011/oct/17/foreign-owners-premier-league-relegation (accessed 6 November 2011).
6. See the White Paper on Sport (European Union, 2006).
7. Related to food, transportation, clothes, footwear, construction and so on, to be consumed in the sports sector.
8. Related to publicity, media, marketing and so on, which consume sports goods.
9. Professional sport is also considered within this segment or production function of high-level performance. All of these sports goods are included in the production at the top of the pyramid.
10. 'Sport England's key policy objectives are developing talent that can progress to elite level (Excel), encouraging participation across the community (Grow) and to enhance the satisfaction of participants of their experiences (Sustain).'
11. Eurostrategies et al. (2011).
12. Described in the US and UK literature as the 'farm system'.
13. In the 2001 version, Article 2 sets out the following definition: 'Sport means all forms of physical activity which, through casual or organized participation, aims at expressing or improving physical fitness and mental well-being, forming social relationships or obtaining results in competition at all levels.'
14. Akerlof (1970) analyses the relationship between the difference of quality and asymmetric information, concluding that in markets in which the guarantees of quality are undefined, the market tends to disappear. Therefore, if the buyer displays a lack of perception with regard to quality, the seller can have an incentive to present low-quality goods to the buyer as if they were of higher quality. An example of a scarcity of quality that leads to a decline in market consumption is found in the Portuguese case, in which sports production is decreasing steadily in the various segments of the sports market.
15. These statistics have been sourced from studies of the general demand for sport among the population Eurobarometer (2010).
16. These figures are extrapolated from football, although there are no definitive figures for this production function.

BIBLIOGRAPHY

Akerlof, G.A. (1970), 'The market for "lemons": quality uncertainty and the market mechanism', *Quarterly Journal of Economics*, **84** (3), 488–500.
Amnyos, Eurostrategies, Centre de Droit et d'Economie du Sport, Deutsche Sporthochschule Koln (2008), 'Study on the funding of grassroots sports in the EU', European Union.
Andreff, W. (2005), 'A Coubertobin tax against muscle drain', Fourth Play the Game Conference, 'Governance in Sport: The Good, the Bad and the Ugly', 6–10 November, Copenhagen.
Andreff, W. and Staudohar, P.D. (2001), 'The evolving European model of professional sports finance', in *Actas*, Conferência Internacional sobre Economia do Desporto, CISEP, Instituto Superior Economia Gestão, Universidade Técnica Lisboa.

Arnaut, J.L. (2006), *Independent European Sport Review 2006*, Nyon, Switzerland: European Union and UEFA.

Barros, C.P., Muradali, I. and Szymanski, S. (eds) (2002), *Transatlantic Sport: The Comparative Economics of North American and European Sports*, Cheltenham, UK and Northampton, MA, USA: Edward Elgar.

Baumgärtner, S. and Jöst, J. (2000), 'Joint production, externalities, and the regulation of production networks', *Environmental and Resource Economics*, **16** (2), 229–251.

Borland, J. (2006), 'The production of professional team sports', in W. Andreff and S. Szymanski (eds), *Handbook on the Economics of Sport*, Cheltenham, UK and Northampton, MA, USA: Edward Elgar, pp. 22–6.

Chapellet, J.-L. (2010), *Autonomy of Sport in Europe*, Brussels: EPAS, Council of Europe.

Coase, R. (1960), 'The problem of social cost', *Journal of Law and Economics*, **3** (October), 1–44.

Coase, R. (1991), Nobel prize speech, available at: http://www.nobelprize.org/nobel_prizes/economics/laureates/1991/coase-lecture.html (accessed February 2012).

Collins, M. (2010), *Examining Sports Development*, Abingdon, UK and New York: Routledge.

Council Europe (2001), *European Sport Charter*, Brussels: Council of Europe.

Downward, P. and Rasciute, S. (2010), 'The relative demands for sports and leisure in England', *European Sport Management Quarterly*, **10** (2), 189–214.

Downward, P. and Riordan, J. (2007), 'Social interactions and the demand for sport: an economic analysis', *Contemporary Economic Policy*, **25** (4), 518–37, available at: http://onlinelibrary.wiley.com/doi/10.1111/j.1465-7287.2007.00071.x/abstract (accessed December 2010).

Downward, P., Dawson, A. and Dejonghe, T. (2009), *Sports Economics: Theory, Evidence and Policy*, Abingdon, UK and New York: Routledge.

Eurobarometer (2010), 'Sport and physical activity, 2010', available at: http://ec.europa.eu/public_opinion/archives/eb_special_en.htm#334 (accessed 31 March 2010).

Eurobarometer (2014), 'Sport and physical activity' survey, Special Eurobarometer 412/Wave EB80.2 – TNS Opinion & Social, European Commission.

European Union (2006), *Sport White Paper*, Brussels: European Union.

Eurostrategies, Amnyos, Centre de Droit et d'Economie du Sport, Deutsche Sporthochschule Koln (2011), *Study on the Funding of Grassroots Sports in the EU – with a Focus on the Internal Market Aspects Concerning Legislative Frameworks and Systems of Financing*, Brussels: European Union.

Fédération international de football association (FIFA) 2007, *Rankings Sobre as Selecções Nacionais (Rankings of National Teams)*, available at: http://www.fifa.com/worldfutebol/ranking/lastranking/gender=m/fullranking.html (accessed November 2007).

Fort, R.D. (2003), *Sports Economics*, Upper Saddle River, NJ: Prentice Hall.

Gratton, G. and Taylor, P. (2000), *Sport and Recreation: An Economic Analysis*, London: Taylor and Francis.

Kesenne, S. (2007), *The Economic Theory of Professional Team Sports: An Analytical Treatment*, Cheltenham, UK and Northampton, MA, USA: Edward Elgar.

Kirkeby, M. (2009), 'The pyramid is history! The real challenges and conflicts between grass-roots and top sport', International Sport and Culture Association, available at: www.isca-web.org (accessed October 2010).

Krugman, P. and Wells, R. (2006), *Introdução à Economia* (*Introduction to Economics*), Rio de Janeiro: Editora Campus.

MacDonald, R. (2008), 'Football in a competitive marketplace', *Sports Economist*, 29 February, available at: http://www.thesportseconomist.com/2008/02/football-in-competitive-marketplace.htm (accessed February 2008).

MacDonald, R. (2010), '(Ir)rational reading', *Sports Economist*, 15 May, available at: http://thesportseconomist.com/wordpress/2010/05/15/irrational-reading/ (accessed February 2008).

Neale, W. (1964), 'The peculiar economics of professional sports: a contribution to the theory of the firm in sporting competition', *Quarterly Journal of Economics*, **78** (1), 1–14.

Petry, K., Steinbach, D. and Tokarski, W. (2004), 'Sports systems in the countries of the European Union: similarities and differences', *European Journal for Sport and Society*, **1** (1), 15–21.

Szymanski, S. and Kuipers, T. (1999), *Winners & Losers*, London: Viking.

Szymanski, S. (2010), 'What future sustainable funding model(s) for grassroots sports in the internal market?', paper presented at the European Union Brussels Conference, 16 February.

Tenreiro, F. (2010), Urban sport: the economy of sport federations approach, Sport, Stad, Okonomik, Sport and Urban Economics, Sportokonomie, 12 (collection of conference papers from a conference held in Berlin, organised by W. Maennig and edited by Hoffmann).

Tenreiro, F. (2011), 'Economia do Desporto: A Competitividade de Portugal na União Europeia, tese de doutoramento', Universidade do Porto, Faculdade de Desporto.

Vrooman, J. (2007), 'Theory of the beautiful game: the unification of European football', *Scottish Journal of Political Economy*, **54** (3), 314–54.

3. The English disease: has football hooliganism been eliminated or just displaced?

Colin Green and Robert Simmons

1 INTRODUCTION

Football hooliganism was recognized as a serious social problem in England and Scotland in the 1970s and 1980s. Football hooliganism is generally taken to mean violence and disorder involving football fans in football stadia and nearby city centres on match days. It can be broken down into two main types: spontaneous disorder, such as fighting and throwing missiles, and organized gang violence between groups of opposing fans. Such behaviour can cause a number of negative externalities. Property may be damaged and people with no interest in the football matches that generate the violence and disorder may be physically and mentally hurt or threatened. Consumers may be deterred from shopping on a matchday occasion, with adverse effects on retailers' revenues. The football industry is affected as non-violent fans may be deterred from attending games and broadcasters will be reluctant to televise games which have the risk of generating violent behaviour inside stadia. Similarly, sponsorship could be reduced as firms tend to associate football with images of violence and disorder.

The term 'English disease' was coined in the 1980s by media reports of high-profile football matches where crowd trouble broke out into full-scale fighting, pitch invasions and many injuries to fans and innocent bystanders. Following a large-scale riot at a Football Association (FA) Cup match between Millwall and Luton in March 1985, Prime Minister Thatcher set up a 'War Cabinet' to tackle hooliganism. Fences at grounds were already in place but apparently did not deter the aggressive behaviour of fans at the Millwall game. Fatalities did occur as a result of hooliganism, in particular at the European Cup Final between Liverpool and Juventus in 1985 at the Heysel Stadium, Brussels, where 39 fans were killed in a riot. As a consequence of the shocking scenes at this game, English clubs were

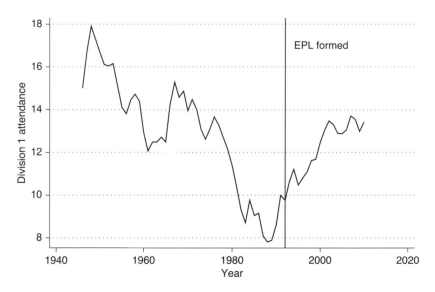

Figure 3.1   English attendance since 1946–47

banned from European competitions until 1990, with Liverpool banned from a further year.

Szymanski and Kuypers (1999) show that football league attendances in England had a downward trend until the mid-1980s, with a turning point at the 1984–85 season then leading into an upward trend, in all divisions, to the present day. They attribute the downward trend to poor quality football played in unsafe and dilapidated stadia with bad facilities. It is likely that the growth of hooliganism in the 1970s and 1980s exacerbated the decline in attendances. Figure 3.1 shows the time pattern of attendances for the English top division over 1946 to 2010.

Conversely, Szymanski and Kuypers (1999) attribute the rising trend in attendances post-1985 to a fashion element (that is, a change in tastes especially by young people), to better, more comfortable and safer stadia, better quality football perhaps related to fewer restrictions on immigration of foreign players and to the decline of football hooliganism.[1] Reduced hooliganism can in turn be determined by a number of factors such as the increased use of closed-circuit television for surveillance, undercover police surveillance activity, more severe penalties for convicted hooligans, a more diverse crowd composition less prone to violence, use of club stewards rather than police and the switch from standing to seated accommodation inside stadia.

By way of contrast, Italian football interestingly shows the opposite

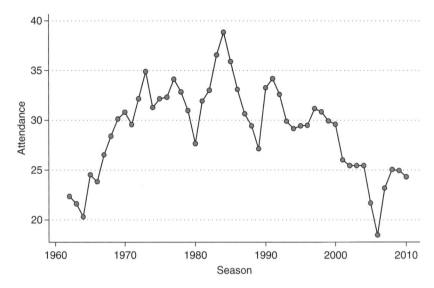

Figure 3.2   Italian attendances 1962–2010

time pattern of attendances in the top tier. Figure 3.2 shows rising attendances in the 1970s and 1980s followed by a declining trend over the 1990s and 2000s. There are many possible reasons for the trend decline but it is likely that hooliganism perpetrated by hardcore and violent Ultra fans, has played an important role alongside scandals and departures of star players (Baroncelli and Lago, 2006).

Currently, the United Kingdom Home Office claims that 'the downwards trend in football-related arrests is continuing, but there is no complacency' (Home Office, 2011). This chapter investigates the patterns of football-related arrests through the four levels (divisions) of English football. Although in aggregate, hooliganism as expressed by numbers of arrests is now at historically low levels, there remains considerable variation in hooligan activity across clubs. Specifically, we find that whereas in the 1980s hooliganism was concentrated in the top division, in recent years it has become more observable in the lower divisions. We assess how and why this changing pattern of displacement has occurred.[2]

2   LITERATURE

In the 1980s and 1990s, football hooliganism was a topic covered at great length by sociologists. See *inter alia* Dunning et al. (1988), Pearson (1999) and Stott and Pearson (2007). These studies cover themes of working-class culture, including tribal identity and attachment to clubs, working-class alienation in an era of high youth unemployment, and the roles of media and police in reporting and confronting hooliganism.

Economists have typically examined crime using the economic model of crime developed by Becker (1968) and Ehrlich (1973). In this model the marginal criminal evaluates the expected costs and benefits of crime, weighing up probabilities of detection and conviction and then the expected costs conditional on conviction. It could be argued that this model is more applicable to property crimes where the returns and costs are both visible and can be estimated. However, Fajnzylber et al. (2002) argued that the economic model of crime could usefully help explain variations in violent crime. That is, an element in cognitive decision-making, albeit instinctive, that is responsive to incentives could take place in committing a seemingly pathological act of violence such as assault or even murder. Similarly, football hooliganism could be argued to be instinctive and pathological but the marginal violent fan could be deterred from acts of aggression by raising the probability of detection and the costs of conviction, given detection.

The economic literature on football hooliganism is somewhat sparse.[3] Some recent literature has examined the impact of increased police surveillance on football-related crime. Priks (2008) examines the introduction of surveillance cameras in areas where fans approach football stadia in Stockholm and finds evidence of reduced football-related violence. The same author (Priks, 2010) investigates determinants of forms of violence in and around Stockholm stadia and finds a key role for a team's league position as a predictor of aggressive behaviour. That is, the lower a team's league standing the greater the incidence of football-related violence on match days. Poor football results generate feelings of frustration and dissatisfied fans then engage in violent behaviour. Note that this argument goes beyond the standard economic model of crime and extends the analysis into behavioural economics with key concepts of norms, reference points and mental anchoring. Departure from reference points (such as worse than 'normal' league performance of a football team) can generate frustration, which it is argued, spills over into violence. In a similar way, referring to North American college sports, Rees and Schnepel (2009) offer evidence that defeats for a local college (American) football team is associated with increased violent and disorderly behaviour in college towns.

3 DATA AND EMPIRICAL APPROACH

This chapter relies on data sourced from two places and two distinct eras. First, we have data by season and by club on the total number of arrests in and around football stadia in England and Wales over the seasons 1984–85 to 1992–93.[4] These data were supplied by the Association of Chief Police Officers, collated by the Sir Norman Chester Centre for Football Research at the University of Leicester and published in the Football Trusts's *Digest of Football Statistics*.

Our second data set covers a later period, 1999–2000 to 2009–10 and comprises United Kingdom Home Office arrests data, comparable to the data from the *Digest of Football Statistics*, together with data on 'banning orders'. The Football (Offences and Disorder) Act of 1999 was a piece of legislation designed to prevent suspected football hooligans from travelling abroad. But it was actually the Football (Disorder) Act 2000 that introduced banning orders 'on complaint', the 1999 legislation really just tinkered around the edges of the earlier Football Spectators Act (for more details on banning orders see James and Pearson, 2006). The motivation for these changes in law was the poor reputation of England national team supporters when following their team abroad. The Act could be, and is, used to prevent fans from attending particular football grounds. The banning order is issued by a local magistrate and was initially applied for a fixed period of two to three years without conviction and between three and five years where a conviction is applied. Currently, banning orders last for five years.

The Home Office publishes both arrests and banning order data for each club in each season and we shall use both types of data in our analysis. We were unable to locate arrests data between the 1992–93 and 1998–99 seasons as these were not officially published. In seasons since 2001–02, the Home Office reports arrests data by category of offence such as violent activity, racist chanting, throwing weapons or objects and pitch invasion. In addition, for this period we observe whether arrests associated with a particular club occurred at home or away games. Although we would prefer to have access to the missing data we would nevertheless argue that the two sample periods represent quite distinct periods in terms of the evolution of football hooliganism in England and Wales.

Arrests are likely to reflect the levels of police resources devoted to policing football matches. Resources will vary by police force area and will be much greater for urban as opposed to rural areas. Rural areas tend to be populated by lower division football teams in England and Wales. Also important for arrests will be the tactical use of police resources. Arrests may reflect the tactical approach of police rather than actual levels of disorder. Stott et al. (forthcoming) develop a case study of Cardiff City Football Club which finds that the single most important predictor of levels of arrests was not the presence of hooligans *per se* but confrontational and high-profile policing tactics. The role of police resources in arrests associated with football matches is a question that we defer to future research.

Our arrests and banning order data are supplemented by attendance and league standings data taken from the *Sky Sports Football Yearbook* (Rollin and Rollin, various years), previously the *Rothmans Football Yearbook*. We also have data on recorded violent crime by locality and police resources, measured by numbers of police officers by police force area, each available from the Home Office.

Our main statistical results are based on the dependent variable, arrest rate. This is defined as arrests per average attendee (thousands) in a given season. This we label as a measure of arrest incidence (A_j) at club j. Our main interest is in estimating variations in arrest incidence across divisions. In doing so, we work our way up to the following empirical specification:

$$A_{jt} = \beta_0 + \beta Season_{jt} + \emptyset Division_{jt} + \gamma X_{jt} + \mu_j + \varepsilon_{jt}$$

where $Season_{jt}$ is a vector of season dummies, $Division_{jt}$ is a vector of divisional dummies, while X_{jt} are club-level time-varying characteristics. The μ_j term is a club-level fixed effect. This club fixed effect specification seeks to deal with underlying time invariant characteristics that lead to clubs being more, or less, prone to trouble. A key point is that the division effects are identified in these models by movers between divisions.[5] Hence, division effects are explicitly identified via the promotion and relegation of teams, which is non-random. We discuss this later. Subsequently, we use this approach to examine a number of other related dependent variables, including arrests for violence and banning orders, for which we observe data for the 2001–02 season onwards.

4   ANALYSIS AND RESULTS

4.1   Preliminary Evidence – 1984–85 to 2007–08

We first examine broad trends in arrests across this long period. The last two seasons are omitted from this part of the analysis as the arrests data is not comparable to the 1980s' data. Figure 3.3 provides average arrests and average attendances per club by season. Two things are noticeable from this. First, there has been a general decline in the number of arrests

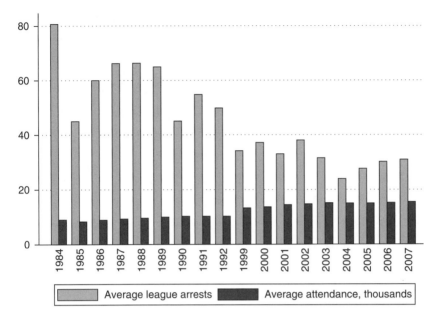

Figure 3.3   *Average club league arrests and attendance, English Football
League, 1984–85 to 1992–93 and 1999–2000 to 2007–08*

occurring at English football games over the past three decades, although
there is some indication of an increase again since the 2004–05 season.
Second, attendances at league games have been steadily increasing over
this period.

Figure 3.4 shows seasonal variations in arrests per capita of attendance
by club. This is shown for each of the four divisions, and to aid comparison we split the data into two frames for the two panels of data we have.
These demonstrate a marked decrease in the number of arrests at both
the top two divisions of English football, but less of a clear pattern for
the lower two divisions. These overall numbers, it could be argued, hide
large changes in the incidence of arrests across the divisions. Consider
the attendance data, average attendances in the top division in the latter
part of our data (1999–2000 to 2007–08) are 66 per cent higher than in
the first half our data (1984–85 to 1992–93). The corresponding percentage changes for divisions 2, 3 and 4 were 59 per cent, 46 per cent and
35 per cent, respectively.

In the following we focus on season arrests per average attendance
(thousands). Table 3.1 provides a series of increasingly more complete
estimates of arrests across our entire sample. The first column reports

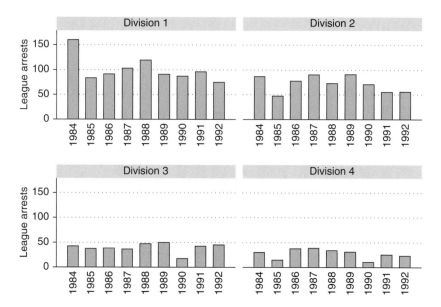

*Figure 3.4a   League arrests/attendance by division, English Football
League, 1984–85 to 1992–93*

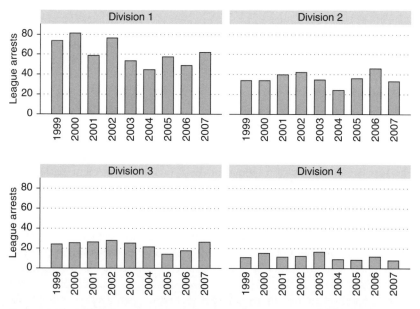

*Figure 3.4b   League arrests/attendance by division, English Football
League, 1999–2000 to 2007–08*

Table 3.1   Average arrests 1984–85 to 1991–92; 1999–90 to 2007–08

	Pooled OLS		Club fixed effects		Scale effects	
	Coef.	Std Err.	Coef.	Std Err.	Coef.	Std Err.
Championship	1.336	0.338	0.760	0.398	0.132	0.435
League 1	2.003	0.337	1.394	0.485	0.465	0.551
League 2	2.100	0.339	0.475	0.549	−0.526	0.617
1985–86	1.155	0.643	0.824	0.599	0.393	0.610
1986–87	4.128	0.645	3.803	0.602	3.424	0.609
1987–88	2.898	0.643	2.475	0.600	2.152	0.605
1988–89	2.492	0.643	2.300	0.600	2.017	0.603
1989–90	2.157	0.645	1.997	0.602	1.744	0.604
1990–91	−1.794	0.650	−1.997	0.607	−2.238	0.608
1991–92	0.562	0.645	0.352	0.602	0.102	0.604
1999–2000	0.296	0.643	0.125	0.600	−0.114	0.601
2000–01	−3.391	0.650	−3.232	0.608	−3.134	0.606
2001–02	−2.975	0.645	−2.828	0.602	−2.679	0.602
2002–03	−3.498	0.643	−3.349	0.601	−3.100	0.603
2003–04	−3.107	0.643	−2.913	0.606	−2.634	0.609
2004–05	−3.503	0.643	−3.219	0.603	−2.905	0.608
2005–06	−4.169	0.643	−3.857	0.601	−3.541	0.606
2006–07	−4.047	0.643	−3.748	0.601	−3.441	0.605
2007–08	−3.699	0.643	−3.440	0.600	−3.107	0.605
Average attendance					−0.105	0.030
Constant	4.604	0.432	5.254	0.477	7.214	0.734
Club fixed effects			✓		✓	
Observations		1825		1825		1825
R squared		0.245		0.391		0.395

Note: * Omitted case is top division (old Division 1/Premier League) and 1984–85 season.

results from a pooled ordinary least squares (OLS) where the only controls are for season and division. The key point to note here is that these show that across this period lower divisions had a 1 to 2 per thousand persons average attendance higher arrest rate than the top division. This in itself is interesting as it seems counter to the typical overt focus on high profile, top division clubs. In the next column, fixed effects at a club level are introduced. This attempts to deal with underlying time invariant characteristics that lead to clubs being more or less prone to trouble. While, smaller in magnitude, the Division 2 and 3 effects are robust to the inclusion of club fixed effects, while the Division 4 effect goes to zero.

In the final column we include average attendance as a control to capture scale effects in arrests. The inclusion of the attendance control reveals that

Table 3.2   Average league arrests by pre- and post-Premier League period

	1984–85 to 1991–92		1999–00 to 2007–08	
	Coeff	Std Err.	Coeff	Std Err.
Championship	−0.398	0.968	0.220	0.243
League 1	−3.054	1.280	1.003	0.311
League 2	−4.867	1.439	1.013	0.345
Average attendance	−0.254	0.112	−0.017	0.021
Constant	15.496	1.721	0.684	0.518
Club fixed effects	✓		✓	
R squared		0.413		0.519
Observations		817		919

Note: All other controls as per Table 3.1, last column.

the rate of arrest decreases with attendance size, and that the inclusion of this control leads to all division effects becoming statistically insignificant. These results across the two data periods suggest that once underlying variations in club arrest propensity and scale effects are controlled for there are no divisional differences in arrest rates.

It is, however, a strong assumption to make that these divisional parameters are constant over the timescale involved, especially with the intervening period of the formation of the Premier League missing. In Table 3.2 we re-estimate our last model from Table 3.1 with the sample split into the earlier and latter periods. This reveals some marked differences in average arrests per division. In the earlier period, the top divisions have clearly higher conditional arrest rates than the two lower leagues. However, for the latter period this switches. Hence, in our later period of analysis after the 'crackdown' on hooliganism there was a conditionally higher rate of arrest in the lower divisions. In the following section we seek to examine this period, where we are fortunate to have more detailed data, and try to determine what this change in pattern represents.

4.2   Lower League Arrests 2001–02 Onwards

From the 2001–02 season onwards, the Home Office reports a more detailed breakdown of arrests data, according to whether fans attached to particular teams are arrested at home or away grounds and also according to type of offence. The types recorded include violent behaviour, public disorder, throwing objects, racist chants, pitch invasions, alcohol related disorder and ticket touting. Table 3.3 reports summary statistics for these types of football-related offences.

Table 3.3   Summary statistics by league, 2001–02 to 2009–10

	Premier League	Championship	League 1	League 2
Average attendance (000s)	34.58	16.68	7.63	4.35
Total arrests	75.88	43.58	25.77	13.21
Arrests at home	36.07	20.72	11.74	6.30
Arrests away	39.82	22.86	14.03	6.91
New banning orders (flow)	15.67	12.71	8.33	4.92
Existing banning orders (stock)	42.43	37.93	24.46	12.68
Arrests – Violence	6.14	7.63	3.03	1.52
Arrests – Public disorder	27.87	16.41	11.58	6.89
Arrests – Throwing objects	1.38	0.82	0.60	0.23
Arrests – Racist chants etc.	0.92	0.93	0.31	0.13
Arrests – Pitch invasions	4.67	4.03	2.09	0.93
Arrests – Alcohol related	26.85	11.48	6.16	2.04
Arrests – Ticket related offences	2.54	0.22	0.04	0.04
Police numbers	12013.23	6773.54	5538.80	4341.27

The United Kingdom government introduced the Football (Offences and Disorder) Act in 1999. A football banning order is a civil order and is intended as a preventative measure as opposed to a penalty for previous behaviour. The Act was intended to prevent known football hooligans from causing trouble at international and club matches at home and abroad. A ban does not just cover attendance at matches but can be extended to prevent an individual from visiting town centres, particular pubs and bars and even from using public transport on match days.[6] Table 3.3 reports descriptive statistics for the stock of banning orders and new banning orders in a given season, each by division.

We regress arrests for violent offences, per attendee, on divisional and seasonal dummies and average home club attendance over the period 2001–02 to 2009–10.[7] Results are shown in Table 3.4. We run similar regressions for new bans and total arrests for comparison. We see an indication of an increase in more serious crimes (per attendance level) as we move down the leagues. As before, with club fixed effects included these divisional effects are identified by promotions and relegations. Specifically, arrests for violent football-related crime are greater in the Championship and League One than in the Premier League. A caveat is that there is no significant difference between per fan arrests for violence in League Two compared to the Premier League. The season dummies do not suggest a downward trend in arrests per fan for violent behaviour over the 2000s.

Turning to new bans, we see a significant and positive coefficient in

The economics of competitive sports

Table 3.4   Arrests, banning orders and violent crime, 2001–02 to 2009–10

	Total arrests (home + away)		New banning orders (2002–03 to 2008–09)		Violent crime (2001–02 to 2008–09)	
	Coeff.	Std Err.	Coeff.	Std Err.	Coeff.	Std Err.
Championship	0.424	0.306	0.222	0.209	0.320	0.119
League 1	1.113	0.386	0.601	0.264	0.327	0.153
League 2	1.410	0.426	0.790	0.291	0.343	0.168
2002–03	0.664	0.220			0.041	0.079
2003–04	0.353	0.220	0.349	0.127	0.060	0.079
2004–05	−0.491	0.220	−0.073	0.126	0.175	0.079
2005–06	−0.426	0.220	0.043	0.126	−0.088	0.079
2006–07	−0.120	0.220	−0.206	0.125	−0.093	0.080
2007–08	−0.026	0.220	0.104	0.124	−0.077	0.080
2008–09	−0.026	0.220	−0.008	0.018	−0.106	0.080
2009–10	−0.202	0.222				
Attendance	−0.018	0.026	−0.007	0.018	0.011	0.010
Constant	2.335	0.616	0.520	0.440	−0.093	0.234
Club fixed effects	✓		✓		✓	
Observations		828		644		736
R squared	0.562		0.471		0.245	

2002–03 compared to 2001–02. This increase in new bans suggests a tough enactment of policy closely following its introduction in the 2000–01 season. New bans are significantly higher in the two lowest divisions (League One and League Two) relative to Premier League and Championship. However, there is no significant difference between new bans in Championship and Premier League. Hence, evidence of detection of football hooliganism (arrests for violent behaviour) and conviction (new bans) is more pronounced for lower divisions in each case, but these patterns are not identical.

The Home Office presents data on arrests in and around stadia by affiliation of fans. Table 3.5 shows results of a fixed effects model of arrests per fan with home and away fan arrests modelled separately. We see no significant variation in home fan arrest rates by division. But we do see significantly increasing arrest rates for away fans as we move down the divisions. In particular, arrest rates for away fans are greater in Leagues One and Two relative to Premier League and Championship. This finding has important policy implications for policing football matches. If away fans are an important source of variations in arrest rates then more careful monitoring and policing of this group of fans is needed to control crowd behaviour in and around football matches.

Table 3.5   Home arrests versus travelling fans, 2001–02 to 2009–10

	Home		Away	
	Coeff.	Std Err.	Coeff.	Std Err.
Championship	0.031	0.203	0.393	0.215
League 1	0.140	0.256	0.991	0.271
League 2	0.247	0.283	1.162	0.300
R squared		0.452		0.476
Observations		828		828

Note: All other controls as per Table 3.4.

Table 3.6   Other types of arrests, 2001–02 to 2008–09

	Public disorder		Alcohol		Throwing	
	Coeff.	Std Err.	Coeff.	Std Err.	Coeff.	Std Err.
Championship	0.002	0.191	−0.012	0.096	−0.008	0.023
League 1	0.559	0.240	0.099	0.120	−0.009	0.029
League 2	0.894	0.266	−0.012	0.133	−0.012	0.032

	Ticket touting		Pitch invasion		Racist	
	Coeff.	Std Err.	Coeff.	Std Err.	Coeff.	Std Err.
Championship	0.002	0.013	0.100	0.062	0.024	0.022
League 1	−0.007	0.017	0.131	0.078	−0.011	0.027
League 2	0.007	0.019	0.100	0.087	−0.032	0.030

Table 3.6 breaks down arrests for illegal acts of non-violent behaviour into public disorder, alcohol related, throwing objects, ticket touting and racist chanting offences. The only statistically significant effects are for public disorder and it is notable that the divisional effects rise markedly as divisional status falls, with coefficients of 0.56 for League One (third tier) and 0.89 for League Two (fourth tier).

As mentioned earlier our fixed effects estimates of division effects are identified by clubs moving between divisions, which are determined in a non-random manner by promotion and relegation. This might be of concern if (a) teams likely who are promoted/relegated in our sample are somehow different to other clubs, and (b) very good or poor performance affects the propensity of supporters to commit crime. With respect to the former, we compared sample statistics of clubs that at some point experienced promotion or relegation in the 2001–02 to 2009–10 period and found no statistical mean differences in arrests or attendance between these and those clubs who at no point were relegated or promoted. Furthermore, we re-estimated our main arrests incidence model on this subsample and, although precision was harmed, the pattern of division estimates mirrored what is reported in Table 3.4. The latter concern is similar to the frustration hypothesis proposed by Priks (2010) whereby poor league standings induce crowd trouble by dissatisfied fans. We attempted to examine this by adding league positions as an additional explanatory variable in our models. We found no evidence in support of the frustration hypothesis, nor any statistically significant effect of league position on arrest incidence in general.

5 CONCLUSIONS

We have presented a simple fixed effects model of arrest rates for football-related offences ('hooliganism') at English league grounds. Examining two distinct data periods, 1984–85 to 1991–92 and 1999–2000 to 2007–08, we find that arrest rates have declined since 1984–85, particularly in the Premier League. In the first sub-period, we find that arrest rates vary negatively with average attendance, so there is a scale effect of crowd size arrests. This scale effect is no longer apparent in the later sub-period. Interestingly, we also find that the relative position of divisional violence switches markedly between the two sub-periods. This is primarily a consequence of a large decrease in hooligan activity at Premier League grounds. It is clear that surveillance and monitoring of fans at Premier League grounds has increased substantially over our sample periods. Also, although Premier League clubs typically hire their own stewards for policing, they can still call on official police resources if crowd trouble is particularly severe. The bigger Premier League clubs are based in large metropolitan police force areas (Greater Manchester, London, Merseyside, Northumbria and West Midlands in particular) and have access to much greater police numbers than, for example, clubs located in West Mercia (say Hereford) or Essex (say Colchester).

Overall we argue that the different divisional pattern in contemporary football hooliganism is at least partly explained by a combination of monitoring (surveillance) and incentives (banning orders). Lower division clubs lack the financial resources to install closed circuit television cameras in multiple locations inside stadia. They also lack resources to hire large numbers of stewards. This lack of financial resources devoted to surveillance and detection of hooliganism at lower division clubs is one factor that explains the greater arrest rates to be found there.

In addition, the crowd composition is probably less diverse at lower division football grounds than at Premier League grounds where women, children and ethnic minorities form a larger part of crowds than was apparent 20 years ago. Thus, the composition of League Two crowds is more closely matched to the profile of typical perpetrators of non-football crimes than is the typical Premier League crowd. As far as incentives are concerned, the loss of access to a Premier League ground could be argued to be a greater cost to the marginally criminal fan than loss of access to a League Two ground.

The answer to our question is in two parts. First, football hooliganism has not been entirely eradicated and the Home Office is correct to warn against complacency. Second, we do find some evidence of displacement effects of hooliganism towards the lower divisions.

ACKNOWLEDGEMENT

We thank Todd Jewell, Geoff Pearson, John Sutherland and the audiences of the Scottish Economic Society and Western Economic Association International (San Diego) for helpful comments on an earlier draft.

NOTES

1. From the 1991–92 season it became mandatory for English football stadia to be all seated. This was a consequence of the Hillsborough disaster of 1989 when 96 Liverpool fans were killed due to overcrowding at the Sheffield Wednesday ground in an FA Cup semi-final. The disaster was not a result of hooligan activity but instead was caused by overcrowding and crushing of people inside the standing areas of the stadium.
2. Football hooliganism is observed in recent years outside England and Wales. In Scotland, the fixtures between Celtic and Glasgow Rangers often generate crowd trouble as these are intense games with religious differences and heavy alcohol consumption giving potential for violence. In the Celtic–Rangers match of March 2011 there were 34 arrests and many unrecorded offences. This led local police and politicians to convene a special summit to discuss the problem. In Italy, an entire weekend set of league matches was cancelled after a policeman was killed during crowd trouble in a game between Catania and Palermo in February 2007 (Pettersson-Lidblom and Priks, 2009). These two teams, and several others, have endured recent spells of playing some games behind closed doors, with no spectators at all, as a punishment for violent fan behaviour.
3. A strand of literature examines the impact of football hooliganism on other forms of criminal activity. Marie (2010) argues that intensive policing of football matches in London creates greater opportunities for criminals to commit property crime on match days as the probability of detection is reduced.
4. 'Arrests' covers all arrests defined in law under schedule 1 of the Football Spectators Act 1989 and includes football specific offences such as violent behaviour, throwing missiles and pitch encroachment, and a wide range of generic criminal offences committed in connection with a football match. Note that the offences need not be committed immediately before, during or after the match; the Home Office states that a football-related arrest can occur 'at any place within a period of 24 hours either side of a match' (Home Office,

2010). This flexibility is designed to capture alcohol-related offences that might occur sometime before or after matches are actually played.

5. Our tables report divisions as Premier League, Championship, League One, League Two which is the current classification. Prior to the formation of the Premier League in 1992, divisions were more simply labelled as Division 1, Division 2, Division 3 and Division 4.

6. The Home Office states that 'banning orders are issued by the courts following a conviction of a football-related offence, or after a complaint by the Crown Prosecution Service or a local police force. For an order to be issued, it must be proved that the accused person has caused or contributed to football-related violence or disorder and that an order will prevent them from misbehaving further' (Home Office, 2010).

7. Although, actual data periods vary by dependent variable owing to differences in reporting and availability.

REFERENCES

Baroncelli, A. and Lago, U. (2006), 'Italian football', *Journal of Sports Economics*, **7** (1), 13–28.

Becker, G. (1968), 'Crime and punishment: An economic approach', *Journal of Political Economy*, **76** (1), 175–209.

Dunning, E., Murphy, P. and Williams, J. (1988), *The Roots of Football Hooliganism*, London: Routledge and Kegan Paul.

Ehrlich, I. (1973), 'Participation in illegal activities: a theoretical and empirical investigation', *Journal of Political Economy*, **81** (3), 551–65.

Fajnzylber, P., Lederman, P. and Loayza, N. (2002), 'What determines violent crime?', *European Economic Review*, **46** (7), 1323–57.

Football Trust (various years), *Digest of Football Statistics*, London: Football Trust.

Home Office (2010), 'Statistics on football-related arrests and banning orders: season 2009–10', available at: www.gov.uk/government/uploads/system/uploads/attachment_data/file/97855/fbo-2009-10.pdf (accessed 19 December 2014).

Home Office (2011), 'Statistics on football-related arrests and banning orders: season 2010–11', available at: www.gov.uk/government/uploads/system/uploads/attachment_data/file/97856/fbo-2010-11.pdf (accessed 19 December 2014).

James, M. and Pearson, G. (2006), 'Football banning orders; analysing their use in court', *Journal of Criminal Law*, **70** (6), 509–30.

Marie, O. (2010), 'Police and thieves in the stadium: measuring the (multiple) effects of football matches on crime', Discussion Paper No. 1012, Centre for Economic Performance, London.

Pearson, G. (1999), 'Legitimate targets? The civil liberties of football fans', *Journal of Civil Liberties*, **4**, 28–47.

Pettersson-Lidborn, P. and Priks, M. (2010), 'Behavior under social pressure: empty Italian stadiums and referee bias', *Economics Letters*, **108** (2), 212–14.

Priks, M. (2008), 'Do surveillance cameras affect unruly behaviour? A close look at grandstands', Working Paper No. 2289, Centre for Economic Studies Ifo Institute (CESifo), Munich.

Priks, M. (2010), 'Does frustration lead to unruly behaviour? Evidence from the Swedish hooligan scene', *Kyklos*, **63**, 450–60.

Rees, D. and Schnepel, K. (2009), 'College football games and crime', *Journal of Sports Economics*, **10**, 68–87.

Rollin, J. and Rollin, G. (various years), *Sky Sports Football Yearbook*, London: Headline.

Stott, C., Hoggett, J. and Pearson, G. (forthcoming), '"Keeping the peace": Social identity, procedural justice and the policing of football crowds', *British Journal of Criminology*.

Stott, C. and Pearson, G. (2007), *Football 'Hooliganism'*, London: Pennant Books.

Szymanski, S. and Kuypers, T. (1999), *Winners and Losers: The Business of Football*, London: Viking Press.

4. Where to play first (away or home) in a best-of-two tournament? An analysis from UEFA competitions

Carlos Varela-Quintana, Julio del Corral and Juan Prieto-Rodríguez

1 INTRODUCTION

The analysis of order in decisions affecting competitive outcomes through psychological pressure and emotions has been addressed previously in the sports economics literature. For instance, Magnus and Klaassen (1999) found that the player who served first in the first set of a tennis match had an advantage over his opponent and Apesteguia and Palacios-Huerta (2010) showed that, during the period 1970–2008, the teams which began the penalty shoot-out had a 60.5 per cent chance of winning a tie in soccer.

Within the framework of behavioural economics, DellaVigna (2009) indicates that individuals could make non-standard decisions because of (1) the frame or context of the situation; (2) limited attention; (3) simplifying heuristics when choosing from a large menu of options; (4) social pressure and persuasion; and (5) emotions. A well-known phenomenon in sports where social pressure and emotions play a crucial role is home advantage. This effect is especially relevant in soccer where, for instance, 48 per cent of the matches played in the Spanish First Division between the 2000–2001 and 2010–11 seasons were won by the local team, while the away percentage of winning was below 28 per cent. Factors related to the referee's behaviour, psychological reasons, location and venue are usually considered the causes for the existence of home advantage. The pressure of the crowd, and how it affects players and referees, is one of the main factors studied in the literature. Several aspects have been analysed, such as size (Dowie, 1982), noise (Nevill et al., 2002), proximity to the field (Dohmen, 2005) or the length of extra time assigned by referees at the end of a match when the local team needs to overcome the away team (Garicano et al., 2005). Regarding psychological factors, some researchers have proposed a sense of territoriality on the part of the home team

(Pollard, 2006) or its confidence (Waters and Lovell, 2002). Of course, factors other than pressure and psychological reasons, such as location and venue, have been proposed by researchers. Thus, for example, familiarity with an artificial pitch at home (Barnett and Hilditch, 1993) or travel time (Recht et al., 2003) are variables that are also considered in the literature.[1]

Given the advantage of playing at home, the order assigned in the tie can crucially affect the final outcome through psychological pressure. Many knockout competitions are set to an odd number of matches. However, in some sports (for example, football, handball and table tennis) the number of matches played is even. Thus, the decision to be made is how to choose the venue for the matches, since it is usual to play the same number of matches in each venue. Page and Page (2007) investigated this question regarding European competitions, and found that teams that play at home in the second leg have an advantage in the knockout rounds. They proposed as possible explanations that the second leg is perceived as the most decisive match in the tie, and this generates a greater home advantage in the second leg. This greater advantage could be a result of referee bias, managerial tactics or the motivation of the players. In this sense, Krumer (2013) elaborates a model with teams of equal ability that combines psychological pressure and home advantage, concluding that if victory in the first stage provides a psychological advantage in the second stage, a team may prefer to play the second stage at home in order to maximize its expected payoff.

Page and Page (2007) analysed second-leg home advantage by controlling the difference in ability between teams, but they assumed that the second-leg advantage is the same for all matches. We argue that the second-leg home advantage could be especially relevant if teams have similar abilities, but the effect could disappear if the contest is really uneven. To do so we analyse the second-leg home advantage separately for even and uneven contests, testing this hypothesis using an econometric model.

The rest of the chapter is organized as follows. Section 2 describes the characteristics of the European tournaments. Section 3 presents the context of the Union of European Football Associations (UEFA) seeding system. Section 4 analyses the data, while section 5 presents the main results. Section 6 concludes.

2 CHARACTERISTICS OF THE EUROPEAN TOURNAMENTS

The database contains the knockout rounds played in six European tournaments: the European Champions' Cup (1956–92), the Champions League (1993–present), the Inter-Cities Fair Cup (1958–71), the UEFA Cup

(1972–2009), the Europe League (2010–present) and the Cup Winners' Cup (1961–99).[2] The European Champions' Cup was created in 1955 on the initiative of the French newspaper *L'Equipe* and was organized by UEFA under the name Coupe des Clubs Champions Européens in order to enable the winners of national leagues to face each other. From the 1992–93 season, the name of the tournament and organization was changed to Champions League. The Inter-Cities Fair Cup was a competition sponsored by the International Federation of Association Football (FIFA) that began in 1955. Under the 'one city, one team' rule, it was not aimed at clubs, but at representative teams from cities that hosted trade fairs; the achievements of these teams in their national competitions had no relevance. In practice, it became a competition between runner-up clubs from the domestic leagues. Thus, in the 1971–72 season, it came under the auspices of UEFA and was replaced by the UEFA Cup. In the 2009–10 season, this competition was renamed the Europa League. Finally, the Cup Winners' Cup was first organized in 1960–61 by the Mitropa Cup committee, and was intended as a competition of domestic cup winners. Recognized by UEFA in 1963, this competition lasted until the 1998–99 season, when it was absorbed into the UEFA Cup.

The format of these tournaments has changed over time. Initially they had only three phases: qualifying rounds, a knockout phase and a final stage. In the qualifying rounds and the knockout phase, teams were removed through two matches, with one played at each team's home ground. The two finalist teams resolved the competition in the final stage, which had a different format depending on the competition: the Inter-Cities Fair Cup and UEFA Cup (until the 1996–97 seasons) maintained the two-leg format, while in the Cup Winner's Cup, European Cup and Champions Cup only one match was contested, usually in a neutral field. With the exception of the first season of the Inter-Cities Fair Cup, this format remained virtually unchanged for over 30 years, with the number of rounds varying between a minimum of four and a maximum of six. In the 1990s, the format changed with the inclusion of the group phase in the European Cup[3] of the 1991–92 season, the incorporation of new federations from Eastern Europe and the absorption of the Cup Winners' Cup by the UEFA Cup in the 1999–2000 season. These changes contributed to increasing the number of rounds to ten, thereby increasing the number of matches necessary to pass in order to win a continental tournament.

The difference in goals scored in both legs of the knockout round determines, in most cases, the winner of it. Several tie-break methods have been used to determine the winner when there is no goal difference after the regulation time of 90 or 180 minutes. From 1956 to 1975, three practices were commonly employed to resolve a tie: added extra time of 30 minutes after the regulation match play time (since 1957), a match on neutral ground (from 1956 to 1974) and the toss of a coin if the draw still persisted (from 1957 to 1970). To reduce the need to use these three systems, the away goals rule began to be applied in 1965. This rule determined that, in the case of equal goals having been scored, the team that scores more goals away from home wins the draw. Finally, the additional match and the coin toss were gradually replaced after 1970 by penalty shoot-outs at the end of extra time. It should be added that these systems did not apply to all of UEFA competitions; their use varied depending on the championship and phase. Only since 1975–76 season, and with minor exceptions, has UEFA had uniform regulation across all their championships.

3 QUALIFICATION AND SEEDING FOR THE EUROPEAN TOURNAMENTS

In order to respond to growing interest, the number of contestants in the European championships increased dramatically over the years, from 16 teams in the 1955–56 season to 270 contestants in the 2010–11 season.

Since 1979, UEFA has published Association Club Coefficient Rankings (also known as Country Rankings) in order to determine the number of teams from each association that will play in the European tournaments. The ranking for a particular country in season t ($ACCR_t$) is computed as the sum of the Association Club Coefficients (ACC_i) of the five preceding seasons, including the current one, t.

$$ACCR_t = \sum_{i=t-4}^{t} ACC_i = \sum_{i=t-4}^{t} \left(\frac{\sum_{k=1}^{N} P_k}{N} \right)_i$$

$$= \sum_{i=t-4}^{t} (Country's\ teams\ average\ number\ of\ points)_i$$

The value of the coefficient for each season i, ACC_i, is the result of adding the P points obtained in the European tournaments by each of the k teams of the country and divide this value by N (the total number of clubs representing the association during that season). The number of points depends on the number of total wins and draws, and bonuses earned by reaching a certain round.[4] This index is not only used to determine how many teams from each country will enter a particular competition, but also it is taken into account to define the Club Coefficient Ranking, *CCR*.

The value in the ranking for a particular club in season t (CCR_t) is based on the sum of the Club Coefficients (CC_i) over the last five seasons, including the season ending in year. t. This coefficient consists of two elements: the team and the country components.

$$CCR_t = \sum_{i=t-4}^{t} CC_i = \sum_{i=t-4}^{t} (Team\,part)_i + \sum_{i=t-4}^{t} (Country\,part)_i$$

$$= \sum_{i=t-4}^{t} P_i' + \alpha \cdot ACCR_t$$

The value of the Team part for each season i, denoted by P_i', depends on the number of the team's wins and ties in the competition (excluding from this calculation the qualifying rounds) and the bonus earned by reaching a certain stage. The Country part is the result of weighting the average number of points of the country, $ACCR_t$, by a percentage α determined by UEFA: 0 per cent in the period 1979–98, 50 per cent in the period 1999–2003, 33 per cent between 2004 and 2008 and 20 per cent from 2009 to the present.

The subsequent pairing of teams is not perfectly random. First, Club Coefficient Rankings published by UEFA are used to determine the seeding of each club in all UEFA competitions. Second, the randomness of the pairing is affected by the UEFA rule which states that teams from the same association cannot face each other until the quarter-finals. Third, teams that share a group in the group stage cannot be together in the next phase. Finally, teams that lead the group at the end of the group stage play the second leg of the next round as hosts.[5]

4   DATABASE

The data with the results of the playoffs and how they were resolved are taken from the following websites: (1) http://www.uefa.com, (2) http://www.rsssf.com, (3) http://wildstat.com/ and (4) http://kassiesa.home.xs4all.nl/bert/uefa/. This last website provided further information on UEFA rankings, which have been reconstructed since season 1959–60 allowing us to know the differences in the ability between the teams. The six UEFA competitions in the database add up to a total of 8612 knockout rounds from the 1960–61 to 2010–11 seasons. However, we have to exclude from the dataset 1396 ties played in the group stages and 118 single-match rounds (105 finals, two semi-finals, seven playoffs in which a team did not show up and four knockouts disputed in a single match by mutual agreement between clubs). Additionally, the present study does not take into account 23 qualifiers whose outcome was decided randomly by the toss of a coin.

Our final base consists of 7075 straight knockout contests with two-legged home and away ties, of which 919 were played in the European Champions' Cup, 813 in the Champions League, 461 in the Inter-Cities Fair Cup, 3324 in the UEFA Cup, 334 in the Europa League and 1224 in the Cup Winners' Cup. The winner was decided in regulation time by goal difference on 6089 occasions, and by the away goals rule 535 times; the rest needed to add extra time (222), a third match (52) or penalty shoot-outs (177).

5   RESULTS

The main objective of the chapter is to analyse the second-leg home advantage, but before this analysis it is worth studying whether there have been home advantages in each match. Figure 4.1 shows the kernel densities of the difference in goals between the local team and the away team.

It can be seen that both kernel densities are biased to the right – that is to say, home teams score more goals than away teams – so there is home advantage. However, the objective of the chapter is not to analyse the well-known home advantage in football, but to analyse second-leg home

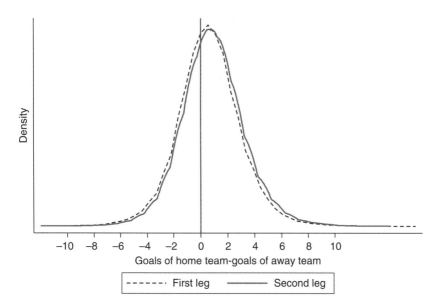

Figure 4.1   Kernel of goal difference in both legs without including the goals scored in added extra time

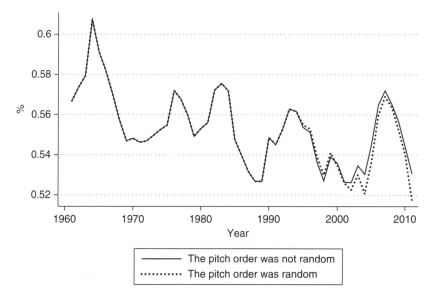

*Figure 4.2   Second-leg home advantage evolution using a moving average
on five observations*

advantage. Figure 4.1 shows the first insight about it given that the kernel
density of the second leg is on the right with respect to the first leg.

Figure 4.2 shows the evolution of the percentage of contests in which
the winning team hosted the second leg. It can be seen that teams that
played as locals in the second leg are more likely to progress to the
following round. It is another insight into the existence of second-leg
home advantage, but it could be due to differences in the teams' quality,
since better teams are more likely to play as home teams in the second
leg.

Table 4.1 shows where the favourite plays in the first leg and who wins.
While the percentage of victories of the favourites is 72 per cent when they
play as local teams in the second leg, this figure falls to only 65 per cent if
they play at home in the first leg. So a small second-leg home advantage
is inferred from Table 4.1. Goodman and Kruskal's gamma[6] value is also
remarkable, at −0.174, showing a negative relation between playing the
first leg at home and winning the contest.

Given that our objective is to analyse second-leg home advantage controlling for different levels of teams' quality, we estimate a logit model to
determine the probability of the victory of the favourite team, taking into
account the difference in the log of the rank of each team. Given that a
huge increase in the number of teams in the European competitions is

Table 4.1   Percentage of favourites' victories by order of play (All)

	Favourite lost		Favourite won		Total	
	Obs.	%	Obs.	%	Obs.	%
Favourite plays at home in second leg	984	(27.78)	2558	(72.22)	3542	(100.0)
Favourite plays at home in first leg	1108	(35.33)	2028	(64.67)	3136	(100.0)
Total	2092	(31.33)	4586	(68.67)	6678	(100.0)

Notes:
All matches excluding those in which there is no favourite.
Pearson χ_2: 44.08, p-value=0.000.
Goodman and Kruskal's gamma: −0.174; asymptotic standard error: 0.026.

Table 4.2   Logit estimates to estimate the probability of the victory of the favourite

Model 1	Coefficient
Constant	0.626***
DIFLRANK1960–1966	0.221**
DIFLRANK1967–1999	0.174***
DIFLRANK2000–2011	0.502***
Log-likelihood	−4254
Number of observations	7075

Note: *, ** and *** indicate significance at the 10 per cent, 5 per cent and 1 per cent levels, respectively.

observed at the 1966 and 1999 seasons, we allow for different coefficients in the logit model. See Table 4.2.

As expected, the coefficient for the difference in the log of the teams' rankings in the three periods is positive, indicating that the larger the difference in the ranking of teams, the higher the probability of a favourite victory. Figure 4.3 shows the kernel density of the probability of the favourite winning derived from the predictions of Model 1. We divide the distribution into five types of matches: (1) matches in which the probability of a favourite's victory is below percentile 10 of the distribution of this probability (PINF10); (2) matches in which the probability of a favourite's victory is below percentile 25 (PINF25); (3) matches in which the probability of a favourite winning is above percentile 75 (PSUP75); (4) matches in which the probability of a favourite winning is above than percentile 90 (PSUP90); and (5) matches with a favourite's winning probability lying

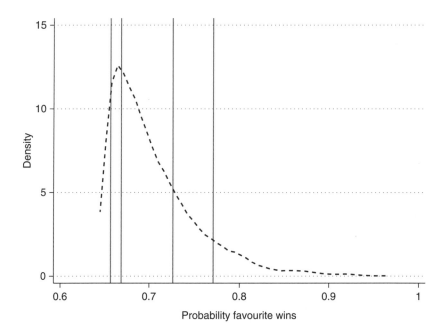

Figure 4.3   Kernel density of the probability of a favourite's victory from Model

Table 4.3   Percentage of favourites' victories by order of play (PINF10)

	Favourite lost		Favourite won		Total	
	Obs.	%	Obs.	%	Obs.	%
Favourite plays at home in second leg	140	(40.6)	205	(59.4)	345	(100)
Favourite plays at home in first leg	169	(52.3)	154	(47.7)	323	(100)
Total	309	(46.3)	359	(53.7)	668	(100)

Notes:
The probability that the favourite wins is lower than the 10th percentile.
Pearson χ_2: 9.25, p-value=0.000.
Goodman and Kruskal's gamma: −0.233; asymptotic standard error: 0.074.

in the two central quartiles (above percentile 25 and below percentile 75). These five groups are proxies of the difference in teams' quality and, therefore, of the evenness of the matches. Moreover, they are not mutually exclusive since, for instance, very uneven matches will be included in both groups PINF10 and PINF25.

Using these groups, in Tables 4.3–4.6 we check if there is a second-leg

Table 4.4   Percentage of favourites' victories by order of play (PINF25)

	Favourite lost		Favourite won		Total	
	Obs.	%	Obs.	%	Obs.	%
Favourite plays at home in second leg	334	(38.4)	536	(61.6)	870	(100)
Favourite plays at home in first leg	380	(47.6)	419	(52.4)	799	(100)
Total	714	(42.8)	955	(57.2)	1669	(100)

Notes:
The probability that the favourite wins is lower than the 25th percentile.
Pearson χ_2: 14.33, p-value=0.000.
Goodman and Kruskal's gamma: −0.185; asymptotic standard error: 0.048.

Table 4.5   Percentage of favourites' victories by order of play (PSUP75)

	Favourite lost		Favourite won		Total	
	Obs.	%	Obs.	%	Obs.	%
Favourite plays at home in second leg	173	(18.6)	756	(81.4)	929	(100)
Favourite plays at home in first leg	181	(24.4)	561	(75.6)	742	(100)
Total	354	(21.2)	1317	(78.8)	1671	(100)

Notes:
The probability that the favourite wins is higher than the 75th percentile.
Pearson χ_2: 8.23, p-value = 0.004.
Goodman and Kruskal's gamma: −0.17; asymptotic standard error: 0.058.

Table 4.6   Percentage of favourites' victories by order of play (PSUP90)

	Favourite lost		Favourite won		Total	
	Obs.	%	Obs.	%	Obs.	%
Favourite plays at home in second leg	68	(17.3)	326	(82.7)	394	(100)
Favourite plays at home in first leg	58	(21.2)	215	(78.8)	273	(100)
Total	126	(18.9)	541	(81.1)	667	(100)

Notes:
The probability that the favourite wins is higher than the 90th percentile.
Pearson χ_2: 1.677, p-value=0.196.
Goodman and Kruskal's gamma: −0.129; asymptotic standard error: 0.098.

home advantage controlling for differences in teams' quality. Obviously, the lower the percentile of the distribution of probability of a favourite's victory, the more equalized the qualifying round. Therefore, we expect a larger percentage of favourites' victories and a lower second-leg home advantage as differences in teams' quality increase.

Given these tables, an alternative way to analyse the second-leg home advantage is to evaluate the difference between the percentage of favourites' victories when playing at home in the second and in the first leg. A positive difference will indicate the existence of second-leg home advantage. We hypothesize that this difference will decrease as parties become more unequal. Moreover, this can be checked using the Goodman and Kruskal's gamma value: a negative value indicates the existence of second-leg home advantage, and our hypothesis will not be rejected if its value (in absolute terms) decreases from more uneven matches to more even matches.

In the very even matches (PINF10), the percentage of victories of the favourites playing the second leg at home is 59 per cent, while it is 48 per cent when they play at home in the first leg, so the difference is about 11 per cent. This difference drops to 9 per cent in the even matches (PINF25), to 6 per cent in the uneven matches (PSUP75) and to 4 per cent in the really uneven matches (PSUP90). Furthermore, the Goodman and Kruskal's gamma takes negative values in the four cases and its absolute value decreases from the more even contests to the more uneven contests, indicating that there exists a greater second-leg home advantage for more even matches: that is, strong teams playing against weak teams are less concerned about the order of play, as their quality advantage is enough to more than offset the advantage of playing the second leg at home. In order to check the robustness of these results, we have estimated logit models to test the effect of the second-leg home advantage where the dependent variable takes value one if the round was won by the favourite and zero otherwise. As independent variables we have included the difference in the log of the ranks of the teams for three different periods (1960–66, 1967–99, 2000–2011), a dummy variable that takes value one if the favourite team plays the first leg at home (FAV PLAY HOME 1st LEG), and this variable interacted with the a priori expected evenness of the match (PINF10, PINF25, PSUP75 and PSUP90). See Table 4.7)

The results of Model 2 show that, at the means of the variables, the marginal effect of second-leg home advantage is −0.103. This result implies that second-leg home advantage is significant and, before controlling for the difference in the teams' ability, the effect is close to 10 per cent – that is, the probability of victory of the favourite team that plays the first leg as the away team increases by ten points. However, it is important to take

Table 4.7 Logit estimates of favourite's victory

	Model 2		Model 3		Model 4		Model 5	
	Coeff.	ME	Coeff.	ME	Coeff.	ME	Coeff.	ME
CONSTANT	1.100***		0.853***		0.877***		0.949***	
DIFLRANK1960–1966			0.210**	(0.043)	0.187**	(0.039)	0.114	(0.023)
DIFLRANK1967–1999			0.189***	(0.039)	0.167***	(0.034)	0.098***	(0.020)
DIFLRANK2000–2011			0.522***	(0.107)	0.474***	(0.098)	0.344***	(0.071)
FAV PLAY HOME 1st LEG	−0.495***	(−0.103)	−0.513***	(−0.106)	−0.490***	(−0.101)	−0.460***	(−0.095)
PINFP10·FAV PLAY HOME 1st LEG					−0.536***	(−0.110)	−0.196	(−0.040)
PSUP90·FAV PLAY HOME 1st LEG					0.100	(0.021)	−0.097	(−0.020)
PINFP25·FAV PLAY HOME 1st LEG							−0.436***	(−0.090)
PSUP75 FAV PLAY HOME 1st LEG							0.330***	(0.068)
Observations	7075		7075		7075		7075	
Log-likelihood	−4251		−4206		−4201		−4187	

Notes:
ME, marginal effect measured at the means of the other variables.
*, ** and *** indicate significance at the 10 per cent, 5 per cent and 1 per cent levels, respectively.

into account the difference in ability between the teams in order to take an accurate measurement of the second-leg home advantage. Once rank differences are taken into account (Model 3), the marginal effect of the relevant variable remains close to negative 10 per cent.

In order to test our hypothesis that the second-leg home advantage effect is different in the even rounds than it is in the uneven contests, in Model 4 we have included the interactions between the relevant dummy and the dummies that proxy really uneven matches (PSU90) and really even matches (PINF10). The results show that the marginal effect for second-leg home advantage for even matches is close to 21 per cent higher than playing the second leg away, which implies a really big advantage. On the other hand, the marginal effect of playing the second leg away for the favourite team in really uneven matches is −0.08 per cent.

Model 2 examines the probability that the favourite team wins the tie, depending on whether it plays at home in the first leg. Model 3 analyses the probability that the favourite team will win the tie based on the difference in ability and whether it plays at home in the first leg. Model 4 includes playing at home in the first leg interacted with the estimated probability lower than the 10th percentile and greater than the 90th percentile. Model 5 includes playing at home in the first leg, interacting with the estimated probability below 10th and 25th percentile and greater than 75th and 90th percentile.

When both teams have the same ranking, it is assumed that the favourite is the winning team.

DIFLRANK is defined as the difference in the log of the ranking between the favourite team and the non-favourite team.

Finally, Model 5 includes all the proxies of quality differences, and again the results are comparable with those obtained in the previous models.

Thus, from both the data analysis and the econometric approach, we have obtained that second-leg home advantage is present in European football and that the second-leg home advantage is larger in even games than in uneven contests, when the second-leg home advantage almost vanishes due to the impact of differences in teams' ability.

So far, we have analysed second-leg home advantage in the tournaments as a whole, but this advantage could be different in extra time or even in the penalty shoot-out. Figure 4.4 shows second-leg home advantage in the matches that needed extra time to be resolved in different periods of time.

It can be seen that, in the four periods considered, the home teams in the second leg were more likely to proceed to the next round. It is important to note that the number of matches considered was 417 and that, for the whole period, the percentage of contests won by the home team in the second leg was 60 per cent, which is significant using a *t*-test for difference of means.

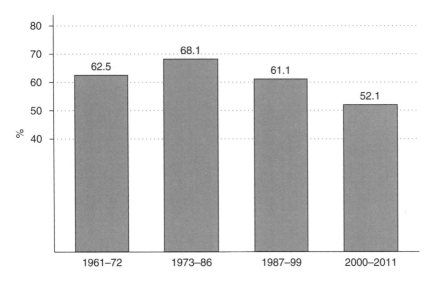

Figure 4.4   *Percentage of victories for second-leg home teams when extra time was needed*

Shoot-outs have been used regularly to try to break the deadlock after extra time. It could be argued that the away teams in the second leg will be less favoured by the crowd, but in addition to that, they could feel less pressure in the penalty shoot-out. Thus, the effect is ambiguous. Figure 4.5 shows that the local teams were more likely to win a penalty shoot-out in the second leg in the four periods analysed. In all, 98 out of 177 contests were won by the local team in the second leg.

In 1986, Real Madrid played against Inter Milan in the semi-finals of the UEFA Cup. The first leg was played in Milan and the result was 3–1 to the Italian team. The second leg was played in the Santiago Bernabéu stadium and the result was 5–1; thus the Spanish team advanced to the final. After this match, Juanito, a Real Madrid player, said to the Italian players a sentence that has become a legend to Real Madrid supporters: '90 minuti en el Bernabéu are molto longo' ('90 minutes in the Bernabéu are very long'). An important element of home advantage for the local team in the second leg is the increased likelihood of recovery from bad results in the first leg. In the subsequent analysis, we analyse this fact. In particular, Table 4.8 shows the relation between the difference in goals in the first match of the round and whether the team that lost in the first leg was able to overcome this result, depending on where the second match was played.

It can be seen that the likelihood of recovery is much higher if the second match is played at home and that good first-leg results for teams playing

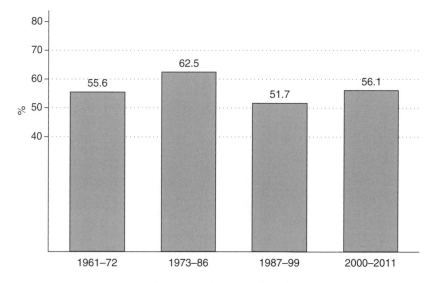

*Figure 4.5   Percentage of victories for second-leg home teams when
penalty shoot-out was used*

Table 4.8   Goal difference in the first leg and recovery

Goal difference	No recovery				Recovery				Total	
	Second leg away		Second leg home		Second leg away		Second leg home			
1 goal	794	(33.7)	806	(34.2)	69	(2.9)	685	(29.1)	2354	(100)
2 goals	438	(32.0)	718	(52.5)	11	(0.8)	200	(14.6)	1367	(100)
3 goals	223	(28.7)	507	(65.3)	1	(0.1)	45	(5.8)	776	(100)
≥ 4 goals	180	(26.0)	509	(73.7)	0	(0.0)	2	(0.3)	691	(100)
Total	1635	(31.5)	2540	(49.0)	81	(1.6)	932	(18.0)	5188	(100)

this match away tend to be definitive (no recoveries), since the second
match is played at home. But in order to get an appropriate measure of
advantage to recover from a bad result in the second leg, it is important to
control for the difference in the teams' ability. Table 4.9 shows the estimates
of two alternative logit models in which the dependent variable takes the
value of one if the team that lost the first leg was able to advance to the
next round of the tournament and zero otherwise.

The results show that once differences in quality are controlled for,
playing the second leg at home is a big advantage in terms of recovery, since
the marginal effect of this dummy is close to 0.3. As expected, there is also

Table 4.9   Logit estimates of recovery

	Coefficient	ME
Constant	−1.727***	
2ND LEG AT HOME	2.405***	0.297
DIFLRANK1960–66	−0.066	−0.008
DIFLRANK1967–99	0.204**	0.025
DIFLRANK2000–2011	0.318***	0.039
GOAL DIFFERENCE	−0.681**	−0.084
GOAL DIFERENCE SQUARED	−0.138*	−0.017
Observations	5188	
Pseudo-R^2	0.232	
Log-likelihood	1.968	

Notes:
ME, marginal effect measured at the means of the other variables.
*, ** and *** indicate significance at the 10 per cent, 5 per cent and 1 per cent levels, respectively.
DIFLRANK is defined as the difference in the log of the ranking between the team that lost in the first leg and the other one.

Table 4.10   Probability of recovery (percentages)

Goal difference	No difference in rank		Big and positive	
	Second leg home	Second leg away	Second leg home	Second leg away
1 goal	47.0	7.0	51.4	8.6
2 goals	21.0	2.0	24.0	2.7
3 goals	7.0	0.7	8.6	0.8
4 goals	2.0	0.2	2.7	0.2
5 goals	0.7	0.1	0.8	0.1

a positive relation between the variable DIFLRANK and the likelihood of a recovery. Moreover, there is a negative exponential relation between goal difference and the likelihood of a recovery. Specifically, assuming that the teams either have the same ranking or the difference is quite big (0.53 in log terms), the probabilities for a recovery are shown in Table 4.10.

As expected, the higher the difference in goals, the lower the probability of a recovery. Moreover, the probability of a recovery at home is much higher than the probability of a recovery away, reinforcing once again the relevance of the home advantage effect. On the other hand, it can be seen that second-leg home advantage changes with the difference in teams' ability. For instance, the probability of a recovery of one goal at home in the second leg is 47.0 per cent if teams have the same ranking, but this probability is 51.4 per cent if there is a large difference between the teams' levels of quality.

6   CONCLUSIONS

In this chapter, second-leg home advantage was analysed. In particular, we studied whether second-leg home advantage is the same regardless of differences in teams' quality. As expected, we found that second-leg home advantage is greater for those tournament rounds between teams of similar ability rather than in uneven matches. When differences in quality are great, playing the second match at home has a smaller influence on the final outcome – that is, strong teams playing against weak teams are less concerned about the order of play, as their quality advantage is enough to more than offset the advantage of playing the second leg at home. We also examined second-leg home advantage linked to the extra time that has to be played when the standard 90 minutes of the second leg end in a tie. In this case, the results hold, given that the host team has a higher probability of victory. Moreover, if the extra time is not enough to break the tie and a penalty shoot-out is required, the host team still has a higher chance of success. Finally, we analysed the probability of recovering from a bad result in the first leg. Results show that recoveries in the second leg are much more likely at home than away.

NOTES

1. An excellent literature review of the home advantage can be found in the Page and Page (2007) article.
2. For simplicity, each season is designated by the year in which it ended, that is, the year 1999 refers to the 1998–99 season.
3. In the case of the UEFA Cup, the inclusion of the group phase occurred in the 2004–05 season.
4. Further details about the points system and the calculation method can be found in http://kassiesa.home.xs4all.nl/bert/uefa/calc.html and http://www.uefa.com/member associations/uefarankings/club/index.html.
5. Giving a total of 433 confrontations characterized by a non-random assignment from 1991–92 to 2010–11.
6. Goodman and Kruskal's gamma is a measure of rank correlation, that is, the similarity of the order of the data when ranked by each of the quantities. It measures the strength of association of the cross-tabulated data when both variables are measured at the ordinal level. It makes no adjustment for either table size or ties. Values range from −1 (100 per cent negative association, or perfect inversion) to +1 (100 per cent positive association, or perfect agreement). A value of zero indicates the absence of association.

REFERENCES

Apesteguia, J. and Palacios-Huerta, I. (2010), 'Psychological pressure in competitive environments: evidence from a randomized natural experiment', *American Economic Review*, **100** (5), 2548–64.

Barnett, V. and Hilditch, S. (1993), 'The effect of an artificial pitch surface on home team performance in football (soccer)', *Journal of the Royal Statistical Society*, **156** (1), 39–50.

DellaVigna, S. (2009), 'Psychology and economics: evidence from the field', *Journal of Economic Literature*, **47** (2), 315–72.

Dohmen, T. (2005), 'Social pressure influences decisions of individuals: evidence from the behavior of football referees', IZA Discussion Paper No. 1595, May.

Dowie, J. (1982), 'Why Spain should win the World Cup', *New Scientist*, **94** (10), 693–95.

Garicano, L., Palacios-Huerta, L. and Prendergast, C. (2005), 'Favoritism under social pressure', *Review of Economics and Statistics*, **87** (2), 208–16.

Krumer, A. (2013), 'Best-of-two contests with psychological effects', *Theory and Decision*, **75** (1), 85–100.

Magnus, J.R. and Klaassen, F.J.G.M. (1999), 'On the advantage of serving first in a tennis set: four years at Wimbledon', *The Statistician (Journal of the Royal Statistical Society, Series D)*, **48** (2), 247–56.

Nevill, A.M., Balmer, N.J. and Williams, A.M. (2002), 'The influence of crowd noise and experience upon refereeing decisions in football', *Psychology of Sport and Exercise*, **3** (4), 261–72.

Page, L. and Page, K. (2007), 'The second leg home advantage: evidence from European football cup competitions', *Journal of Sports Sciences*, **25** (14), 1547–56.

Pollard, R. (2006), 'Worldwide regional variations in home advantage in association football', *Journal of Sports Sciences*, **24** (3), 231–40.

Recht, L.D., Lew, R.A. and Schwartz, W.J. (2003), 'Baseball teams beaten by jetlag', *Nature*, **377** (6550), 583.

Waters, A. and Lovell, G. (2002), 'An examination of the homefield advantage in a professional English soccer team from a psychological standpoint', *Football Studies*, **5**, 46–59.

5. Long-term and short-term causes of insolvency and English football

Stefan Szymanski

1 INTRODUCTION

Insolvency is a common problem among European football clubs. While the Union of European Football Associations' (UEFA's) Financial Fair Play initiative is often discussed in relation to controlling wealthy individuals (the so-called 'sugar daddies') who bankroll expensive teams, an alternative interpretation is that it is intended to reduce the incidence of insolvency. The Union of European Football Associations' 'no overdues payable' rule is a way of imposing a sporting sanction on financial delinquency. UEFA's own research reveals that the problem is significant. In their 2011 survey of the accounts of clubs in the top division of each of its 53 member associations (679) they found that over the past five years net losses had increased from €0.6 billion to €1.7 billion, that 63 per cent of clubs reported an operating loss and 55 per cent reported a net loss overall. Thirty-eight per cent of clubs reported negative net equity, and 16 per cent of club accounts reviewed contained a qualification expressed by the auditors as to financial viability of the company.

Insolvency means the incapacity to meet one's debt obligations (when referring to a person we talk of bankruptcy, but insolvency when talking about a corporation). In this situation the law allows creditors to take action to recover their debts, effectively removing control of the company from the board of directors. Frequently there is bargaining between creditors and the company prior to triggering a formal legal intervention, but here I discuss only formal legal insolvencies, since these are clearly recorded events. Between 1945 and 1982 there were no such formal insolvency events in the four English professional league divisions. Between 1982 and 2010 there were 67 insolvency events involving clubs who were at the time participating in the four divisions.[1]

This chapter does two things. First it discusses the reason for the pattern of insolvency events since 1945, and second it examines some of the underlying factors that might account for individual insolvencies.

2   INSOLVENCY IN ENGLISH LAW

The starting point for thinking about corporate insolvency is limited liability. Most modern businesses are organized as limited liability companies, meaning that those who own the company (the shareholders) are not personally liable for the debts of the company beyond the extent of their existing investment in the company. When an individual is bankrupt, his creditors can seize all of his assets to recover their debts, when a company is insolvent, it is only the assets of the company that can be seized – the owners themselves have no further liability. The problem for creditors is that the shareholders and managers of the company may continue to operate the business while knowing that it will not ultimately be able to repay its debts. Creditors can protect themselves by requiring a mortgage – a specific, valuable asset that can be claimed in the event that repayments are not made. But other creditors cannot always identify a specific asset associated with the debt they are owed – this would be true of a trade creditor who is owed money for services supplied, a bank that has lent money on overdraft or the tax authorities that are owed payments for social security or other taxes.

Until the 1980s English law provided essentially two routes for creditors – either a compulsory winding-up or receivership. Winding-up involved finding a liquidator to sell off assets and pay off as much as possible to the creditors and then close the company down.[2] Receivership was similar, but allowed a specific creditor protected by a mortgage or similar legal charge to appoint an individual to manage the company on their behalf in order to ensure that the monies owed to them were repaid. Otherwise a receiver acted like a liquidator.

By the end of the 1970s this law was deemed to be flawed because it allowed too many viable companies to be shut down just to meet the demands of creditors. This was a particular problem in the deep recessions of the 1970s, when many companies failed. The US changed their system in the 1970s to allow Chapter XI bankruptcy, whereby a company can be protected from its creditors, giving it the time to find a way to pay off as much debt as possible while ensuring that the company could survive. The British government decided to follow suit and the Insolvency Acts of 1985 and 1986 introduced the idea of administration for insolvent companies. The model allowed for an insolvent company to appoint an administrator, a role played by licensed insolvency practitioners, to act as an honest broker between the company and the creditors with a view to the long-term survival of the business where possible.

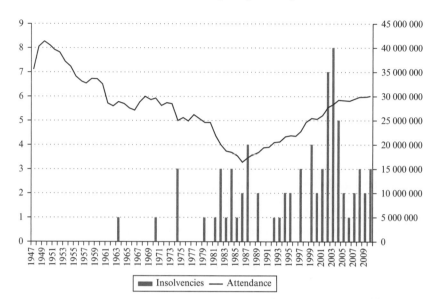

Figure 5.1   The frequency of English football club insolvencies (left hand scale) and total attendance at League football (right-hand scale)

3   THE LONG-TERM TREND OF INSOLVENCIES IN ENGLISH FOOTBALL

The striking feature of insolvencies in English football is that they are a relatively recent phenomenon. As Figure 5.1 shows, prior to the 1980s they were a relatively rare, while the greatest frequency is observed in the last three decades or so. This seems paradoxical, since as Figure 5.1 also shows that insolvency was rare in the era when attendance at English football was declining, and became commonplace in the era of rising attendance. The trend in attendance reflects a significant positive change in the economic fortunes of English football but, seemingly, an adverse trend in financial stability.

The era of declining attendance, between 1949 and 1985, was an era of mounting financial crisis for English clubs. The most important change occurred in 1961, when the maximum wage was abolished. The maximum wage kept wages so low (around the level of a semi-skilled industrial labourer) that clubs at all levels could generate a profit. Moreover, the financial gap between the divisions was small, since even teams in the Fourth Division could afford to hire some of the best players. Abolition of the maximum wage led both to rapid wage inflation and growing inequality between the divisions.

This growth in inequality was observed to generate financial pressure from the late 1960s. A government report, published in 1968, speculated that within a decade several clubs would go to the wall.[3] The perception that only teams in the top two divisions were likely to prosper intensified economic competition with clubs extending their spending on players to their financial limits. This in turn led most clubs to neglect investment in other aspects of the business, such as stadium quality. As leisure spending grew in the post-war boom many people turned away from dilapidated stadiums and found alternative pursuits. The phenomenon of hooliganism became an issue for concern in the 1960s, seemingly perpetrated by young men on low incomes who could afford the still low ticket prices and enjoyed the freedom of open terraces. Alarm about hooliganism certainly kept away many potential fans, but probably as important was concern about safety, as crumbling stadiums put fans at risk.

Yet despite the financial pressure that accompanied the period of decline, insolvencies were rare. The most famous case of the period was Accrington Stanley, which quit the league in 1961 because of looming insolvency and was liquidated a couple of years later. Likewise some other clubs during this era failed after they had left the league, but until the 1980s there were no cases of legal insolvency proceedings while a club was still in the league.

It was the severe UK recession between 1980 and 1982, following which unemployment rose from 5.3 per cent to a peak of 11.9 per cent in 1984, that caused several clubs to go into insolvency proceedings. Bristol City was the first, followed by Hull City, Wolverhampton Wanderers, Bradford City, Charlton Athletic and Derby County. In Bristol City's case the club was saved at the last minute by fans creating a new company to buy up the ground from the liquidator. Under the insolvency law of the time, these clubs were at genuine risk of being closed down, since the appointment of a liquidator limited the opportunity to save the business as a going concern.

The recovery of football club attendance dates from 1986, but in reality the late 1980s were still difficult times for many clubs. The first club to take advantage of the 1985 and 1986 Insolvency Acts was Tranmere Rovers, which went into administration in February 1987. The restructuring of the club's finances was successful and the club emerged from administration within two months. Three other clubs entered administration in the same year and for the next decade there continued to be insolvencies at the rate of one per year. Yet by the 1990s the economic conditions for clubs had much improved. The advent of the Premier League in 1992 generated a large increase in income for the larger clubs, while the government provided substantial funding for stadium refurbishment following the Taylor Report. Greater investment in security at grounds, and arguably rising ticket prices, caused the incidence of hooliganism to decline. Following the recession of 1990–92 the economy recovered strongly, and football was once again considered fashionable. Football clubs were even seen as potential investments by the financial markets.

Yet despite these positive trends insolvencies continued, and became increasingly frequent at the end of the 1990s. The peak of insolvencies occurred in 2002, following the collapse of the ITV Digital, a broadcaster which had contracted to pay significant sums to broadcast lower-division football but collapsed one year into its contract. What became apparent in this period was that clubs were using administration strategically, as a means of writing off debts, only to re-emerge as a stronger competitor in the league. As a result, in 2004 the Football League instituted a points penalty for clubs going into administration. Many fans wonder why insolvent clubs are penalized when they are already facing problems – the answer is that the Football League believes the system is being manipulated strategically.

Thus it appears that a rise in insolvencies in English football over the long term is dependent on the incentives that clubs face. The Insolvency Acts of 1985 and 1986 made it easier for clubs to write off debts while remaining a going concern, and so they have taken advantage of this opportunity. The change in the law seems to have encouraged more risk-taking by clubs in the knowledge that if things go wrong there will be no long-term damage to the club.

4   THE SHORT-TERM CAUSES OF INSOLVENCIES IN ENGLISH FOOTBALL

The causes of football club insolvency are imperfectly understood. Much is written in the media at the time that insolvencies occur about poor management, but these effects are hard to quantify. Moreover, there have been no attempts to examine formally the underlying causes. The typical narrative portrayed in the media might be called the 'Icarus syndrome' – owners and managers have ambitions to rise to a higher position in the league, invest heavily in paying talent but then fail to produce results. As a result income does not match expenditure and there is a collapse into insolvency.

This section reports some preliminary analysis based on financial data from English football club accounts. Financial accounts are available for inspection for a small fee from Companies House,[4] and around 85 per cent of complete financial reports are available going back to 1974.

Figure 5.2 shows the relationship between average league position of clubs that enter insolvency proceedings. '0' represents the season in which

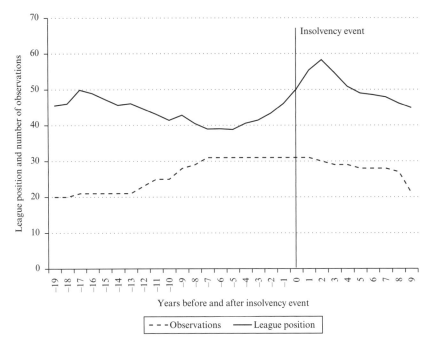

Figure 5.2   League position before and after insolvency event

the event occurred. Some clubs have been through insolvency events more than once, but Figure 5.2 only shows the results for the first insolvency event. Figure 5.2 also shows the number of observations. There are 31 observations for year zero, but the number of observations falls as one moves further back or forward in time. League position is measured between 1 and 92, where for example the top of the Premier League is position 1, the bottom is currently 20, so the top of the Football League Championship is position 21, the bottom is position 44, and so on.[5] Note that in Figure 5.2 a higher number means a lower position in the league.

The data does not appear to confirm the Icarus hypothesis. The key feature, on average, for clubs entering insolvency is that their league position is deteriorating. In the five seasons leading up to the insolvency event the average team falls by around 11 places in the league, and this decline typically involves a relegation to a lower division. In the five years before this (that is, up to a decade before the insolvency event) average league position is relatively within a range of two or three places. It is true that if one goes further back, in the period 10–20 years before insolvency, clubs seem on average to experience an increase in league performance of around ten places, and this might be associated with the Icarus effect, but this seems a

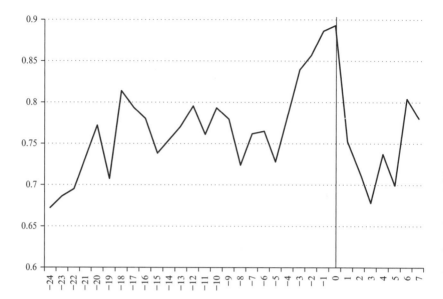

Figure 5.3   *The wage–revenue ratio for clubs before and after insolvency*
            events

much longer time frame for such an effect than one might expect, and it is
worth noting that the sample size also deteriorates over this period.

Equally interesting is the post-insolvency history. The chart suggests
that performance continues to deteriorate for two seasons after the insolvency event, but then recovers sharply, so that league position rises to
pre-insolvency levels within five seasons and tends to continue upward
thereafter (although, again, the sample size diminishes quite rapidly seven
or eight years after the insolvency event). This suggests that there is some
regression to the mean. One interpretation of the data is that insolvency
results from a series of poor league performances. These negative shocks
might be considered bad luck which triggers insolvency but, after the
insolvency event, performance returns to its long-term trend.

Support for this conjecture is provided by Figure 5.3 which illustrates
the wage to revenue ratio of clubs before and after the insolvency event.

Again the data suggests a sharp rise in the wage to revenue ratio in the
five years leading up to the insolvency event but a relatively stable ratio in
the decade before that. This is consistent with the notion that as league
performance deteriorates revenues also deteriorate but clubs find it hard
to keep spending in line with revenues. This is likely to be the case since
players have contracts which can be expensive to break, and while it is
possible to sell players on the market, the perception that a club may be

in distress often makes it difficult to obtain the best possible price. There is little evidence here of unrealistic spending in the decade before the ratio starts to rise, which is also inconsistent with the Icarus hypothesis.

Finally, Figure 5.3 also suggests that exiting from administration produces a rapid improvement in the wage revenue ratio. It is to be expected that in a process such as administration, wages should be cut to match the spending power of the club, and while this may cause a continuing deterioration in league position, as we observed in the Figure 5.2, once the club's finances have stabilized it appears feasible to improve league performance at the same time as sustaining a viable wage policy.

5   CONCLUSIONS

This chapter has presented some preliminary results concerning the insolvency of English football clubs. It highlights two important issues. First, taking the long term into consideration, it shows that insolvency has been a relatively recent phenomenon, and has accompanied a period in which the fortunes of English football have recovered. By contrast in the long period of decline between 1950 and 1985 insolvencies were relatively rare. This apparent paradox may be explained by changes in English insolvency law, especially the Insolvency Acts of 1985 and 1986 which enabled businesses to negotiate write-offs of debts of the company without jeopardizing their long term survival. English football clubs appear to have been particularly adept at this procedure, and despite frequent insolvencies, all the clubs that play in the top four English divisions have survived.

The second contribution of this chapter has been to examine some common trends of clubs entering into insolvency proceedings. The data suggests that clubs entering insolvency are not those that have recently overspent in the attempt to rise up the leagues, a narrative which is frequently presented in the media, but clubs that have dropped suddenly down the league. This appears to be confirmed by the data on wage to revenue ratios, which shows that the ratio deteriorates in line with the fall in league position. Moreover, the evidence of a rebound after the insolvency events could be interpreted that insolvencies are generally caused by random negative shocks which drive clubs away from the long term-performance levels, and that after insolvency there is regression back to the mean.

NOTES

1. There are further cases where clubs have become insolvent after exiting the fourth tier, but those cases are not considered here. For a list of all known insolvencies in English football see Beech at: http://footballmanagement.wordpress.com/no-of-clubs/ (accessed 19 July 2013).
2. Shareholders could also choose to enter a voluntary liquidation when they decided they no longer wanted the company to continue.
3. Chester, N. (1968), *Report of the Committee on Football*, London: HMSO.
4. http://wck2.companieshouse.gov.uk//wcframe?name=accessCompanyInfo (accessed 24 July 2013).
5. The drop off in post-insolvency observations reflects the fact that many insolvencies are recent. The drop off in pre-insolvency observations arises because data only runs as far back as 1974.

PART II

Competition: Competitive Balance, Rewards
and Outcome

6. The optimal competitive balance in a sports league?

Stefan Késenne

1 INTRODUCTION

A well-known peculiarity of the industry of professional team sports is the simple fact that at least two firms (that is, two teams) are needed to produce and supply the final product which is a game or the championship. Moreover, a minimum degree of uncertainty of outcome in the game or the championship is necessary. If not, games and championship can become boring, and public interest and attendance fade (see Rottenberg, 1956; Neale, 1964). However, the empirical evidence is not convincing regarding the positive impact of the competitive balance in a league on spectator interest (see Borland and Macdonald 2003; Szymanski, 2003; Szymanski and Leach, 2005). It has been shown that a perfect competitive balance, that is, every team has an equal chance of winning, is not optimal (see Rascher 1997; Rascher and Solmes, 2007). The empirical evidence shows that supporters prefer a winning home team, but they also want to watch a close competition. If there is no competition, and the best team wins the championship by a landslide, things can get boring. So, the optimal winning percentage of a team should be somewhere between 0.5 and 1. The question is if the welfare optimal competitive balance can somehow be derived, and what are the most important parameters, affecting the optimal competitive balance.

In this short chapter, section 2 considers only the interests of the team and the league, with total league revenue as the optimality criterion. In section 3, we try to derive theoretically what the optimal competitive balance in a league should be from a welfare economic point of view, concentrating on the preferences of the spectators and the parameters that can affect this optimum.

2   THE OPTIMUM LEAGUE REVENUE AND THE NASH EQUILIBRIUM

Starting from the following concave club revenue functions in a simple two-team league, where x is the large-market club and y is the small-market club ($m_x > m_y$):

$$R_x = R(m_x, w_x) \quad \text{with} \quad w_x = \frac{t_x}{t_x + t_y}$$

$$R_y = R(m_y, w_y) \quad \text{with} \quad w_y = \frac{t_y}{t_x + t_y} \tag{6.1}$$

In this model, the winning percentages are determined by the relative talents (t) of the teams.

Assuming profit maximization, the non-cooperative Nash equilibrium with a given unit cost of talent (c) is given by the reaction functions:

$$\frac{\partial R_x}{\partial w_x}\frac{\partial w_x}{\partial t_x} = c = \frac{\partial R_y}{\partial w_y}\frac{\partial w_y}{\partial t_y} \Rightarrow \frac{\partial R_x}{\partial w_x}t_y = \frac{\partial R_y}{\partial w_y}t_x$$

$$\text{So:} \quad \frac{t_x}{t_y} = \frac{\dfrac{\partial R_x}{\partial w_x}}{\dfrac{\partial R_y}{\partial w_y}} \quad \text{and if } t_x > t_y \frac{\partial R_x}{\partial w_x} > \frac{\partial R_y}{\partial w_y} \tag{6.2}$$

Because the optimum league revenue is only reached if $\frac{\partial R_x}{\partial w_x} = \frac{\partial R_y}{\partial w_y}$, it follows from (6.2) that the Nash equilibrium is not efficient. Total league revenue can be increased by making the competition more unbalanced. Indeed, if one starts from the following well-behaved[1] marginal revenue functions:

$$\frac{\partial R_i}{\partial w_i} = m_i - m_i w_i \tag{6.3}$$

It can be derived that the Nash equilibrium is: $\frac{w_x}{w_y} = \sqrt{\frac{m_x}{m_y}}$ which is more equal than the optimal competitive balance $\frac{w_x}{w_y} = \frac{m_x}{m_y}$, which maximizes total league revenue.

Under the win-maximization assumption, the Nash equilibrium results in an even more unequal competitive balance: $\frac{w_x}{w_y} = \frac{m_x - 0{,}5m_y}{m_y - 0{,}5m_x} > \frac{m_x}{m_y}$.

3   THE WELFARE ECONOMIC APPROACH

In this section we start from the preferences of the supporters of both teams, who want their home team to win, as well as from the interests of the more neutral spectators, who want the watch a close competition. We assume here that the number of more neutral supporters has increased by the rise of televised sports.

In section 3.1, we first derive the optimal winning percentage for the supporters of one particular team. By using a simple welfare function in section 3.2, we then try to derive the social optimum. Section 4 concludes.

3.1 The Optimal Winning Percentage of a Team

Among the most important variables, affecting attendance, are the size of the market and the winning percentage of the team, apart from the absolute quality of the league and the ticket price which are exogenously determined in this analysis. Teams with a high drawing potential, in large markets or densely populated areas, attract more spectators than teams with a limited drawing potential in small towns. But the empirical research also shows that spectators prefer a winning home team, and that they turn away from a losing home team. However, if some degree of uncertainty of outcome is necessary in sports, the question is if an optimal competitive balance can be derived, taking into account the interest of all supporters and spectators.

In order to analyse this, we again start from a simplified two-team league with one large-market team x and one small-market team y, so: $m_x > m_y$. In this case, the terms 'uncertainty of outcome' and 'competitive balance' can be used interchangeably. The utility function of the supporters of both teams, with a given market size, depends on the team's winning percentage (w) and on the uncertainty of outcome (uo) in the league which is measured in its most simple way by:

$$uo = w_x w_y \tag{6.4}$$

Indeed, this indicator is zero if $w_i = 0$ and if $w_i = 1$, and it reaches its highest value for $w_i = 0.5$. Assuming that the utility function of the supporters of a team can be approached by the weighted product of the winning percentage and the uncertainty of outcome, this can be written for a two-team league as:

$$U_x = w_x^{1-\alpha} uo^\alpha = w_x w_y^\alpha \text{ with } 0 \leq \alpha \leq 1 \tag{6.5}$$

$$U_y = w_y^{1-\beta} uo^\beta = w_y w_x^\beta \text{ with } 0 \leq \beta \leq 1$$

The weights α and β are assumed to be different in the two teams, because it is reasonable to assume that the supporters of a strong large-market team value winning and competitive balance differently compared with the supporters of a weak small-market team.

Based on these utility functions, one can derive the optimal winning percentage for both teams from the first-order condition $\frac{\partial U_i}{\partial w_i} = 0$ as:

$$\frac{\partial U_x}{\partial w_x} = w_y^\alpha - \alpha w_x w_y^{\alpha-1} = 0$$

$$\frac{\partial U_y}{\partial w_y} = w_x^\beta - \beta w_y w_x^{\beta-1} = 0 \qquad (6.6)$$

which, after some rearrangements, can be written as:

$$w_y^{\alpha-1}(w_y - \alpha w_x) = 0$$

$$w_x^{\beta-1}(w_x - \beta w_y) = 0 \qquad (6.7)$$

Because $w_y^{\alpha-1}$ *and* $w_x^{\beta-1}$ are both different from zero, we can derive that the optimal competitive balance for the supporters of both teams are:

$$w_x/w_y = 1/\alpha$$

$$w_y/w_x = 1/\beta \qquad (6.8)$$

So, if $\alpha = \beta = 0.5$, the optimal winning percentage the supporters prefer for their home team can be found as:

$$\frac{w_x}{w_y} = 2 \text{ or } w_x^* = 2/3 = 0.67$$

$$\frac{w_y}{w_x} = 2 \text{ or } w_y^* = 2/3 = 0.67 \qquad (6.9)$$

The more the supporters value winning (that is, the smaller is α and β), the higher the optimal winning percentage of their home team will be. It is obvious that both teams prefer a winning percentage that is larger than 0.5, but this is impossible because the sum of the winning percentages in a 2-team league has to equal unity.

3.2 The Welfare Optimum

In order to find the optimal competitive balance from a welfare economic point of view, we need to specify a welfare function which could be the weighted product of the utilities of the supporters of the large- and small-market team:

$$W = U_x^{m_x} U_y^{m_y} U_n^{m_n} = U_x^m U_y U_n^n \tag{6.10}$$

where the weight m is the ratio of the market sizes because a large-market team has more supporters than a small-market team, so $m = \frac{m_x}{m_y} > 1$. We also add a third utility function of the neutral (television) spectators which is:

$$U_n = uo = w_x w_y \tag{6.11}$$

Assuming that the more neutral television spectators are not supporters of one of the teams, the winning percentages of the teams do not matter to them. So, the utility of the neutral supporters is only determined by the uncertainty of outcome, and its weight in the welfare function is given by the parameter n, which equals to ratio of the number of neutral (television) spectators m_n and the number of supporters of the small-market team (m_y).

So, we can derive that:

$$W = U_x^m U_y U_n^n = (w_x w_y^\alpha)^m (w_y w_x^\beta) (w_x w_y)^n = w_x^{m+\beta+n} w_y^{\alpha m+n+1} \tag{6.12}$$

The first order condition for the optimal winning percentage of the large-market team x can be found as:

$$\frac{\partial W}{\partial w_x} = (m + \beta + \gamma) w_x^{m+\beta+n-1} w_y^{\alpha m+n+1}$$

$$- (\alpha m + \gamma + 1) w_y^{\alpha m+n} w_x^{m+\beta+n} = 0 \tag{6.13}$$

which, after some rearrangements, can be written as:

$$w_y^{\alpha m+n} w_x^{m+\beta+n-1} [(m + \beta + n) w_y$$

$$- (\alpha m + n + 1) w_x] = 0 \tag{6.14}$$

Because the product before the parentheses is non-zero, the expression between the parentheses has to equal zero. So, we can find that the optimal competitive balance is:

$$\frac{w_x}{w_y} = \frac{m + \beta + n}{\alpha m + 1 + n} \tag{6.15}$$

Based on these simple utility and welfare functions, we can derive that the optimal competitive balance depends on the preferences of the supporters of the large- and the small-market team, on the relative size of the markets of the two clubs, and on the number of neutral spectators or the importance of televised sport.

We can also derive from (6.15) that:

$$\frac{\partial(w_x/w_y)}{\partial m} > 0 \quad \frac{\partial(w_x/w_y)}{\partial \alpha} < 0 \quad \frac{\partial(w_x/w_y)}{\partial \beta} > 0 \tag{6.16}$$

The larger the difference in market size, the more unequal the competitive balance should be. The more the large-team supporters value the uncertainty of outcome, the more equal the competitive balance should be. The more the small-team supporters value uncertainty of outcome, the more unequal the competitive should be. These findings can hardly be called unexpected.

Also, it does not come as a surprise that if $m = 1$ and $\alpha = \beta$, for whatever value of n, that is, the relative size of the group of neutral supporters, we find that both teams should have the same winning percentage $(\frac{w_x}{w_y} = 1)$.

More interesting is the result that even a very large difference in market size or drawing potential does not justify a very unbalanced competition or a strong large-team dominance in the league. Indeed:

$$\lim_{m\to\infty} \frac{w_x}{w_y} = \lim_{m\to\infty} \frac{m + \beta + n}{\alpha m + 1 + n} = 1/\alpha. \tag{6.17}$$

So, if $\alpha = 0.5$, that is: the supporters of the large-market team value winning and uncertainty of outcome equally, whatever the difference between the market sizes of the teams in a league, and whatever the preferences of the small-market team supporters, the optimal competitive balance should always stay below 2, which implies that on no account should the optimal winning percentage of a large-market team be larger than $w_x = 0.67$.

Only if the supporters of the large-market team show a strong preference for winning, relative to uncertainty of outcome, can the optimal competition be very unbalanced.

As can be illustrated by simulation results in Table 6.1, large differences in preferences for winning between the supporters of two teams with the same market size do not strongly affect the optimal competitive balance, The winning percentage of the large-market team should again not be larger than $w_x = 0.67$.

One can also derive from (6.12) that:

$$\frac{\partial(w_x/w_y)}{\partial n} = \frac{(\alpha m + 1 + n) - (m + \beta + n)}{(\alpha m + 1 + n)^2} < 0 \text{ for } w_x > w_y \tag{6.18}$$

Table 6.1   Optimal values for w_x for $n = 0$ (and $n = 100$)

α/β	$m = m_x / m_y$	1	2	10	50	100	
						$n = 0$	$n = 100$
0.1/0.9		0.63	0.70	0.84	0.89	0.99	0.64
0.5/0.5		0.50	0.55	0.63	0.65	0.66	0.57
0.9/0.1		0.36	0.42	0.50	0.51	0.52	0.51

It follows that the larger the group of more neutral television spectators becomes, the more balanced the competition should be from a welfare economic perspective.

Finally, if we combine the interests of the teams in section 2 and the interests of the spectators in section 3, and try to find a compromise between the two preferred competitive balances, we can derive that for most sensible values of the parameters it holds that:

$$\frac{m + \beta + n}{\alpha m + 1 + n} < m = \frac{m_x}{m_y} \qquad (6.19)$$

which means that the optimum competitive balance should be more equal than the ratio of the market sizes.

4   CONCLUSION

In this short chapter, we have shown that the welfare optimal competitive balance in a league is not only affected by the relative size of the markets of the teams and the preferences of the supporters of the teams, but also by the number of more neutral spectators, watching the games on television. We conclude from the results that only the unique combination of large differences in market size, a strong preference for winning by the large-market supporters and a low number of neutral spectators result in a very unequal optimal competitive balance.

We did not investigate to what extent these results are robust or sensitive to alternative specifications of preferences and welfare function. The multiplicative form of the welfare function assumes that the utilities of the different groups of spectators are complements, which affects the optimal degree of competitive imbalance. Also, we did not take into consideration explicitly the interests of the players, who are important stakeholders as well.

The more important televised sport and broadcast rights become, the more balanced the competition should be. Moreover, the optimum competitive balance should be more equal than the ratio of the market sizes.

We conclude from this theoretical approach that the optimal winning percentage of the dominant team should be between 0.5 and 0.67, and closer to 0.5 depending on the relative size of the growing group of neutral television spectators, unless the supporters of the large-market team have a much stronger taste for winning than the supporters of the small-market team.

NOTE

1. We call these revenue functions well-behaved because they are downward sloping in winning percentage and because it holds that the marginal revenue of winning approaches zero if the winning percentage approaches 100 per cent.

REFERENCES

Borland, J. and R. Macdonald (2003), 'Demand for sport', *Oxford Review of Economic Policy*, **19** (4), 478–503.
Neale, W. (1964), 'The peculiar economics of professional sports', *Quarterly Journal of Economics*, **78** (1), 1–14.
Rascher, D. (1997), 'A model of a professional sports league', in W. Hendricks (ed.), *Advances in the Economics of Sport*, vol. 2, Greenwich and London: JAI Press, pp. 27–76.
Rascher, D. and J.P.G. Solmes (2007), 'Do fans want close contests? A test of the uncertainty of outcome hypothesis in the National Basketball Association', *International Journal of Sport Finance*, **2** (3), 130–41.
Rottenberg, S. (1956), 'The baseball players' labor market', *Journal of Political Economy*, **64** (3), 242–58.
Szymanski, S. (2003), 'The economic design of sporting contests', *Journal of Economic Literature*, **41** (4), 1137–87.
Szymanski, S. and S. Leach (2005), 'Tilting the playing field: why a sports league planner would choose less, not more, competitive balance?', working paper, Tanaka Business School, Imperial College, London.

7. Live football demand

Ruud Koning[1] and Jeroen Achterhof

1 INTRODUCTION

Live attendance at football games in the Netherlands is higher than attendance at any other sport. In this chapter we study the determinants of live attendance at football games. In particular, we focus on the effect of a variable that measures match significance. A match between two teams can be very contentious, independent of the relevance of the match for the top of the final ranking. However, a particular match may be highly significant for one of the teams if that team could, say, win the title if it were to win that particular game. Both variables are related to competitive balance, a feature of sports that is assumed to yield utility to fans. In fact, the relevance of maintaining some level of balance in competition has been underlined recently in a report by the European Commission, see KEA Economics Affairs and Centre de Droit et Economie du Sport (2013). In our empirical analysis, we take the maximum size of live attendance (due to the maximum capacity of the stadium) into account, and estimate marginal effects of the variables in a tobit model. To assess whether determinants of live attendance vary by level, we estimate the same specification both for the highest level of football in the Netherlands (Eredivisie) and for the second-tier level (Jupiler League).

2 FOOTBALL DEMAND AND MATCH SIGNIFICANCE

In this section we give a short review of earlier results, but only as far as relevant to our particular case. Excellent reviews on the determinants of attendance of sports matches are available in Downward et al. (2009) and Dobson and Goddard (2011). The latter reference focuses on football in particular.

One of the key characteristics of sports is the externality that one needs an opponent to produce the contest. Even though fans of one particular team may prefer that their team wins all the time, fans of other teams (and football fans not affiliated to any particular team) will lose interest in that case. As a consequence, maintaining a certain level of competitive balance in a league has been one of the main goals by the league organization for a long time. In fact, Fort (2006) argues that four scarce goods are produced in a sporting contest, and fans (consumers) have a preference over these scarce goods. The goods are:

1. Athletic prowess: football players possess technical and tactical skills that the average fan does not possess.
2. Quality of teams and competition: fans enjoy a competitive league, both in an absolute sense (Champion League matches usually attract a larger audience than matches in the Europa League), and in a relative sense (a closely contended competition is better appreciated than one where one team wins all its games).
3. Commonality: sports provides a bond between people, it is a common reference.
4. Winning: fans like to associate themselves with winning teams.

These dimensions, together with income, the relative price of attendance, and population density determine the demand for sports contests in a particular locality. In a slightly different setting, Dobson and Goddard (2011, p. 322) distinguish between four factors determining demand: short-term team loyalty, team performance, admission price, and entertainment. The determinants we use below can all be put under these headings.

In some empirical analyses, fixed effects (or home dummies if only one season is considered) are included to accommodate for all time-invariant variation that may be correlated with the other explanatory variables. An early example of this approach is Dobson and Goddard (1992). Examples of such time-invariant variables are local per capita income, local unemployment, demographic composition of the fan base. Even though we have a short panel (three seasons), it seems reasonable to consider variables that could change over time as being constant. An important variable that we also assume to be captured by a fixed effect is the price level of the tickets. Obviously, one could model the fixed effects using these covariates, but even then, it seems that data on potentially important determinants may not be available, so in the end inclusion of fixed effects is needed.

We focus on the effect of match significance on attendance. This is different from uncertainty of outcome, the variable that is usually included in attendance equations: the outcome of a particular match may be very uncertain, but that particular match may not have any material effect on the final ranking. Final ranking itself has been included as a determinant of attendance of individual matches during the season (Dobson and

Goddard, 1995; Simmons, 1996; Szymanski and Smith, 1997), but then it is interpreted as a measure of the quality of the teams. We measure the effect of the outcome of a particular match on the final ranking, and hypothesize that attendance increases if a team stands to gain in the final ranking, should it win the next game. Note that this approach is different from the well-known approach of Jennett (1984) who essentially assumes the number of points needed for a championship to be known. In the approach sketched below, the number of points needed to win the title is an endogenous outcome of the season, and that number may vary week by week, depending on results so far and the remaining schedule of play.

Our measure of significance of a match as a determinant of attendance follows Bojke (2007). His approach has been slightly adapted in Koning (2007), and we follow that approach here. Consider a game played at (calendar) time s. Assuming fans have a probability distribution over all possible outcomes of the games that remain to be played in the season, they can calculate the probability distribution of the end-of-season ranking. This probability distribution of the end-of-season ranking is conditional on all information available at time s, I_s. Once this probability distribution is known, one can also calculate the probability distribution of functions of this ranking. It is difficult to measure or estimate the relevant probability distribution of all remaining results, that is, of all matches played between time s and the end of the season. Bojke (2007) uses betting odds that are observed shortly before each match to estimate the probability distribution of the outcome of that match. A disadvantage of that approach is that odds at, say, $s + 3$ are based on information available at that moment, and not on information available at s only. Here, we use the approach in Koning (2007). At each moment s in the season, we estimate an ordered probit rating model (Koning, 2000) using results of the last 306 games played before s. The estimated parameters of the rating model are then used to calculate the probability distribution of outcomes of each match that remains to be played. These probabilities reflect information available at s only. Using the ranking at s, and integrating with respect to all probability distributions of outcome, one obtains the probability distribution of the final ranking, estimated at time s. This approach allows us to calculate relevance of a game as well: what is the probability distribution of ranking if the next match is won by the home team, and what is it when the next match is won by the away team?

This approach is perhaps best illustrated by considering the last weekend of the 2010–11 season in the Eredivisie. All games were played simultaneously on Sunday 15 May 2011. The top of the ranking before the start of the games is given in Table 7.1. The most relevant game on that last day was Ajax–Twente. According to the rating model, the

Table 7.1   Ranking 15 May 2011, Eredivisie

	P	W	D	L	Points	Programme
1. Twente	33	21	8	4	71	Ajax–Twente
2. Ajax	33	21	7	5	70	Groningen–PSV
3. PSV	33	20	8	5	68	...

Table 7.2   Probability distribution of final ranking 15 May 2011, Eredivisie

	1	2	3
Twente	0.45	0.41	0.14
Ajax	0.55	0.33	0.12
PSV	0	0.26	0.74

probability distribution of the outcomes of Ajax–Twente is 0.55/0.27/0.18 (home win/draw/away win), and that of Groningen–PSV is 0.45/0.29/0.26. Using these probabilities, and the ranking of Table 7.1, the probability distribution of the final ranking for each team is easily calculated assuming independence of results between matches. The distribution is given in Table 7.2, with any ties between the teams determined by the superior goal difference of PSV.

The significance of the match Ajax–Twente can be assessed by making tables similar to Table 7.2 conditional on a home win and conditional on an away win. The effect of a home win is then measured by the change in title probability, or the change in expected ranking. In the example, Ajax wins the title with probability 1 if it wins, and with probability 0 if it does not win, so the game Ajax–Twente is very significant. Significance of this match is an extreme case, but in general this approach tends to quantify the importance of matches. Moreover, other characteristics can be measured, for example, the probability that the away team will win the title. The calculations above are simple because only one round was left to play, in our empirical analysis we calculate the probability distribution of the final ranking for every match in the season, and we calculate the conditional (on home win or away win) probability distributions as well. Because the relation between outcomes and final ranking is not one to one, we estimate the probability distribution of the end-of-season ranking by simulation.

3 EMPIRICAL RESULTS

The dependent variable in our analysis is the occupancy rate of a particular match: the number of people who attend the match in the stadium (live attendance) divided by the maximum capacity of the stadium. We choose this measure over live attendance by itself because in that case we would have to account for possible endogeneity of the truncation point, and the truncation point would vary between teams. By focusing on the occupancy rate, all observations are truncated at 1 (or a number slightly less than 1, say 0.97), and this truncation point does not vary between teams. For this reason, the model that we estimate is a tobit model, with truncation at 1. To introduce notation, consider a match between teams i (home team) and j (away team) in season t ($t = 2009$–10, 2010–11, 2011–12).

The latent occupancy rate is y_{ijt}^*, given by:

$$y_{ijt}^* = \alpha_i + \beta' x_{ijt} + \varepsilon_{ijt} \qquad (7.1)$$

and the observed occupancy rate y_{ijt} is:

$$y_{ijt} = \begin{cases} y_{ijt}^* & \text{if } y_{ijt}^* < 1, \\ 1 & \text{if } y_{ijt}^* \geq 1. \end{cases} \qquad (7.2)$$

In equation (7.1), α_i is a fixed home team effect that reflects all variables that are constant between matches and seasons. The variables in x_{ijt} are variables specific to the particular match (for example, rankings at the moment the match is played), or to the season. Finally, ϵ_{ijt} is an error term that is assumed to follow a normal distribution, and is assumed to be independent between all matches. Variance of this error term is σ^2.

3.1 Data and Variables

Data on attendance and capacity in the seasons 2009–10, 2010–11 and 2011–12 were obtained from a website (www.fcupdate.nl), and checked against other sources (Voetbal International, 2010, 2011, 2012). Capacity of all stadiums considered was constant during these three seasons, with the exception of Twente; their stadium was significantly expanded in the summer of 2011. Because the reconstruction was not finished when the 2011–12 season started, we removed the first four home games of Twente of that season. Box plots of attendance are given in Figures 7.1 (Eredivisie) and 7.2 (Jupiler League). Some teams in the Eredivisie show little variation in attendance, which suggests that the capacity constraint will be binding in many cases. If the capacity constraint is binding for all observations, the

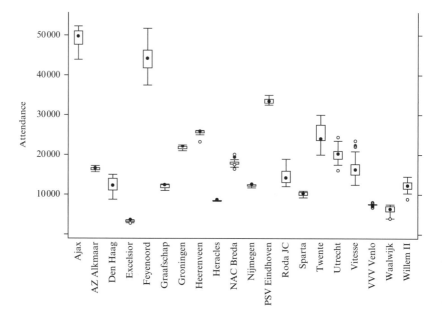

*Figure 7.1   Box-whisker plots of attendance by team, 2009–10 to 2011–12
           (Eredivisie)*

team fixed effect α_i in equation (7.1) is not identified. For this reason, we removed teams from our analysis that showed consistently very high occupancy rates: Nijmegen, Heerenveen, and Heracles. For each of these teams, the occupancy rate exceeded 97.5 per cent in three out of four matches. The issue of all too frequent sell-outs is not relevant in the Jupiler League, as is evident from Figure 7.2.

A dummy variable indicates whether or not a match is a derby. Usually, a derby would be a match between two teams that are close to each other geographically, but since the density of teams varies by region, we use a list of derby matches that is partly based on geographic proximity, and partly on the number of competing teams nearby. A derby is expected to attract a higher audience because of fan interest and relatively small travel costs for fans of the away team to attend the match.

To measure the expected quality of the match, we calculated the position of the home team and the position of the away team for each match. Weather conditions (obtained from www.weerstatistieken.nl) may induce less-committed fans not to attend a game. Weather conditions will be less important for attendance of home games of Ajax and Vitesse, since their stadiums have a roof. Weather conditions are measured by the temperature.

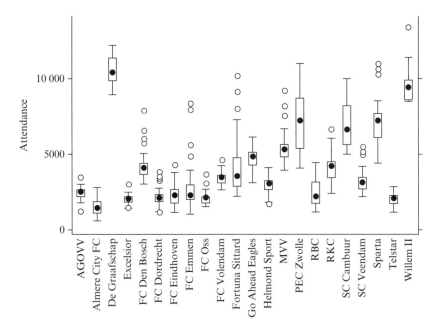

Figure 7.2 Box-whisker plots of attendance by team, 2009–10 to 2011–12 (Jupiler League)

One type of variable that is hard to measure, but possibly a determinant of live attendance, is form of the home team and the away team. If a team is on a winning streak, it may attract additional spectators. Many different variables have been proposed to measure form, for example, the moving average of the number of goals scored, the moving average of the number of points obtained, return on bets on the team during the last few matches. To avoid discussion on specific measures, we calculated eight different indicators of form (six in the case of the Jupiler League), both for the home team and the away team. These measures were condensed into a single measure using principal components analysis. The single measure can be interpreted as a weighted average of the indicators, and captures 60 per cent of the total variance of all indicators. Details are in Appendix 7A.1.

Finally, using the approach discussed in section 2, we calculated the effect of the outcome of a match on the expected ranking for both the home team and the away team. Furthermore, since live attendance is mainly support of the home team, we calculated the increase in title probability should the home team win. Potential of the away team is measured by a dummy to indicate they are a serious title contestant (that is, their probability of winning the title at the moment of the match exceeds 0.10).

3.2 Results

In Table 7.3 we present point estimates of the slope coefficients of tobit model (7.1).[2] Estimates of the fixed effects α_i are given in Appendix 7A.2. In the results of the baseline model without match significance variables, the dummy for a derby is significantly larger than 0: occupancy is higher by 3.4 per cent if a match is a derby. Here and in the sequel we interpret the marginal effects under the assumption that the capacity constraint is not binding. Furthermore, recent performance as measured by our form constructs have a positive effect on occupancy: if the home team or the away team have been doing well in recent games, occupancy is higher. Since the scale of our form constructs is not easily interpretable, the magnitude of the effects is assessed as follows. If form of the home team (form.H) increases from its first sample quartile to its third sample quartile (that is, it covers the middle 50 per cent of the observed values in the sample), occupancy is expected to increase by 1.35 per cent.

A similar calculation for form of the away team gives an increase in the occupancy rate of 2.7 per cent.

Some variables are not significant: the effects of home team position and away team position are not significantly different from 0. Also, the temperature does not determine the occupancy rate in the Eredivisie, and there are no systematic shifts in the occupancy rates between seasons.

In Table 7.4 we extend the specification by including the variables for match significance. The effects discussed above still hold. We include the expected improvement in final ranking of the home team if they were to

Table 7.3   Estimation results model 1, Eredivisie (estimated fixed effects in Appendix 7A.2)

	Estimate	sd	z	p
derby	3.427	1.176	2.915	0.004
ht.pos	−0.008	0.055	−0.140	0.888
at.pos	0.097	0.052	1.856	0.063
temperature	−0.063	0.045	−1.400	0.162
season2010–2011	−0.760	0.680	−1.118	0.264
season2011–2012	−0.616	0.679	−0.907	0.364
form.H	0.623	0.211	2.957	0.003
form.A	1.037	0.166	6.250	0.000
σ	7.051	0.202	34.873	0.000

Table 7.4   Estimation results model 2, Eredivisie, (estimated fixed effects in Appendix 7A.2)

	Estimate	sd	z	p
derby	3.194	1.160	2.755	0.006
ht.pos	0.006	0.055	0.100	0.920
at.pos	0.083	0.052	1.615	0.106
temperature	−0.064	0.045	−1.424	0.155
season2010–2011	−0.852	0.678	−1.256	0.209
season2011–2012	−0.773	0.673	−1.149	0.251
form.H	0.578	0.209	2.764	0.006
form.A	0.687	0.178	3.857	0.000
ΔR_H	−0.295	0.839	−0.351	0.725
ΔR_A	−0.104	0.723	−0.144	0.886
$\Delta \Pr(R_H = 1)$	3.370	4.648	0.725	0.468
$I_{\{\Pr(RA = 1) \geq 0.10\}}$	4.226	0.926	4.563	0.000
σ	6.951	0.199	34.935	0.000

win that game (ΔR_H) and a similar measure for the away team (ΔR_A). These two variables are not significant. Also, occupancy rates do not increase significantly with the probability that a home win would increase the probability of the home team to win the title ($\Delta \Pr(R_H = 1)$). However, the occupancy rate is significantly increased by 4.2 per cent if the away team is a serious contestant for the title. Home fans may want to see a possible champion, and away fans will attend away games to support their team to the title.

All variables are jointly significantly different from 0, as is obtained from a likelihood ratio test ($p = 0$). The estimate of the residual standard deviation in the model with only fixed effects is 7.42, which is reduced to 7.05 by including the covariates in Table 7.3. The fixed effects themselves vary significantly between teams (again, $p = 0$ by a likelihood ratio test). These effects capture variables that are team specific, and do not vary over time. Since our time series is very short, many variables that vary over time in the long run can be treated as (almost) constant in our sample. Examples are per capita income in the city of the team, drawing power and artificial turf. The effect of some of these variables could be identified using between-team variation in occupancy rates, but considering the limited number of teams in our dataset, we do not attempt to do so.

We summarize: occupancy rates in Eredivisie are determined by the derby effect, recent performance of both the home and away teams, and the prospect of the away team to win the title.

Table 7.5   Estimation results model 1, Jupiler League (estimated fixed effects in Appendix 7A.2)

	estimate	sd	z	p
derby	11.709	1.869	6.264	0.000
ht.pos	−0.022	0.080	−0.270	0.787
at.pos	0.001	0.076	0.007	0.994
temperature	0.465	0.076	6.104	0.000
season2010–2011	−1.261	1.038	−1.215	0.224
season2011–2012	−0.103	1.044	−0.099	0.921
form.H	2.250	0.333	6.751	0.000
form.A	1.223	0.301	4.067	0.000
σ	12.075	0.285	42.302	0.000

We estimate similar models for the Jupiler League. As is clear from our description of occupancy rates in that league above, the capacity constraint is hardly ever binding. Hence, we could estimate the model using least squares, but for ease of comparison, we use the same estimation procedure as in the case of the Eredivisie.

Baseline estimation results are in Table 7.5, fixed effects are given in Appendix 7A.2. Again, we find a strong, positive derby effect. Form of both the home team and the away team have a significant, positive effect on the occupancy rate. The rate is increased by 4.4 per cent and 2.2 per cent respectively, if form increases from its first quartile to its third quartile in the sample distribution. Interestingly, weather conditions have a significant, positive effect as well, just as reported for Spain by García and Rodríguez (2002).

Also in this case the other variables from the fixed effects are jointly significant: $p = 0$ and the standard deviation of the error term is reduced from 12.8 to 12.1. The fixed effects themselves vary significantly between teams ($p = 0$).

Estimation results with the match significance variables included are given in Table 7.6. Possible improvement in ranking of the away team increases the occupancy rate. Unlike in the case of the Eredivisie, teams in the Jupiler League tend to have enough capacity to host fans of the away team. A possible increase in the title probability of the home team increases the occupancy rate, and so does the fact that the away team is a serious title contestant. To interpret the relative magnitudes of the effects, Table 7.7 gives the expected change of the occupancy rate, when each variable increases from its first sample quartile to its third sample quartile.

Table 7.6   Estimation results model 2, Jupiler League (estimated fixed effects in Appendix 7A.2)

	estimate	sd	z	p
derby	12.268	1.822	6.735	0.000
ht.pos	−0.005	0.078	−0.065	0.948
at.pos	0.011	0.074	0.149	0.882
temperature	0.389	0.075	5.175	0.000
season2010–2011	−0.907	1.012	−0.896	0.370
season2011–2012	0.381	1.020	0.374	0.709
form.H	2.278	0.325	7.011	0.000
form.A	0.685	0.321	2.137	0.033
ΔR_H	−1.754	1.235	−1.420	0.156
ΔR_A	2.691	1.183	2.276	0.023
$\Delta \text{Pr}(R_H = 1)$	61.776	11.674	5.292	0.000
$I_{\{\text{Pr}(RA = 1) \geq 0.10\}}$	7.090	1.746	4.060	0.000
σ	11.753	0.278	42.305	0.000

Table 7.7   Effects of a change from first quartile to third quartile on occupancy rate, model 2, Jupiler League

Temperature	form.H	form.A	ΔR_A	$\Delta \text{Pr}(R_H = 1)$
3.190	4.450	1.215	1.371	0.106

Clearly, temperature and form of the home team have a stronger effect than the other variables. The effect of form of the home team is much larger than in the case of the Eredivisie. The effect of a change in the title probability of the home team seems to be of limited empirical relevance (though statistically significant).

4   CONCLUDING REMARKS

In this chapter, we have analysed attendance (measured by occupancy rates) at individual matches in the two levels of professional football in the Netherlands. Especially at the highest level, attendance is often close to capacity of the stadium, so we allowed for censoring by using a tobit model. At both levels, fixed team effects are important, and they vary significantly between teams. Besides the significance of team effects, we found that occupancy rates are positively related to form of both the home and away team, and to a derby match effect. Also, attendance is higher when the away team is a serious title contender, probably because fans of the away team will use the tickets allocated to them in that case. Only in the Jupiler League we found that the occupancy rate responds to match significance. The variation explained by this effect is small, though, especially compared to the variation explained by the derby match effect, and recent form of both teams. Since occupancy rates in the Jupiler League are usually noticeably smaller than 1, fans are not discouraged to visit the stadium and buy a ticket. These teams are not operating near the capacity limit, and therefore, are better able to offer a seat to a fan who wants to visit a single game. Unsurprisingly, matches in the Jupiler League are better visited when the temperature is higher.

NOTES

1. The computations to estimate match significance were performed on the millipede multi-core cluster of the University of Groningen.
2. The models are estimated using the censReg package in R (Henningsen, 2012; R Core Team, 2012).

REFERENCES

Bojke, C. (2007), 'The impact of post-season play-off systems on the attendance at regular season games', in J. Albert and R.H. Koning (eds), *Statistical Thinking in Sports*, London: CRC Press, pp. 179–202.

Dobson, S. and J. Goddard (2011), *The Economics of Football*, 2nd edn, Cambridge: Cambridge University Press.

Dobson, S.M. and J.A. Goddard (1992), 'The demand for standing and seated viewing accommodation in the English Football League', *Applied Economics*, **24** (10), 1155–63.

Dobson, S.M. and J.A. Goddard (1995), 'The demand for professional league football in England and Wales, 1925–92', *The Statistician*, **44** (2), 259–77.

Downward, P., A. Dawson and T. DeJonghe (2009), *Sports Economics*, Abingdon: Routledge.

Fort, R.D. (2006), *Sport Economics*, 2nd edn, Upper Saddle River, NJ: Prentice-Hall.

García, J. and P. Rodríguez (2002), 'The determinants of football match attendance revisited', *Journal of Sports Economics*, **3** (1), 18–38.

Henningsen, A. (2012), *censReg: Censored Regression (Tobit) Models*, R package version 0.5-16.

Jennett, N. (1984), 'Attendance, uncertainty of outcome and policy in Scottish league football', *Scottish Journal of Political Economy*, **31** (2), 176–98.

KEA Economics Affairs and Centre de Droit et Economie du Sport (2013), 'The economic and legal aspects of the economic and legal aspects of the transfers of players', available at: http://ec.europa.eu/sport/library/documents/f-studies/ study-transfers-final-rpt.pdf (accessed 15 December 2014).

Koning, R.H. (2000), 'Competitive balance in Dutch soccer', *The Statistician*, **49** (3), 419–31.

Koning, R.H. (2007), 'Post-season play and league design in Dutch soccer', in P. Rodríguez, S. Késenne and J. García (eds), *Governance and Competition in Profesisonal Sports Leagues*, Oviedo: Ediciones de la Universidad de Oviedo, pp. 191–215.

R Core Team (2012), *R: A Language and Environment for Statistical Computing*, Vienna: R Foundation for Statistical Computing. ISBN 3-900051-07-0.

Simmons, R. (1996), 'The demand for English league football: a club-level analysis', *Applied Economics*, **28** (2), 139–55.

Szymanski, S. and R. Smith (1997), 'The English football industry: profit, performance and industrial structure', *International Review of Applied Economics*, **11** (1), 135–53.

Voetbal International (2010), *Voetbaljaarboek 2010*, Gouda: Voetbal International.

Voetbal International (2011), *Voetbaljaarboek 2011*, Gouda: Voetbal International.

Voetbal International (2012), *Voetbaljaarboek 2012*, Gouda: Voetbal International.

APPENDIX 7A.1   PRINCIPAL COMPONENT ANALYSIS

Form of a team is considered by the following eight indicators (six in the case of Jupiler League). For the home team, we use:

- points obtained in last three matches;
- goals scored in last three matches;
- goals against in last three matches;
- financial return on bets on home team in last three matches (not available for Jupiler League);
- points obtained in last three home matches;
- goals scored in last three home matches;
- goals against in last three home matches
- financial return on bets on home team in last three home matches (not available for Jupiler League).

For each variable, a three match moving average is calculated. To avoid incomplete observations in the beginning of the season, the moving average is calculated with data of the preceding season, if necessary. Factor loadings and the variance composition are given in Tables 7A.1–7A.4.

Table 7A.1   Principal components form home team, Eredivisie

	Comp.1	Comp.2	Comp.3	Comp.4	Comp.5
ma.points.h.imp	−0.368	0.116	0.298	−0.275	−0.069
ma.goals.s.h.imp	−0.340	−0.294	0.393	−0.027	0.459
ma.goals.a.h.imp	0.256	−0.451	−0.347	0.085	0.618
bet.return.h.imp	−0.195	0.062	−0.021	−0.773	0.270
ma.points.home.h.imp	−0.498	0.084	−0.303	0.197	−0.139
ma.goals.s.home.h.imp	−0.488	−0.563	0.084	0.274	−0.171
ma.goals.a.home.h.imp	0.285	−0.606	0.047	−0.396	−0.524
bet.return.home.h.imp	−0.280	−0.037	−0.731	−0.220	−0.078
st. dev	1.607	0.863	0.644	0.563	0.359
prop. var.	0.593	0.171	0.095	0.073	0.030
cum. prop.	0.593	0.764	0.859	0.932	0.962

Table 7A.2   Principal components form away team, Eredivisie

	Comp.1	Comp.2	Comp.3	Comp.4	Comp.5
ma.points.a.imp	−0.355	0.069	0.254	−0.431	0.151
ma.goals.s.a.imp	−0.295	−0.188	0.529	−0.262	−0.534
ma.goals.a.a.imp	0.292	−0.416	−0.028	0.191	−0.635
bet.return.a.imp	−0.226	−0.187	−0.202	−0.557	0.015
ma.points.away.a.imp	−0.461	−0.013	0.006	0.332	0.049
ma.goals.s.away.a.imp	−0.337	−0.380	0.377	0.486	0.290
ma.goals.a.away.a.imp	0.384	−0.666	0.144	−0.229	0.442
bet.return.away.a.imp	−0.421	−0.404	−0.672	0.017	−0.083
st. dev	1.642	0.837	0.806	0.539	0.364
prop. var.	0.583	0.151	0.140	0.063	0.029
cum. prop.	0.583	0.734	0.875	0.937	0.966

Table 7A.3   Principal components form home team, Jupiler League

	Comp.1	Comp.2	Comp.3	Comp.4	Comp.5
ma.points.h.imp	−0.383	−0.087	0.517	0.389	0.227
ma.goals.s.h.imp	−0.317	0.319	0.475	0.185	−0.572
ma.goals.a.h.imp	0.297	0.453	−0.391	0.546	−0.352
ma.points.home.h.imp	−0.552	−0.039	−0.472	0.464	0.342
ma.goals.s.home.h.imp	−0.479	0.608	−0.196	−0.534	0.050
ma.goals.a.home.h.imp	0.362	0.561	0.305	0.126	0.614
st. dev	1.413	0.893	0.501	0.372	0.332
prop. var.	0.601	0.241	0.075	0.042	0.033
cum. prop.	0.601	0.842	0.917	0.959	0.992

Table 7A.4   Principal components form away team, Jupiler League

	Comp.1	Comp.2	Comp.3	Comp.4	Comp.5
ma.points.a.imp	−0.390	0.111	0.512	−0.242	−0.355
ma.goals.s.a.imp	−0.256	0.440	0.482	0.596	0.019
ma.goals.a.a.imp	0.377	0.330	−0.359	0.515	−0.392
ma.points.away.a.imp	−0.518	0.123	−0.463	−0.157	−0.589
ma.goals.s.away.a.imp	−0.330	0.592	−0.349	−0.153	0.579
ma.goals.a.away.a.imp	0.513	0.565	0.201	−0.522	−0.195
st. dev	1.350	0.830	0.551	0.369	0.349
prop. var.	0.589	0.223	0.098	0.044	0.039
cum. prop.	0.589	0.811	0.909	0.953	0.993

APPENDIX 7A.2   FIXED EFFECTS

The estimated fixed effects are given in Tables 7A.5 and 7A.6. The effects differ significantly between teams. In the case of Eredivisie, no fixed effects were estimated for Heerenveen, Heracles, and Nijmegen.

Table 7A.5   Fixed effects, Eredivisie

	Estimate	sd	Estimate	sd
Ajax	91.59	1.44	91.02	1.67
AZ Alkmaar	95.01	1.34	94.68	1.54
Den Haag	82.87	1.29	82.39	1.63
Excelsior	95.47	1.68	95.18	1.81
Feyenoord	84.35	1.31	84.10	1.56
Graafschap	97.50	1.67	97.24	1.86
Groningen	98.25	1.40	98.17	1.66
NAC Breda	94.28	1.33	94.24	1.66
PSV Eindhoven	95.68	1.42	95.25	1.62
Roda JC	72.55	1.35	72.53	1.62
Sparta	92.93	2.07	93.24	2.31
Twente	98.84	1.50	98.42	1.79
Utrecht	82.45	1.36	82.44	1.62
Vitesse	66.15	1.35	66.02	1.64
VVV Venlo	95.83	1.43	95.53	1.62
Waalwijk	87.79	1.54	87.39	1.72
Willem II	84.24	1.75	83.87	1.86

Table 7A.6   Fixed effects, Jupiler League

	Estimate	sd	Estimate	sd
AGOVV	71.02	2.22	69.17	2.69
Almere City FC	46.88	2.30	45.27	2.73
De Graafschap	78.07	3.46	67.49	3.92
Excelsior	48.97	3.23	46.81	3.54
FC Den Bosch	44.48	2.30	43.23	2.86
FC Dordrecht	47.76	2.23	46.23	2.77
FC Eindhoven	47.54	2.27	46.56	2.79
FC Emmen	29.62	2.28	28.24	2.66
FC Oss	42.08	2.59	40.36	2.94
FC Volendam	42.35	2.30	40.88	2.83
Fortuna Sittard	28.55	2.24	26.74	2.64
Go Ahead Eagles	65.52	2.29	62.51	2.86
Helmond Sport	67.28	2.25	65.77	2.75
MVV	48.36	2.26	47.30	2.84
PEC Zwolle	51.89	2.22	45.07	2.65
RBC	46.39	2.53	45.30	2.95
RKC	50.00	3.50	40.96	3.81
SC Cambuur	61.59	2.24	57.93	2.71
SC Veendam	43.90	2.31	42.66	2.76
Sparta	58.80	2.72	57.07	3.17
Telstar	62.27	2.31	60.80	2.65
Willem II	61.36	3.53	57.42	3.82

8. Sport talent, media value and equal prize policies in tennis

Pedro Garcia-del-Barrio and Francesc Pujol

1 INTRODUCTION AND METHODOLOGY

Given the economic and commercial implications of sports, the media value of players and teams is considered a major asset in professional sports businesses. In addition to sport talent, professional players possess other skills that the general public find attractive and are considered potential revenue sources. In so far as both sport and non-sport related skills are appreciated in the media, the task of evaluating the intangible talents of players can be performed by appraising their media value.

The notion of media value is thus used to designate the economic value that individuals and institutions achieve thanks to their recognition in the mass media. In professional sports, as well as in other entertainment industries (such as cinema, art and music), media value has become a major asset on the basis of which an increasing number of firms develop their businesses.

This chapter assesses the economic value of intangible assets in the tennis industry. More specifically, it establishes procedures to measure the intangible talent of players based on their exposure in the mass media. In addition to ranking the media value of professional tennis players (both men and women), we examine some issues related to the competitive structure of tennis. Then, we explore whether policies regarding prize money could be more efficiently designed to account for the economic contribution of the players who produce spectacle in sporting events.

Building on the economics, sports and intangibles (ESI) methodology, we have developed indexes to assess the economic value of talent, as captured by the degree of interest expressed by fans and the exposure achieved in the media. As mentioned previously, the ESI media value approach permits an evaluation of the players' personal talents and attractiveness beyond the contribution directly linked to sport performance.

The basic guidelines of the ESI methodology consist of analysing two complementary elements: popularity and notoriety. The ESI comprehensive index of media value is then computed by combining the popularity and notoriety indexes. Based on the individual appraisal of media value, it is also possible to develop measures of media value for teams, leagues, institutions, and so on.

The popularity index captures the interest that a given player or team generates among people around the world. To measure the popularity of individuals or institutions, we analyse the share of attention that the protagonists draw from supporters and the general public (as captured by the Internet traffic: websites, specialized sites, blogs, home pages, and so on). Then, to obtain the popularity indexes of teams or leagues, we simply compute aggregate figures based on individual records.

Similarly, the notoriety index reflects the mass media exposure of individuals or teams. To evaluate the notoriety rank, we examine the number of news articles published, in the selected prominent languages, associated with each player in a given period of time. Therefore, the notoriety element reflects the mass media exposure of individuals that results from their sport performance or is attached to the social recognition of their personal characteristics.

The strength and broad scope of the ESI methodology derives from its capacity to provide homogeneous indicators of media value. These ratings can be applied to examine sport disciplines, as well as other entertainment industries. The homogeneous and reliable nature of ESI rankings permits accurate comparisons between individuals and over time, based on comparable records on media value.

Depending on the type of analysis, records are gathered on a monthly or weekly basis. To describe changes in the media's perceptions of a player over the course of a season, for instance, collecting records twice a week may be appropriate. Instead, if the aim is to calculate annual rankings, the meaningful procedure consists of computing the average for the entire year. The ESI methodology has been successfully applied in recent years and has permitted evaluations of the media values of professional sport competitions within the context of football (European domestic leagues, UEFA Champions League, the World Cup, and so on), basketball (National Basketball Association, Liga ACB and Basketball World Cup), and Formula 1. Economics, sports and intangibles data-sets also include other fields, such as golf, cycling and baseball.

In addition to providing information on the levels of media value and popularity of prominent tennis players, our analysis permits us to address questions within the fields of labour and industrial economics. Consider, for instance, the relationship between productivity (both sport performance and media value) and earnings in tennis or the competitive structures of the main tournaments.

Once the main aspects of the ESI methodology have been described, the following pages address various aspects related to media value in professional tennis. The most relevant issue that we examine here is perhaps the extent to which policies regarding prize money could be more efficiently implemented. From an economic point of view, the structure and organization of sport industries should be arranged to reward the agents involved in entertainment provision in keeping with their economic contributions.

2   RELATED LITERATURE

Nowadays, an increasing number of economic activities are based on the exploitation of intangible assets. Thus, there is an urgent need to devise tools for evaluating intangibles, especially in businesses where assets of this kind are the most valuable revenue source (Hall, 1992). Some papers highlight the complexity of this endeavour, owing to the nature of the assets to be evaluated (see, for instance, Lev, 2006). To address this issue, we adopt an innovative methodology, the description of which is one of the relevant contributions of these pages.

First, note that the tennis industry is a peculiar market within the entertainment business. Considering the large size of the professional sports industry, it must be understood as one of the most significant entertainment providers. As a business, the tennis industry builds on the talent of its players, whose performances generate sport success and awards. Therefore, measuring sport talent (largely intangible) is critical to explore the potential sources of revenues.

Second, the professional tennis market has been drastically transformed recently through technological progress. Owing to the development of mass media, large numbers of new 'consumers of leisure' have gained access to the tennis (media) industry. As a result, a tremendous increase in the size of the market (and consequently, in the amount of revenues) has taken place.

Attempts at approximating the value of the players' economic contribution have generally been restricted to their sport performance, as for instance in the works by Scully (1974) or Berri (1999).[1] However, given that the actual contribution of players is also related to their skills as media leaders, we must go beyond mere sports achievements to obtain a complete picture of the matter. In other words, most studies conducted thus far have not managed to accurately evaluate the overall contribution of players, as they neglect essential aspects of the business linked to mass media power.

Besides, there are other aspects of the sports industry that should be considered. As mentioned previously, owing to the economic implications of modern sports, the media value of players is a key asset for organizing professional sports as a business. On the one hand, this type of industry is characterized by the typical contest system, which draws attention from the fans through the uncertainty attached to the unpredictable outcomes of matches (see Szymanski, 2001, 2003).

On the other hand, the tennis industry is a winner-take-all market. According to the winner-take-all hypothesis, proposed by Frank and Cook (1995), workers who are slightly better than others become winners in the market and receive much higher earnings than the losers (the wages of the former group exhibit a more than proportional size with respect to its productivity). Typically, in this type of industry, a limited number of leaders achieve 'superstar' status, thereby attracting extra high earnings.

In the economics literature, Noll (1974) and Rosen (1981) have already referred to the phenomenon of superstars. More recently, Dobson and Goddard (2001) stressed again that skewed earnings distributions might stem from the scarce supply of outstanding talent, along with the large audiences they attract. Thus, a reduced number of people dominate the activities they engage in and earn enormous rewards. Frank and Cook (1995) remark that these markets (professional sports, pop culture, arts, and so on) exhibit similar reward structures, in which many individuals compete for a few large prizes at the top. As pointed out by Garcia-del-Barrio and Pujol (2007, 2009), the winner-take-all element is at work in several sports industries.

Moving into a different area, we must be aware that sports are also present in the field of brand development and sponsorship. The reputation of a brand is typically constructed on the basis of strategic intangible assets that, in the context of sports, essentially consist of player talent and sport achievements. Brand development is also closely linked to merchandising, broadcasting rights, and other commercial sources of revenues.[2]

3   DATA DESCRIPTION AND MEDIA VALUE RANKINGS

In this study, we use weekly data on the number of news articles and the cumulative Internet exposure of the top 1400 professional tennis players: 700 women from the WTA and 700 men from the ATP in 2007. (ATP denotes the Association of Tennis Professionals, formed in 1972; WTA is the Women's Tennis Association, founded one year later). The data come from different sources: the data on media value are calculated by the authors, while the information on the other variables, such as money prizes and tournaments, was obtained from the official web pages of the

The economics of competitive sports

Table 8.1   Ranking of media value of professional tennis players (men)

Rank	Player	Country	ESI index of media value	Points, ATP 2007
1	Roger Federer	SUI	43.5	7205
2	Rafael Nadal	ESP	36.9	5385
3	Andy Roddick	USA	21.3	2430
4	Novak Djokovic	SRB	19.9	4470
5	Nikolay Davydenko	RUS	15.3	3250
6	James Blake	USA	12.4	2110
7	Lleyton Hewitt	AUS	11.5	1365
8	Carlos Moya	ESP	10.8	1620
9	Fernando Gonzalez	CHI	10.6	1905
10	David Ferrer	ESP	10.2	2130
11	Richard Gasquet	FRA	10.2	1680
12	Andy Murray	GRB	10.0	1705
13	Tommy Robredo	ESP	9.9	1965
14	Tomas Berdych	CZE	8.8	1735
15	Guillermo Canas	ARG	8.7	1678
16	Marat Safin	RUS	8.6	735
17	Andre Agassi	USA	8.6	–
18	Tommy Haas	GER	8.2	1870
19	David Nalbandian	ARG	7.7	1375
20	JuanCarlos Ferrero	ESP	7.7	1335

Sources: ESI own calculations and ATP (http://www.atptennis.com, accessed 10 April 2009).

ATP (http://www.atptennis.com) and the WTA (http://www.sonyericsson wtatour.com).

Table 8.1 reports the media value rankings of the top male tennis players in 2007. The magnitude of this index indicates the multiple by which an individual player multiplies the media value level of the normal (average) individual in our sample.

First, we identify Federer and Nadal as the undisputed leaders of tennis media value in 2007. This conclusion refers to the men's rankings but also applies to the comprehensive mixed ranking with all 1400 players (reported in Table 8.3 and computed using records of all players either in the ATP or WTA tour). According to our estimations, Federer received (on average throughout the year 2007) a degree of attention 43.5 times larger than the interest achieved by the average tennis player in the sample, which in this case consists of 700 players. Similarly, Rafael Nadal receives 37 points in

Table 8.2   Ranking of media value of professional tennis players (women)

Rank	Player	Country	ESI index of media value	Points, WTA 2007
1	JUSTINE HENIN	BEL	41.1	5930
2	MARIA SHARAPOVA	RUS	33.3	2861
3	SERENA WILLIAMS	USA	32.2	2767
4	VENUS WILLIAMS	USA	31.4	2470
5	JELENA JANKOVIC	SRB	25.5	3475
6	SVETLANA KUZNETSOVA	RUS	24.1	3750
7	AMELIE MAURESMO	FRA	21.7	1906
8	ANA IVANOVIC	SRB	20.7	3175
9	MARTINA HINGIS	SUI	16.9	1502
10	MARION BARTOLI	FRA	14.1	2096
11	PATTY SCHNYDER	SUI	12.2	1704
12	ELENA DEMENTIEVA	RUS	11.8	2022
13	ANNA CHAKVETADZE	RUS	11.8	2625
14	ANNA KOURNIKOVA	RUS	11.6	–
15	DANIELA HANTUCHOVA	SVK	10.5	2027
16	NADIA PETROVA	RUS	10.0	1976
17	NICOLE VAIDISOVA	CZE	9.9	1904
18	TATIANA GOLOVIN	FRA	8.5	1882
19	MARY PIERCE	USA	8.3	–
20	DINARA SAFINA	RUS	8.3	1820

Sources: ESI own calculations and WTA (http://www.sonyericssonwtatour.com, accessed 10 April 2009).

the ESI ranking, meaning that he enjoys a level of media value 37 times greater than the average player.

Similarly, Table 8.2 presents the results for the top 700 women players. Justine Henin is the leader among women, while Maria Sharapova (sixth in the combined ranking of Table 8.3) holds the second position, receiving a share of attention that clearly exceeds the predicted level that one should expect if relying exclusively on sport performance. This particular feature will be examined and further explained in sections 4 and 5.

One significant finding of this analysis is the large distance found – in terms of media value – between the few leaders in the rankings and the remaining players. In the ATP tour, a large gap separates the top two superstars (Federer and Nadal) from Andy Roddick, who is the third player in the ranking. A similar situation holds for the upper part of the women's WTA tour.

This feature suggests that the winner-take-all element is present in tennis.

Table 8.3 Joint ranking of media value in professional tennis (both men and women)

	Player	ATP/WTA rank	Country	ESI index of media value	Prize money*	Grand Slam 2007	Masters 2007
1	Federer, Roger	ATP (1)	SUI	54.3	7 405 620	3	2
2	Nadal, Rafael	ATP (2)	ESP	48.4	4 395 185	1	3
3	HENIN, JUSTINE	WTA (1)	BEL	28.4	4 367 086	2	2
4	Roddick, Andy	ATP (5)	USA	25.6	1 232 070	0	0
5	Djokovic, Novak	ATP (3)	SRB	24.2	3 313 700	0	2
6	SHARAPOVA, MARIA	WTA (5)	RUS	22.9	1 258 550	0	1
7	WILLIAMS, SERENA	WTA (6)	USA	22.4	2 066 641	1	1
8	WILLIAMS, VENUS	WTA (8)	USA	21.6	1 843 187	1	0
9	Davydenko, Nikolay	ATP (4)	RUS	19.0	1 576 775	0	0
10	JANKOVIC, JELENA	WTA (3)	SRB	17.9	1 685 387	0	2
11	KUZNETSOVA, SVETLANA	WTA (2)	RUS	16.9	1 962 487	0	0
12	Blake, James	ATP (7)	USA	15.9	941 585	0	0
13	MAURESMO, AMELIE	WTA (13)	FRA	14.8	580 104	0	0
14	Hewitt, Lleyton	ATP (23)	AUS	14.7	662 075	0	0
15	Moya, Carlos	ATP (16)	ESP	14.5	853 315	0	0
16	IVANOVIC, ANA	WTA (4)	SRB	14.3	1 660 354	0	1
17	Gonzalez, Fernando	ATP (9)	CHI	14.3	1 219 330	0	0
18	Murray, Andy	ATP (12)	GBR	13.0	830 155	0	0
19	Ferrer, David	ATP (6)	ESP	13.0	1 206 252	0	0
20	Robredo, Tommy	ATP (8)	ESP	12.6	928 147	0	0

Note: * Prize money in $US.

Sources: ATP (http://www.atptennis.com, accessed 10 April 2009); WTA (http://www.sonyericssonwtatour.com, accessed 10 April 2009) and ESI own calculations.

Moreover, as will soon be illustrated, it affects the monetary rewards as well as the distribution of media value concentration. That is precisely why, when conducting the empirical analysis, we include qualitative variables to account for 'superstar' players.

A cursory inspection of the tables also demonstrates the close correlation between media value and sport performance (captured by WTA or ATP points). This is corroborated by the usual statistical tools, as the correlation coefficient is 0.94, very high indeed.

Thus far we have computed separate rankings for men and women. This choice seems to be imposed by the structure of tennis competition itself, as the tournaments are typically organized by grouping men and women separately. The same can be said of the rating systems: the WTA and ATP rankings. At this point, it must be noted that among the advantages of the ESI approach is precisely the homogeneous character of its rankings, which permits conducting a joint analysis of men and women.

The joint mixed index (for the full sample) is then computed by including both the 700 men and 700 women. In line with this new arrangement, the ESI index is now expressed with respect to the average value of the representative player in the data-set of 1400 players. Table 8.3 presents the results of this exercise, which enable us to fairly compare the index for all the players, either men or women.

First, note that five women are found in the group of the top ten most popular tennis players in the world. Notice further that Henin's prominence in 2007 (she has more than twice the points of Sharapova in the WTA ranking) does not correspond to an equivalent proportion with respect to their relative positions in terms of media value. It is also noteworthy that Hewitt (twenty-third in the ATP) displays a greater level of media value than Anna Ivanovic, despite her being the fourth player in the WTA ranking. The reasons behind these outcomes are discussed in section 5.

Second, we found evidence again of the winner-take-all effect, which may help to explain the high degree of media value concentration in tennis. This phenomenon especially affects individuals situated in the upper tier of the distribution, an assertion that can be inferred from the substantial distance that separates the leaders in the rankings and their direct rivals. The economic and media status of Nadal or Federer is far beyond the levels of other tennis players. Additionally, a similar feature applies, albeit to a decreasing extent, all along the media value distribution function.

Moreover, as the following sections demonstrate, the winner-take-all structure affects the media value distribution as well as the distribution of tennis players' earnings. That is to say, the media value of tennis players – and hence the total money prizes – grows more than proportionally compared to sport performance or productivity.

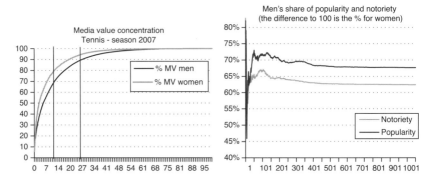

Figure 8.1   Concentration and share of media value by sex – tennis 2007

Our analysis also reveals that most of the attention in the mass media is absorbed by a limited number of superstars. Some information may help to illustrate this point: the top 20 players (out of 1400) generate 30 per cent of the total media value in tennis, even if the degree of concentration differs in the WTA and ATP tours. The left diagram in Figure 8.1 summarizes the analysis by dividing the sample into two groups by sex.

The group of the top ten women accounts for more than 37 per cent of the overall media value generated by female players, whereas the corresponding figure is approximately 27 per cent for men. By examining the 70 most relevant women and the top 70 men (the top 10 per cent of each group), we conclude that they are responsible for 77 and 67 per cent, respectively, of the overall media value in tennis. Similarly, to account for nearly all of the media attention generated by the tennis industry, one only needs to consider 25 per cent of the players, as they represent more than 90 per cent of the media value of tennis.

Another important matter seems to be the different structures in the level and share of media value in tennis exhibited by men and women. The right-side diagram in Figure 8.1 conveys information that is useful in two respects. First, it enriches the approach by distinguishing between the two elements that define media value: the notoriety and popularity indexes. Second, it presents a full account of the percentage of notoriety and popularity that correspond to men or women at every stage of the cumulative distribution (starting from the player with the highest rating and moving down to the player in position 1000).

One conclusion of this analysis is that both notoriety and popularity exhibit a similar evolution, with respect to the percentage shares corresponding to men and women. However, the most interesting feature disclosed here is that ATP players attract a much higher level of interest than women (from fans and the public) in the mass media. The share of popularity produced by male players is above 70 per cent for top players and tends to stabilize at approximately 68 per cent when more than 200 players are considered (implying that women are responsible for only 32 per cent of the overall popularity of tennis). Similarly, the share of notoriety attached to men ranges from between 67 per cent for small samples and 62.5 per cent if considering more than 200 players. This point motivates the empirical analysis in section 5 and is considered perhaps the main contribution of the present study.

4   SOURCES OF MEDIA VALUE IN TENNIS

It has already been stressed that, in markets such as the tennis industry, the media value of players is a major revenue source. Some individuals are endowed with outstanding performance skills (exclusive factors that are considered irreplaceable), which allow these individuals to accrue large economic revenues.

This section examines the sources of media value in tennis, focusing on the extent to which sport performance enriches the media value status of players. In line with the previous results, we find that the sport achievements of tennis players largely determine the sizes and changes in their media value figures.

Some reports produced by ESI revealed a strong statistical relationship between sport success and media value, a feature occurring for individual sports and for team sports.[3] The specific direction of the causal link (from sport performance to media value), although not easily verifiable through empirical analysis, is solidly based on theoretical arguments and common sense. Previous studies have recognized media value as a critical factor to predict potential revenues in sports industries.[4]

Before presenting the results of the regression analysis, Table 8.4 reports the summary statistics of the main variables. The empirical analysis in this section aims to identify the primary factors that are at the root of media value in tennis. Moreover, it explores whether there are significant differences between men and women in this regard.

For this purpose, and provided that the structures of the tournaments and the rating system is separated by sex, the regressions are run separately for the two sub-sample groups of men and women. Note also that, although the data-set initially comprised 700 men and 700 women, missing values of some variables have forced the sample to be restricted to 680 and 698 players, respectively.

In the estimations we present hereafter, our baseline model adopts the

Table 8.4   Summary statistics of the main variables

	Sample	Mean	Std Dev. Deviation	Min.	Max.
Women					
MediaValue	698	1.03	3.53	0	40.9
Popularity	698	1.03	3.04	0	31.7
Notoriety	698	1.00	4.13	0	52.1
PointsWTA_2007	698	209.42	467.94	0	5930.0
PointsWTA_Past	698	167.93	384.54	0	3932.8
MoneyPrize_2007*	698	90.82	267.96	0	4367.1
RankPosit_2007	698	603.10	346.01	1.0	1390.0
NoTourn_2007	698	10.98	7.87	3.0	34.0
NoTourn_Past	698	13.12	7.93	0	31.2
Men					
MediaValue	680	1.01	2.92	0	42.7
Popularity	680	0.99	2.03	0	21.1
Notoriety	680	1.03	4.01	0	64.2
PointsATP_2007	680	247.95	509.59	1.0	7205.0
PointsATP_Past	680	206.23	404.55	3.4	5679.0
MoneyPrize_2007*	680	125.19	400.07	0	7405.6
RankPosit_2007	680	397.76	296.18	1.0	1461.0
NoTourn_2007	680	13.57	5.87	1.0	28.0
NoTourn_Past	680	13.63	7.76	0.4	33.2

Note: * Earnings expressed in thousands of $US.

'MediaValue' index as the dependent variable. However, bear in mind that the ESI media value ranking is constructed by combining the notoriety and popularity indexes, reflecting mass-media exposure and the number of news articles associated with the players. Hence, we can always take the option of using either 'Notoriety' or 'Popularity' as alternative dependent variables; this approach permits the exploration of aspects that would otherwise remain unknown. (The three alternative dependent variables must, of course, enter separately into the regressions.)

As for the explanatory variables, current and past performances are the main factors to be examined. Among the various ways to evaluate sport performance in tennis, we initially employed the total cumulative points accrued over the season by players in the WTA or ATP tours. These variables were denoted 'PointsWTA_2007' or 'PointsATP_2007', for 2007, and 'PointsWTA_Past' or 'PointsATP_Past', to account for the average (annual arithmetic mean) of the points accrued between 2002 and 2006.[5]

Although the estimations of this model were satisfying, we prefer reporting the results of an alternative approach that captures sport performance by calculating the sport achievement per tournament. The results were nonetheless essentially similar.

The chosen explanatory variable is thus defined as the ratio of the cumulative number of points (WTA or ATP) accrued in the season over the number of tournaments played. The variables are denoted 'PointPerT_2007', for year 2007 records, and 'PointPerT_Past', for the average computed for the previous five seasons.

To complement the variables for sport performance, and due to the presumed winner-take-all element, dummy variables are also included in the regressions. They take a value of 1 for the winners in the market (tennis superstars) and 0 for the other players. We consider superstars to be the players who receive the highest levels of exposure in the media, as measured by the 'MediaValue' index. The names of these qualitative variables are 'WinT-All_mv2', for the two men or women with largest media values; and 'WinT-All_mv4' for the two second-best players (the third and fourth superstars of WTA or ATP tour). We have run the regressions using two variables of this type, although the number of superstars is of course a matter of choice.[6]

The set of explanatory variables also includes the number of tournaments played in the 2007 season: 'NoTourn_2007' and the average number of competitions in which the players have participated in the previous five tennis seasons: 'NoTourn_Past'. These two variables are potentially relevant, as the more exposed a player is in the mass media, the greater attention he actually receives.

Finally, in addition to the main variables, one auxiliary variable is included to correct for some deficiencies in the measurement process of the dependent variable. As explained in the methodological introduction, the procedure for computing the notoriety levels of players consists of quantifying the number of news articles associated with them over the season. In doing so, we include articles in some of the most relevant languages: English, Spanish, French, German, Italian, Portuguese and Dutch. However, other important languages – such as Chinese or Russian – were ignored. As a consequence, measurement errors may be relevant, and this problem ought to be addressed to avoid bias and distorted results. Because no better way to address the matter was feasible, we include a qualitative dummy variable to control for players whose languages were neglected in the searching stage.

Other technicalities must be noted. First, to avoid heteroskedasticity problems, we have computed robust standard errors estimations. Second, to compare the weight of each explanatory variable relative to the others, elasticity ratios ('ey/ex', computed at the mean of the respective variable) are reported at the bottom of the tables.[7]

Table 8.5 gathers the estimation results of the regressions for men and women. The existence of four models (reported in four columns) is the result of estimating both regressions for the full sample (700 players) and for the top 300 players; a procedure that is suitable to cross check the validity of the results.

The similarity of the estimations made for the four models indicates that the results are conclusive. Moreover, the respective R-squared values (0.9 or greater) are very high for a cross-sectional analysis, indicating the strong explanatory power of the models.

There is no question that – among all the explanatory variables – the most important factor is sport achievement, both at the present time and in the past. This conclusion is evident from the observation of the sign and significance of the estimated coefficients (as reported by the t-statistics). It is also corroborated by comparing elasticity ratios.

As we had already accounted for sport performance, we expect the two variables accounting for the number of tournaments to be positively correlated with media value status. This is the case regarding the year 2007, as 'NoTourn_2007' shows a positive coefficient that is statistically significant for women. However, for 'NoTourn_Past' (annual average of tournaments in the last five years), the relationship is statistically insignificant, and (implausibly) negative in the case of men.[8]

Regarding the qualitative variables for superstar players, the expected outcomes hold for the women's model and to some extent in the case of men. The estimated coefficients are consistently positive and generally significant (except for the two ATP leaders), providing support for the winner-take-all hypothesis.

The results in Table 8.5 contain similar outcomes regardless of sex. Accordingly, one may argue that the empirical analysis conveys essentially identical conclusions in all regards for WTA and ATP players. Moreover, the results undergo no substantial changes when the regressions are performed for the group of the top 300 men or top 300 women, rather than using the full sample of 700 individuals.

The estimation of our basic model, with 'MediaValue' as the dependent variable, will now be replicated to deliver the 'Notoriety' and 'Popularity' models. This analysis is performed by separately employing the two components of the initial dependent variable. This further refinement of the analysis leads to a better understanding of the behaviour of media value in the short and long runs (which is what we refer to when speaking of notoriety and popularity, respectively).

The estimation results of these models are presented in Table 8.6 and

Table 8.5 Estimation results of the 'MediaValue' model

	Median value Women			Median value Women 300			Median value Men			Median value Men 300		
	Coeff.	at	t-stat	Coeff.	at	t-stat	Coeff.	at	t-stat	Coeff.	at	t-stat
WinT-All_mv2	14.9854***		(6.80)	14.1969***		(5.73)	5.0586		(1.22)	4.2385		(0.95)
WinT-All_mv4	8.2017**		(2.05)	7.4746*		(1.70)	5.4428***		(3.27)	5.1167***		(2.94)
PointPerT_2007	0.0223***		(7.20)	0.0238***		(7.09)	0.0661***		(8.08)	0.0685***		(7.44)
PointPerT_Past	0.0696***		(6.47)	0.0719***		(5.66)	0.0490***		(6.56)	0.0491***		(5.90)
NoTourn_2007	0.0262***		(3.70)	0.0482***		(3.73)	0.0006		(0.08)	0.0273		(1.59)
NoTourn_Past	−0.0038		(−0.58)	0.0157		(1.18)	−0.0191***		(−2.97)	−0.0056		(−0.58)
No_language	−0.2527***		(−3.25)	−0.4557***		(−2.85)	−0.2875***		(−4.36)	−0.4063***		(−3.09)
Constant	−0.4685***		(−4.96)	−1.1567***		(−3.90)	−0.1843*		(−1.77)	−0.9597***		(−2.85)
Number obs.	696			300			680			300		
R-squared	0.8987			0.9151			0.9190			0.9301		
	ey/ex	at	mean	ey/ex	at	mean	ey/ex	at	mean	ey/ex	at	mean
WinT-All_mv2	0.0417		0.003	0.0423		0.006	0.0147		0.003	0.0137		0.006
WinT-All_mv4	0.0228		0.003	0.0223		0.006	0.0159		0.003	0.0166		0.006
PointPerT_2007	0.5714		26.465	0.5622		52.960	0.9605		14.662	0.8877		26.654
PointPerT_Past	0.7044		10.444	0.5964		18.567	0.5287		10.880	0.4333		18.158
NoTourn_2007	0.2787		11.004	0.2814		13.090	0.0077		13.573	0.2205		16.603
NoTourn_Past	−0.0480		13.159	0.1171		16.692	−0.2582		13.630	−0.0503		18.344
No_language	−0.1174		0.479	−0.1051		0.516	−0.0867		0.304	−0.0547		0.276

Note: Statistical significance: *** p-value < 0.01; ** p-value < 0.05; * p-value < 0.1; (t-statistic) in parenthesis.

Table 8.6 Estimation results of the 'Notoriety' model

	Notoriety Women		Notoriety Women 300		Notoriety Men		Notoriety Men 300	
	Coeff.	t-stat.	Coeff.	t-stat.	Coeff.	t-stat.	Coeff.	t-stat.
WinT-All_mv2	21.4592***	(3.89)	19.1700***	(3.58)	14.5421***	(3.63)	12.7149***	(2.91)
WinT-All_mv4	13.2766***	(2.80)	10.7876**	(1.99)	9.4283***	(4.67)	8.6837***	(3.96)
PointPerT_2007	0.0308***	(6.20)	0.0325***	(6.02)	0.0944***	(7.92)	0.1007***	(7.78)
PointPerT_Past	0.0570***	(4.47)	0.0668***	(4.32)	0.0427***	(4.31)	0.0412***	(3.68)
NoTourn_2007	0.0427***	(4.64)	0.0725***	(4.36)	0.0043	(0.57)	0.0469***	(2.58)
NoTourn_Past	-0.0114	(-1.52)	0.0125	(0.72)	-0.0306***	(-4.57)	-0.0100	(-0.85)
No_language	-0.2751***	(-2.81)	-0.4125*	(-1.85)	-0.1295	(-1.45)	-0.2405	(-1.33)
Constant	-0.6927***	(-4.80)	-1.8136***	(-3.81)	-0.4875***	(-4.64)	-1.8210***	(-4.60)
Number obs.	696		300		680		300	
R-squared	0.8621		0.8734		0.9399		0.9473	

	ey/ex	at mean	ey/ex	at mean	ey/ex	at mean	ey/ex	at mean
WinT-All_mv2	0.0613	0.003	0.0557	0.006	0.0414	0.003	0.0371	0.006
WinT-All_mv4	0.0379	0.003	0.0313	0.006	0.0268	0.003	0.0254	0.006
PointPerT_2007	0.8113	26.465	0.7509	52.960	1.3397	14.662	1.1759	26.654
PointPerT_Past	0.5917	10.444	0.5410	18.567	0.4501	10.880	0.3278	18.158
NoTourn_2007	0.4667	11.004	0.4138	13.090	0.0563	13.573	0.3409	16.603
NoTourn_Past	-0.1494	13.159	0.0907	16.692	-0.4043	13.630	-0.0800	18.344
No_language	-0.1312	0.479	-0.0929	0.516	-0.0382	0.304	-0.0292	0.276

Note: Statistical significance: *** p-value < 0.01; ** p-value < 0.05; * p-value < 0.1; (t-statistic) in parenthesis.

Table 8.7 and yield interesting findings. On the one hand, these new results corroborate the previous ones, thereby leading us to more resolutely support the conclusions previously mentioned. On the other hand, the regression analyses performed with the 'Notoriety' and 'Popularity' models provide additional implications, as the following paragraphs examine in greater detail.

First, note that current performance is more relevant than past performance in explaining the media value rank in the short run (the 'Notoriety' dependent variable). This conclusion is the expected outcome and is deduced through two findings: (1) the statistical significance of the estimated coefficient of 'PointPerT_2007' compared to that of 'PointPerT_Past' (the former is higher than the latter); and (2) the relative magnitudes of the elasticities reported at the bottom of Table 8.6. (The elasticities of present performance and past performance are: 0.8113 compared with 0.5917 for the model of women and 1.3397 compared to 0.4501 for men.)

Conversely, with respect to the long lasting recognition of players ('Popularity'), past performance is found to be the most relevant explanatory variable. (The respective elasticity, in Table 8.7, is now 0.3761 compared to 0.7744 for women and 0.5629 compared with 0.6112 for men.) Again, the outcome is not surprising, given that popularity can only be accumulated over time.

Second, according to the estimated results, it seems that the 'Notoriety' regressions work better in the case of men; whereas the opposite applies to the sample of women, where the explanatory power of the model is higher when we use 'Popularity' as the dependent variable. This can be seen by comparing the respective significance levels and R-squared coefficients.

In summary, the estimation results are satisfying and indicate that media value in tennis primarily depends on current and past sport performance.

To briefly describe the conclusions reached so far, we can enumerate the factors that are identified as the most relevant to explain the origin of media value:

1. Current sport performance, as captured by the number of ATP or WTA points obtained in the present year.
2. Past sport achievements, approximated by the five-years annual average of the number of points accumulated in the ATP or WTA tour.
3. The number of tournaments in which the player has participated in the current season. (Apparently, the number of past tournaments is less relevant, especially in the case of the ATP tour.)

Table 8.7 *Estimation results of the 'Popularity' model*

	Popularity Women		Popularity Women 300		Popularity Men		Popularity Men 300	
	Coeff.	t-stat.	Coeff.	t-stat.	Coeff.	t-stat.	Coeff.	t-stat.
WinT-All_mv2	9.5689**	(2.52)	9.2238**	(2.24)	-4.4251	(-0.89)	-4.2380	(-0.81)
WinT-All_mv4	4.5479	(1.36)	4.1615	(1.13)	1.4574	(0.95)	1.5498	(1.01)
PointPerT_2007	0.0146***	(9.36)	0.0150***	(8.65)	0.0378***	(5.62)	0.0362***	(4.51)
PointPerT_Past	0.0761***	(7.88)	0.0770***	(6.71)	0.0554***	(8.44)	0.0569***	(8.12)
NoTourn_2007	0.0138**	(2.20)	0.0238**	(2.07)	-0.0031	(-0.37)	0.0077	(0.39)
NoTourn_Past	0.0057	(0.88)	0.0190	(1.55)	-0.0076	(-0.96)	-0.0013	(-0.12)
No_language	-0.2532***	(-3.67)	-0.4989***	(-3.39)	-0.4455***	(-6.99)	-0.5721***	(-4.73)
Constant	-0.2999***	(-4.64)	-0.4999**	(-2.57)	0.1189	(0.89)	-0.0985	(-0.26)
Number obs.	696		300		680		300	
R-squared	0.902		0.9115		0.7694		0.8042	

	ey/ex	at mean	ey/ex	at mean	ey/ex	at mean	ey/ex	at mean
WinT-All_mv2	0.0268	0.003	0.0281	0.006	-0.0132	0.003	-0.0154	0.006
WinT-All_mv4	0.0127	0.003	0.0127	0.006	0.0043	0.003	0.0056	0.006
PointPerT_2007	0.3761	26.465	0.3641	52.960	0.5629	14.662	0.5281	26.654
PointPerT_Past	0.7744	10.445	0.6545	18.567	0.6112	10.880	0.5650	18.158
NoTourn_2007	0.1474	11.004	0.1425	13.090	-0.0433	13.573	0.0703	16.603
NoTourn_Past	0.0730	13.159	0.1448	16.692	-0.1050	13.630	-0.0132	18.344
No_language	-0.1183	0.479	-0.1180	0.516	-0.1376	0.304	-0.0865	0.276

Note: Statistical significance: *** p-value < 0.01; ** p-value < 0.05; ** p-value < 0.1; (t-statistic) in parenthesis.

4. The winner-take-all element, involving top superstar players. This is relevant for both men and women, but still requires a more detailed examination.
5. Other personal characteristics that refer to non-sport-related factors, especially those that the public and the mass media find attractive.

We consider that having been able to approximate, in a statistical way, the relative importance of each of the five features mentioned above is an important contribution of this study. Additionally, in the case of certain individuals, the special skills mentioned in the fifth point are a major source of media value, which allow them to attract substantial additional revenues. Given the relevance of the issue, we devote a complete section to analyse this point.

5   SPORT TALENT AND MEDIA VALUE PREMIUM

The previous section has developed an empirical model for studying the origin and sources of media value. The specifications of the models in section 4 are based on the notion that media value (of tennis players) is largely determined by sport achievements.

Nonetheless, a number of non-sport related factors – such as the nationality or personal characteristics of the players – significantly affect their media value status. This is clear from the awareness that R-squared is never equal to 1, meaning that several aspects fall beyond the explanatory capacity of the variables linked to sport quality and performance.

Building on the baseline model in section 4, this section investigates the size of the personal aspects that are not captured by the indicators of the sport contributions of players. The task of defining these qualitative traits is difficult to achieve, but the ESI approach can help to approximate their magnitudes for a given level of sport performance. Therefore, we use the residuals of the models in Table 8.5 to identify the players who enjoy a media value level that exceeds their potential sport talent.[9]

Moreover, the residuals can be treated as a means of quantifying the players' ability to attract additional media value, in addition to the recognition that is directly related to their sport achievements.

First, it must be noted that residuals from the models estimated for men and women differ. To illustrate this point, the two diagrams in Figure 8.2 plot actual media value against predicted media value. The latter is derived from the sport performance model, thereby indicating the expected media value that players would achieve strictly on the basis of sport performance records.

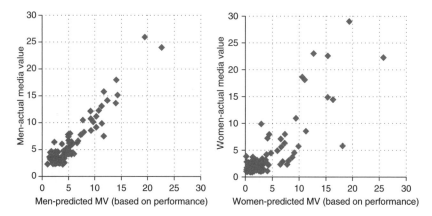

Figure 8.2   Deviations in the predicted outcomes of players' media values by sex

A cursory glance at Figure 8.2 reveals that observations for women deviate, from the 45-degree line, to a greater extent than those of men. In other words, the absolute value of the residuals (especially in the top part of the distribution) is generally larger for women than it is for male players. This is corroborated by a comparison of the R-squared values of the models: 0.919 for the men's and 0.8987 for the women's regression.

Furthermore, if we focus on the 'Notoriety' model, the conclusion seems even more undisputable. Given the respective R-squared values (in this case: 0.94 for men and 0.862 for women) one may interpret, albeit not in an entirely conclusive manner, that approximately 14 per cent of the variance in 'Notoriety' among women tennis players cannot be explained on the basis of sport achievements; whereas the figure is just 6 per cent in the case of men. This contrasting finding invites us to individually examine the case of the top players in both the WTA and ATP tours.

Having described the general behaviour of the residuals by sex, we now turn our attention to the top tennis players.

The main outcomes, resulting from this detailed analysis, are displayed in Figures 8.3 and 8.4 for men and women, respectively. A simple inspection of the figures reinforces the idea that dissimilar effects, in terms of notoriety and popularity, are operative for men and women; this feature is all the more evident when focusing on the superstar tennis players (at the upper end of the media value distribution).

The residuals are represented in white if they take negative values and in black whenever they are positive. To make the interpretation of the graphics more intuitive, we have performed some limited calculations such that:

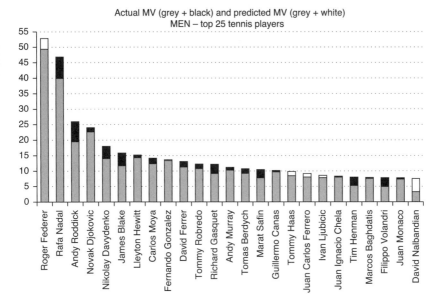

Figure 8.3   Actual and predicted media value (MV) – men tennis players

1. The actual media value (as measured and calculated by the ESI methodology) is defined in the figures by the sum of the grey and black areas.
2. The predicted media value is represented by the union of the areas in grey and white. Bear in mind that the predicted (or expected) media values result from the estimations of the sport performance model, which was based on the sport performance variables referred to in section 4.

Accordingly, the black area represents the extra amount of media value that is not directly linked to sport talent of players but could be due to personal skills and attractiveness to the media. Similarly, the white shadow captures the degree to which tennis players fall short of what they should have achieved according to their sport performance.

Hence, the interpretation of these figures reveals that some players actually enjoy greater media value status than they deserve on the grounds of their athletic merits alone. This is the case for male players, such as Nadal, Roddick and Blake; but the effect is far more significant for women such as Sharapova, Venus and Serena Williams, Jankovic, Ivanovic, Hingis and, especially, Kournikova. Again, Figures 8.3 and 8.4 illustrate – at the individual level – the extent to which some male and female players deviate from the normal pattern of the sport-based model in Table 8.5.

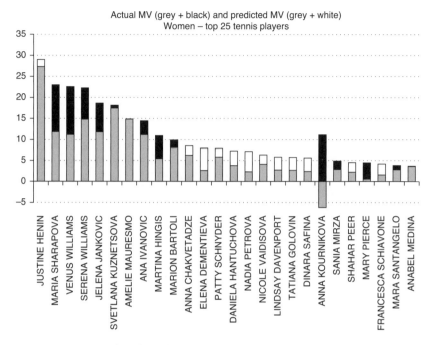

Figure 8.4   Actual and predicted media value (MV) – women tennis players

To summarize, consider the meaningful findings we have obtained by examining the deviations of current (or effective) media value from the predicted (or expected) media value; the latter being the estimated media value one should expect by exclusively considering to sport performance and achievements.

Notice further that the comparison of the two figures immediately provides support for the notion that the personal characteristics of players are more relevant for women than they are for men. This bias, even if statistically not very large, hints at the existence of stereotypes that could be affecting the incorporation of women into particular labour markets.

6   MEDIA VALUE AND 'EQUAL PRIZE' POLICIES

All four Grand Slam tournaments pay equal prize money to male and female tennis players. In 2007, the organizers of the Wimbledon Open decided to adopt this policy, just one year after the French Open began awarding the same prize money to the men's and women's singles champions. The other two (the US Open and Australian Open) had already followed this policy for years. The debate on the subject seems an endless argument that has become more notorious since the last Grand Slam implemented an equal prize policy.

The arguments in support of the current arrangement (of equal prize money in tennis) are varied. On one side, people invoke social reasons, the modern sensitivity towards historical discrimination against women and the desire to ensure that they occupy an equal role in society, a view that is becoming increasingly predominant. The following quote made in June 2012 by Stacey Allaster, the chief executive officer of the women's tour, may be a good summary of this viewpoint:

> Tennis, including the Grand Slams, is aligned with our modern, progressive society when it comes to the principle of equality. I cannot believe in this day and age that anyone can still think otherwise. This type of thinking is exactly why the WTA was founded and we will always fight for what is right. (Daily News, 2012)

Of course, these may be good reasons for establishing equal prize policies in tennis tournaments.

Nevertheless, if the goal is to confront the issue from an economic perspective exclusively, we must then leave aside any argument that is not strictly of an economic nature. The aim of this study is to respond to questions such as: to what extent are money prizes in tennis in accordance with the economic contributions of the players? Is there room for efficiency improvements in the tennis industry?

Thus, adopting an economic-centred approach leads to a different view and even to somewhat contradictory conclusions. In line with this, Gilles Simon, who in 2012 was elected to the ATP Player Council, has argued that men should be paid more than women at tennis tournaments. Two types of argument support his position and may help to characterize people's opinions on the matter:

1   '[M]en spend twice as long on court as women do at Grand Slams'.
2.   '[Men] provide a more attractive show' in their matches (Daily News, 2012)

It is true that, at the Grand Slam tournaments, men play best-of-five-set matches; whereas women play best-of-three matches. Moreover, even if in the majority of the other tournaments, all matches for both genders are best-of-three matches, the duration of the ATP games may still be generally longer than those of women.

Yet, we believe that arguments of this kind are rather weak, as money prizes are nonetheless fixed in advance, without actually knowing the duration of the games. Moreover, from an economic perspective, the critical issue is determining the spectators' willingness to pay for a tennis match, regardless of its duration.

Ultimately, in keeping with economic rationality and to ensure that the events are organized with an efficient structure, attention must be focused on studying whether men's or women's tournaments arouse greater interest among the general public, and examining to what extent.

The basic model developed thus far has proven to be reliable and provided us with a valid framework for responding to these types of question. Given the internal consistency of the previous specifications of the empirical model, we are in a position to address several topics in this industry. In particular, in this section we argue that the ESI methodology is an appropriate tool for addressing the controversial issue of equal money prize rewards in tennis.

Economic theory recommends employing more intensively those inputs that are more productive. This general principle also applies in the sports industry, as shown, for instance, by Szymanski and Smith (1997) or Hoehn and Szymanski (1999).[10] The first purpose of this section is to examine whether this feature holds in the tennis industry and to establish the extent to which it applies.

We have found that media value level (of tennis players) is primarily accrued through sport success, although other factors are also involved. Additionally, tennis players generate economic added value (and hence revenues) through their media value status. Many companies are then happy to pay large amounts of money for the support, in their marketing and sponsorship campaigns, of the most popular superstar players. In summary, the media attention attracted by the individuals is an essential factor in determining their potential capacity for attracting earnings through various sources: prizes, merchandising, television contracts, publicity, sponsorships, and so on.

The issue under examination here is the degree of efficiency in the equal prize money policy now prevailing in the four major tennis tournaments. To determine whether this policy is supported by economic rationality, we estimate a model where the dependent variable is the money prize per tournament 'PrizePerTourn_2007'. Then, the main explanatory variable is the joint index of media value ('MediaValue_Mixed', as shown in Table 8.3, which is reported in more detail in Appendix Table 8A.1). Both variables are perfectly comparable for all tennis players, regardless of their sex, which is a critical strength of this empirical model.

However, in addition to implementing the most revealing empirical

Table 8.8   Summary statistics of the main variables

	Sample	Mean	Std Dev.	Min.	Max.
PrizePerTourn_2007*	1378	9.25	28.69	0	462.9
MoneyPrize_2007*	1378	107.78	339.94	0	7405.6
WinTakeAll_2	1378	0.00	0.05	0	1.0
WinTakeAll_4	1378	0.00	0.05	0	1.0
MediaValue_Mix	1378	1.01	3.16	0	52.9
Popularity_Mix	1378	1.00	2.40	0	28.1
Notoriety_Mix	1378	1.01	4.17	0	78.8
PointPerTourn_2007	1378	20.60	50.93	0	793.8
PointPerTourn_Past	1376	10.66	22.08	0.6	311.8
NoTourn_2007	1378	12.26	7.07	1	34.0
NoTourn_Past	1378	13.37	7.85	0	33.2
Women_Dummy	1378	0.51	0.50	0	1.0
No_language	1378	0.39	0.49	0	1.0

Note: * Earnings expressed in thousands of $US.

model (that is to say, the one described in the above paragraph), it is informative to examine the relationship between money prizes per tournament (the same dependent variable as before, 'PrizePerTourn_2007') with respect to current sport productivity, 'PointPerTourn_2007'; or to the two variables 'WTAperTourn' and 'ATPperTourn', if the number of points in the WTA or ATP tour are allowed to have different slopes in the estimations. Table 8.8 reports the summary statistics of the available variables, including the winner-take-all dummies for the top two and top four superstar players.

Table 8.9 presents the estimation results of the models relating the amount of money prizes per tournament with respect to the sport performance records of tennis players. The R-squared values are very high in all the models, which is not surprising given the existing rewards structure employed in both the ATP and WTA tours.

One obligatory comment, prior to anything else, is to clarify that the models in Table 8.9 are not perfectly legitimated, as men and women play in entirely separate competitions. Thus, a joint comparison in terms of sport performance is inadequate, insofar as half of the players in the sample have never played against the other half. Irrespective of this shortcoming, some comments may still be relevant.

To simplify the explanations, let us focus on the observations of model (3) and model (4), which only differ in the use of dummy variables:

Table 8.9 Regression of the model: money prize per tournament against sport performance

	Model (1) Coeff.	t-stat	Model (2) Coeff.	t-stat	Model (3) Coeff.	t-stat	Model (4) Coeff.	t-stat
WinTakeAll_2	82.684 ***	(3.86)			114.94 ***	(2.78)		
WinTakeAll_4	37.485 *	(1.76)			51.691 ***	(3.37)		
ATPperTourm	0.6550 ***	(8.81)	0.7989 ***	(8.23)				
WTAperTourm	0.4469 ***	(21.50)	0.4694 ***	(25.41)				
PointperTourm					0.4604 ***	(25.27)	0.5150 ***	(15.47)
Women_Dum	0.5265	(0.47)	2.0322	(1.48)	-2.6808 ***	(-4.86)	-3.3340 ***	(-3.91)
Constant	-2.0741 **	(-2.00)	-3.830 ***	(-2.90)	0.6424	(1.37)	0.3316	(0.72)
Number obs.	1378		1378		1378		1378	
% Women	50.65		50.65		50.65		50.65	
R-squared	0.8860		0.8673		0.8736		0.8271	

	Model (1) ey/ex	at mean	Model (2) ey/ex	at mean	Model (3) ey/ex	at mean	Model (4) ey/ex	at mean
WinTakeAll_2	0.0259	0.003			0.0361	0.003		
WinTakeAll_4	0.0118	0.003			0.0162	0.003		
ATPperTourm	0.5121	7.235	0.6247	7.235				
WTAperTourm	0.6455	13.367	0.6781	13.367				
PointperTourm					1.0250	20.603	1.1467	20.603
Women_Dum	0.0288	0.506	0.1112	0.506	-0.1467	0.506	-0.1825	0.506

Note: Statistical significance: *** p-value < 0.01; ** p-value < 0.05; ** p-value < 0.1. (t-statistic) in parenthesis.

'WinTakeAll_2' and 'WinTakeAll_4'. Note that, in both models, we only include a single variable for sport achievements, 'PointPerTourn_2007', implying that the same estimated slope is enforced for men and women. Within this framework, the negative sign, along with the statistically significant level of the estimator for 'Women_Dummy' (a qualitative variable collecting the women in the sample) indicates that the women's money prizes are smaller in size compared to those of men for a similar number of points in the respective WTA and ATP tours.

The interpretation of this empirical finding may be simply due to the fact that there are many tennis tournaments where equal price policies are not adopted. We believe that this may of course be the case; nonetheless, the result is inconclusive for several reasons:

1. As has already been mentioned, men and women play separately in two groups, implying that the number of points accumulated by individuals in each group is not perfectly comparable with those of the other group.
2. According to the elasticities (estimated at the mean) for 'ATPperTourn' and 'WTAperTourn' of models (1) and (2), the result seems to be the opposite: in proportional terms, women receive larger increases in money prizes than men in response to a percentage point increase in sport attainment.
3. Finally, and most importantly from an economic perspective, the critical issue is not so much about matching money rewards to the number of points, but rather to determine whether the earnings of tennis players are congruent with the amount of business and economic added value they actually produce, which can be much better appraised by the ESI media value index.

As a result of the above reflections, we prefer the empirical estimations in Table 8.10, which deliver meaningful and reliable outcomes.[11] The structure of these models is essentially based on the relationship between money prizes per tournament (again the same dependent variable) and a set of explanatory variables, where the main one consists of media value ratings and is denoted 'MediaValue_Mix' (or 'mv_Mix'). We have already clarified that this measure of media value, entering into the regressions, is the joint index shown in Table 8.3 and reported in Appendix Table 8A.1.

The specification of this preferred model overcomes all the drawbacks associated with the approach based solely on the sport performance records. The model is presented in four versions, to robustly determine whether women or men are paid in excess of their contribution to the business, which is the question of interest.

Table 8.10   Regression of the model: money prize per tournament against media value

	Model (5)		Model (6)		Model (7)		Model (8)	
	Coeff.	t-stat	Coeff.	t-stat	Coeff.	t-stat	Coeff.	t-stat
mvMix_Men	5.4982***	(5.47)						
mvMix_Wom	9.9247***	(6.84)						
mvMix			6.8913***	(9.56)	6.7212***	(8.79)	6.6947***	(8.30)
Women_Dum	2.0047	(1.52)	5.9421***	(5.49)	13.5081***	(5.69)	19.0748***	(5.40)
No_language	5.2001***	(4.77)	5.4187***	(4.45)	12.1679***	(4.09)	15.5907***	(3.43)
Constant	0.9226	(−0.81)	−2.8192***	(−2.71)	−5.5216***	(−2.91)	−8.0732***	(−3.02)
Number obs.	1378		1378		600		400	
% Women	50.65		50.65		39.67		37.50	
R-squared	0.6240		0.5733		0.5815		0.5843	

	ey/ex	at mean	ey/ex	at mean	ey/ex	at mean	ey/ex	at mean
mvMix_Men	0.3852	0.648						
mvMix_Wom	0.3842	0.358						
MVmix			0.7495	1.006	0.8127	2.264	0.8633	3.248
Women_Dum	0.1097	0.506	0.3252	0.506	0.2861	0.396	0.2839	0.375
No_language	0.2206	0.392	0.2299	0.392	0.1960	0.301	0.1733	0.280

Note: Statistical significance: *** p-value < 0.01; ** p-value < 0.05; ** p-value < 0.1. (t-statistic) in parenthesis.

Moreover, the results are checked for robustness by using diverse specifications of the model. The first procedure is shown in model (5), where two variables for the players' media value ('mvMix_Men' and 'mvMix_Wom') are included to separately treat the groups of men and women. The estimated slopes – positive, significant and statistically very different – predict that women tennis players receive higher earnings than men, at any given level of media value: the coefficients are, respectively, 9.924 and 5.498.

More revealing than a deeper examination of model (5) is to review the estimations of the other three models. Strictly speaking, all three are actually a single case, given that model (7) and model (8) are mere replications of the same specification of model (6) for different sub-samples. As can be seen subsequently, the regressions when using smaller sample sizes, of either 600 or 400 players, yield similar results.

The specification of model (6) is more suitable, than model (5), for comparing the new estimations with those in Table 8.9. More importantly, its interpretation is straightforward, and the similarity of the results, across the three versions of the model, supports the soundness of the conclusions. Under this approach, instead of dividing the main explanatory variable (using both 'mvMix_Men' and 'mvMix_Wom' permitted the estimation of different slopes for men and women), we include a single 'mvMix' variable, accompanied by a dummy variable capturing all the women in the sample.

This is possibly the simplest and most convincing procedure to provide a truthful answer to our question. The whole point consists of testing if the estimated coefficient of 'Women_Dummy' (a qualitative variable controlling for female players) is statistically significant. A negative and significant coefficient indicates that women are paid less than the amount their media value deserves, and the opposite interpretation follows if the sign is positive and significant. Table 8.10 presents the regressions for 3 different sample sizes of the model. The explanatory power in all the cases is high (R-squared of approximately 0.58). More importantly, the estimated coefficient of 'Women_Dummy' is statistically positive and highly significant, implying that women are paid above the economic value they generate, at least according to the perceptions of the public and the media.

Regarding the quantitative interpretation, the estimations of the elasticity convey very informative outcomes. In model (6), the elasticity is as high as 0.3252, meaning that the earnings of a tennis player increase by approximately 33 per cent simply by the player being a woman.[12] Notice also that constraining the sample to the 600 or 400 most relevant players does not alter this conclusion (in this case the figure is approximately 28 per cent). The results reported in Table 8.10 do not seem to permit another interpretation.

In conclusion, the current situation in the tennis industry is such that women are typically overpaid with respect to men, at least according to the media value approach adopted here. Provided that media value status determines the potential capacity to attract revenues, this finding implies that the current situation of the tennis industry is in clear disagreement with the usual economic views and recommendations. Therefore, our study called into question equal prize policies, provided there is some concern for not compromising the rules of economic rationality and efficiency.

7 CONCLUDING REMARKS

In this study, we have pursued various objectives. First, we have presented and described the principal aspects of the ESI methodology, which we consider a reliable procedure to evaluate the economic value of intangible assets in sports. We have explained how the ESI approach establishes rankings of the intangible talent of players, a task carried out by appraising the level of a player's exposure in the mass media. In this way, ESI calculations provide individual assessments on the media value of players participating in a wide variety of sporting competitions, at any moment in time.

Among the other strengths of the ESI methodology, the homogeneity of its rankings must be stressed. Thanks to the accurate and comparable ratings of media value generated by ESI, we can easily compute rankings and make comparisons (in terms of media value) between players and over time. Then, from individual figures, we can also infer the overall media value of tournaments or leagues, as well as the collective media value of groups of individuals who meet specific criteria or belong to particular teams.

To study the tennis industry, we have used ESI data-set, which comprises weekly records of the top 1400 professional tennis players (700 women in the WTA and 700 men in the ATP in the 2007 season). To rank the media value of tennis players, we follow the basic guidelines of the ESI methodology by combining the notions of notoriety and popularity.

Having computed the ESI media value index for the 1400 most relevant tennis players in the world, our analysis reveals that, in 2007, Roger Federer was the absolute leader in terms of media value; while Rafael Nadal, who was second, came close to him. Among the women, Justine Henin received the third position in the mixed raking, and is considered the most valuable female player in 2007. Then, note that Sharapova is the second-ranked woman (in spite of ranking only fifth in the WTA tour) and even holds sixth position in the mixed ranking. Sharapova received a share of attention that exceeds the rank she would deserve in terms of sport performance. Additionally, five women are found among the top ten players in the world.

Our study has provided insights on other relevant aspects, such as the concentration of media value. Some information may help to summarize the finding that a small number of superstar players absorb most of the attention in the media: The top 20 tennis players (out of 1400) generate 30 per cent of the total media value in tennis. If the analysis is restricted to the leading ten players of each sex, we find that just ten individuals account for 27 per cent of the total interest generated by men (700 men in the data-set, which is less than the 1.8 per cent of the sample), while this figure is approximately 37 per cent for women.

To reach a better understanding on the topic, we have also investigated the sources of media value in tennis. In this context, we have estimated the extent to which sport performance explains the media value level (as well as the popularity and notoriety) of players. In line with previous studies conducted for other sports industries, we find that sport performance largely determines the media value status of tennis players.

The investigation of the size and significance of the estimated coefficients reveals interesting aspects. On one side, sport achievements have a decisive influence on the media value levels of players. On the other side, current performance is found to be relatively more relevant (compared to past performance) for predicting the notoriety level than it is for the popularity level.

The study also examines the influence of non-sport related factors on the media value status of individuals, revealing that women are more dependent than men on their personal characteristics. This bias, even if not enormous, hints at the existence of factors not directly related to sport quality and to stereotypes that could be affecting the opportunities offered to women in certain labour markets.

Once the rankings of media values of the tennis players had been determined, we were well positioned to explore other relevant issues related to the competitive structure of the tennis industry. For instance, as previous ESI reports had found for other sports, we find that the potential earnings of tennis players can be better predicted using media value records rather than sport performance indicators alone.

Finally, the richness of ESI data-set has allowed us to confront the current debate on equal money prize policies in tennis tournaments. The issue has been examined in light of the contribution to spectacle that tennis players generate, as evaluated by the ESI media value index. Interestingly, we find that men are responsible for 65 per cent of the total media value generated in tennis. Accordingly, female players competing in the WTA only represent 35 per cent of the worldwide global interest in the mass media. The estimations from the regression models provide empirical evidence that the gap in money prizes between men and women is smaller than the difference in terms of media value contribution. Therefore, by stressing the uneven contribution to the spectacle by men and women, our study calls into question the prevailing equal prize practices in Grand Slam tournaments.

In conclusion, from an economic perspective, policies of equal money prizes are unlikely to be compatible with economic efficiency. This is because women contribute to the provision of spectacle (by tournament) to a lesser degree than do men, despite the winners for each sex receiving identical money prizes. This statement seems conclusive, as similar results have been obtained through various models. Although there might be a number of good reasons for defending equitable reward schemes, our point is simply to consider this to be incongruent with economic efficiency and rationality. For instance, from the perspective of the organizers of tennis tournaments or sponsorship companies, reward systems of money prizes could be more efficiently designed if the actual (effective) contribution of the agents involved in the spectacle are taken into account.

ACKNOWLEDGEMENTS

We would like to thank Javi Reguart, Pablo Hinojo, Jordi Fábrega and Jorge Álvarez-Campana for their valuable work as research assistants. At the stage of collecting data, we thank: Bruno Mateu, Bernd Frick, Shannon McSween, Aarthi Rajaraman, Peter von Allmen, Francois Rycx and Uwe Sunde.

We have also benefited from comments made by Toni Mora and the participants in the: XIV Encuentro de Economía Aplicada, June 2011, Huelva (Spain), and the: VII GIJON Conference on Sports Economics, 4–5 May 2012, Gijón (Spain). Finally, we gratefully acknowledge financial support from the MEC: Ministerio de Educación y Ciencia (SEJ 2007-67295/ ECON). All remaining errors lie with the authors.

NOTES

1. Among the papers that have clarified the framework for analysing the sports industry, it is worth mentioning the contributions by Rottenberg (1956), Neale (1964) and Sloane (1971). These studies also provide pertinent lessons on good entrepreneurial practice.
2. The economic exploitation of brands in sports has been analysed for the case of Manchester United (Szymanski, 1998) and Real Madrid (Blanco and Forcadell, 2006).
3. For instance, Pujol and Garcia-del-Barrio (2008) analyse the football industry and provide evidence that improved sport achievements imply higher media value levels. As reported by Pujol and Garcia-del-Barrio (2010), the correlation is stronger for the case of individual disciplines, such as Formula 1.

4. The media value of football players seems to be an accurate predictor of their potential capability to generate revenues. This feature is examined for the football industry by Pujol and Garcia-del-Barrio (2008, 2009). These studies report a strong empirical relationship between earnings and media value, to the extent that the latter variable explains nearly 90 per cent of the variance in football clubs' revenues.

5. This feature could be accurately captured either by the cumulative sport performance points (ATP for men and WTA for women) or the total 'prize money' obtained throughout the season. This is because money prizes in tennis are strictly granted on the basis of sport achievements in the various tournaments; hence to capture the level of sport performance, one can in theory choose between these two alternative proxy variables. Ultimately, in the regressions in this section, we preferred the number of points accumulated in the ATP or WTA tours (and these expressed in relative terms per tournament). However, had we employed 'money prizes', instead of using ATP points, the same essential results would have been achieved.

6. However, grouping the superstar players in pairs is not casual, as the structures of tennis contests typically entail rivalries in which the two protagonists share the level of interest generated by the game in a similar fashion. This is particularly the case at the top, for the players who reach the finals, but also applies to earlier stages of the tournaments.

7. Elasticity is a ratio expressing the percentage change in one variable with respect to the percentage change in another variable. Applied economists often resort to elasticity, as it is independent of units and permits direct comparisons. However, because elasticity is evaluated at a point, its interpretation is valid only for small (infinitesimal) changes in the variable. The STATA manual explains that social scientists would informally explain the meaning of ey/ex () $= 1$ as 'y increases 100% when x increases 100%' or as 'y doubles when x doubles', although neither statement is literally true. Instead, for the statement to be accurate, it must incorporate an additional assumption (highlighted in italics): ey/ex () $= 1$ means that 'y increases with x at a rate such that, *if the rate were constant*, y would double if x doubled'.

8. This unexpected result could be due to a correlation between the quality of the players and the number of tournaments played. It is reasonable to imagine that poor performing players attempt to compensate for their weak media value exposure by participating more often in tournaments than high-quality players do.

9. To avoid spoiling the individual residuals of superstar players (Federer, Nadal, Henin, and so on) we use the residuals of the model in which the winner-take-all element is not considered; that is to say: 'MediaValue' against 'PointPerT_2007', 'PointPerT_Past' and 'No_language'. We have performed robust standard errors estimations and run the regressions separately for men and women. In Figure 8.2 the observations for Federer and Nadal have been deleted to retain the same scale for the ATP and WTA tours, thus simplifying a comparison on the basis of a visual inspection of the graphs.

10. A full discussion of the issue requires additional comments. In sports economics, players or clubs are typically considered to be profit maximizing agents. However, following the earlier work of Sloane (1971), Késenne (1996, 2000) argued that, in the world of European soccer, clubs can be treated as win maximizers (subject to a profit constraint) rather than profit maximizers, leading to different conclusions about competitive restraints. Similarly, Garcia-del-Barrio and Szymanski (2009) find consistent evidence of win maximizing (subject to a zero profit constraint) behaviour in both the Spanish and English leagues.

11. In this case, we have not included 'WinTakeAll_2' or 'WinTakeAll_4' as regressors, as they are not statistically significant. This is not surprising because the winner-take-all effect is already implicitly taken into account, as section 4 shows, by the inclusion of 'MediaValue_Mix' in the set of independent variables.

12. Remember that, to be precise, an elasticity is not a fixed number but varies along with the different values taken by the variables involved. Thus, if in model (6) ey/ex () $= 0.3252$, this means that earnings (money prizes per tournament) would increase by approximately 33 per cent. However, this is only true under the assumption that the percentage rate is constant, which is not precisely the case.

REFERENCES

Berri, J. (1999), 'Who is "most valuable"? Measuring the player's production of wins in the National Basketball Association', *Managerial and Decision Economics*, **20** (8), 411–27.

Blanco, M. and Forcadell, F.J. (2006), 'Real Madrid: a new management paradigm for a sport company', *Universia Business Review*, **11**, 36–61.

Daily News (2012), 'France's Gilles Simon says men should be paid more than women at tennis' Grand Slam tournaments', *Daily News*, 27 September, available at: http://www.nydailynews.com/sports/more-sports/france-gilles-simon-men-paid-women-tennis-grand-slam-tournaments-article-1.1103224 (accessed 18 December 2014).

Dobson, S. and Goddard, J. (2001), *The Economics of Football*, Cambridge and New York: Cambridge University Press.

Frank, R. and Cook, P. (1995), *The Winner-Take-All Society: How More and More Americans Compete for Ever Fewer and Bigger Prizes, Encouraging Economic Waste, Income Inequality, and an Impoverished Cultural Life*, New York, London and Toronto: Simon and Schuster, Free Press and Martin Kessler Books.

Garcia-del-Barrio, P. and Pujol, F. (2007), 'Hidden monopsony rents in winner-take-all markets', *Managerial and Decision Economics*, **28** (1), 57–70.

Garcia-del-Barrio, P. and Pujol, F. (2009), 'The rationality of under-employing the best performing soccer players', *Labour: Review of Labour Economics and Industrial Relations*, **23** (3), 397–419.

Garcia-del-Barrio, P. and Szymanski, S. (2009), 'Goal! Profit maximization and win maximization in football leagues', *Review of Industrial Organization*, **34** (1), 45–68.

Hall, R. (1992), 'The strategic analysis of intangible resources', *Strategic Management Journal*, **13** (2), 135–44.

Hoehn, T. and Szymanski, S. (1999), 'European football. The structure of leagues and revenue sharing', *Economic Policy: A European Forum*, **0** (28), 203–40.

Késenne, S. (1996), 'League management in professional team sports with win maximizing clubs', *European Journal for Sport Management*, **2** (2), 14–22.

Késenne, S. (2000), 'Revenue sharing and competitive balance in professional team sports', *Journal of Sports Economic*, **1** (1), 56–65.

Lev, B. (2006), *Intangibles: Measurement, Management and Reporting*, Washington, DC: Brookings Institution Press.

Neale, W.C. (1964), 'The peculiar economics of professional sports', *Quarterly Journal of Economics*, **78** (1), 1–14.

Noll, R.G. (1974), 'Attendance, prices, and profits in professional sports business', in R. Noll (ed.), *Government and the Sports Business*, Washington, DC: Brookings Institution, pp. 115–57.

Pujol, F. and Garcia-del-Barrio, P. (2008), 'Report on media value in football. June 2008', ESI – Universidad de Navarra.

Pujol, F. and Garcia-del-Barrio, P. (2009), 'Biannual report on media value in football. February 2009', ESI – Universidad de Navarra.

Pujol, F. and Garcia-del-Barrio, P. (2010), 'Report of media value in Formula 1. Season 2009', March, ESI – Universidad de Navarra.

Rosen, S. (1981), 'The economics of superstars', *American Economic Review*, **71** (5), 845–58.

Rottenberg, S. (1956), 'The baseball players' labor market', *Journal of Political Economy*, **64** (3), 242–58.

Scully, G.W. (1974), 'Pay and performance in major league baseball', *American Economic Review*, **64** (6), 915–30.

Sloane, P. (1971), 'The economics of professional football: the football club as utility maximiser', *Scottish Journal of Political Economy*, **18** (2), 121–46.

Szymanski, S. (1998), 'Why is Manchester United so successful?', *Business Strategy Review*, **9** (4), 47–54.

Szymanski, S. (2001), 'Income inequality, competitive balance and the attractiveness of team sports: some evidence and a natural experiment from English soccer', *Economic Journal*, **111** (469), F69–F84.

Szymanski, S. (2003), 'The economic design of sporting contests', *Journal of Economic Literature*, **41** (December), 1137–87.

Szymanski, S. and Smith, R. (1997), 'The English football industry: profit, performance and industrial structure', *International Review of Applied Economics*, **11** (1), 135–53.

APPENDIX

Table 8A.1   *Joint index of media value of tennis players: April to October and annual average for 2007*

Ranking	Joint media value 2007		April	May	June	July	Aug.	Sept.	Oct.	2007 average
1	Roger Federer	ATP	63.5	55.2	58.6	51.8	48.1	57.4	35.3	52.9
2	Rafael Nadal	ATP	64.0	51.1	68.6	54.0	43.8	27.3	19.2	46.8
3	JUSTINE HENIN	WTA	27.2	28.1	35.4	27.4	28.6	36.8	19.5	29.0
4	Andy Roddick	ATP	17.7	20.5	25.6	32.4	33.7	33.5	18.3	25.9
5	Novak Djokovic	ATP	18.4	17.9	27.6	17.8	26.1	34.7	25.4	24.0
6	MARIA SHARAPOVA	WTA	16.6	21.4	31.5	29.0	25.1	24.1	13.5	23.0
7	VENUS WILLIAMS	WTA	12.7	16.3	20.1	33.8	26.1	29.0	20.1	22.6
8	SERENA WILLIAMS	WTA	18.9	22.3	27.3	24.8	23.1	24.9	14.6	22.3
9	JELENA JANKOVIC	WTA	14.0	21.2	27.6	11.9	18.7	23.0	14.2	18.7
10	SVETLANA KUZNETSOVA	WTA	16.6	17.1	16.2	12.3	18.2	27.9	18.9	18.2
11	Nikolay Davydenko	ATP	18.4	18.4	20.0	10.8	20.4	22.5	15.4	18.0
12	James Blake	ATP	12.3	13.5	12.2	13.5	22.0	21.3	15.9	15.8
13	Lleyton Hewitt	ATP	14.9	21.0	22.6	13.2	12.6	11.2	10.8	15.2
14	AMELIE MAURESMO	WTA	21.6	21.2	21.8	19.2	6.3	6.0	8.1	14.9
15	ANA IVANOVIC	WTA	12.6	14.3	27.7	14.1	12.9	11.4	8.0	14.4
16	Carlos Moya	ATP	17.4	17.7	19.0	12.1	12.9	12.4	7.7	14.2
17	Fernando Gonzalez	ATP	22.4	21.1	12.7	8.2	8.0	10.0	13.3	13.7
18	David Ferrer	ATP	16.1	12.0	7.1	8.4	15.6	19.5	13.0	13.1
19	Tommy Robredo	ATP	18.4	16.7	17.0	8.9	8.2	7.5	9.2	12.3
20	Richard Gasquet	ATP	17.0	13.9	11.9	17.1	6.7	7.2	11.4	12.2
21	Andy Murray	ATP	12.2	9.1	8.3	9.3	11.0	11.2	17.2	11.2
22	MARTINA HINGIS	WTA	14.7	12.4	10.9	10.0	11.3	10.7	6.6	10.9

23	Tomas Berdych	ATP	17.8	12.4	9.5	10.0	6.9	8.5	10.1	10.7
24	Marat Safin	ATP	13.8	14.1	12.8	12.5	7.7	6.0	6.5	10.5
25	Andre Agassi	ATP	14.1	13.4	13.9	9.3	7.2	7.4	7.7	10.4
26	Guillermo Canas	ATP	18.1	15.5	15.5	6.7	5.3	4.0	5.9	10.2
27	MARION BARTOLI	WTA	6.0	7.6	10.7	19.9	9.0	8.2	7.8	9.9
28	Tommy Haas	ATP	9.2	7.9	7.0	10.0	10.7	12.6	11.7	9.9
29	Juan Carlos Ferrero	ATP	15.9	12.6	10.2	11.6	5.2	3.5	5.1	9.2
30	Ivan Ljubicic	ATP	10.6	11.9	12.0	5.3	4.9	6.4	8.7	8.5
31	ANNA CHAKVETADZE	WTA	5.1	5.6	8.0	9.8	11.7	13.0	6.7	8.5
32	Juan Ignacio Chela	ATP	13.0	11.8	6.7	5.5	8.4	8.1	4.4	8.3
33	Tim Henman	ATP	6.7	6.4	8.9	9.9	8.2	8.5	7.3	8.0
34	ELENA DEMENTIEVA	WTA	9.2	12.0	9.5	5.7	6.1	4.6	8.8	8.0
35	PATTY SCHNYDER	WTA	10.5	12.3	9.7	8.3	6.8	3.8	4.2	7.9
36	Marcos Baghdatis	ATP	11.5	10.4	11.6	8.5	4.4	4.3	4.3	7.8
37	Filippo Volandri	ATP	20.8	16.6	7.7	4.0	2.3	1.6	1.6	7.8
38	Juan Monaco	ATP	7.3	9.8	6.5	6.7	9.1	8.4	6.5	7.8
39	David Nalbandian	ATP	9.8	9.8	11.0	6.2	6.3	4.8	4.6	7.5
40	Igor Andreev	ATP	10.5	10.9	12.5	4.8	3.2	3.4	6.4	7.4
41	DANIELA HANTUCHOVA	WTA	7.0	8.4	8.0	6.9	4.3	6.5	9.3	7.2
42	NADIA PETROVA	WTA	10.5	8.3	6.2	7.5	6.6	4.8	5.8	7.1
43	Philipp Kohlschreiber	ATP	13.2	9.6	6.4	3.4	2.9	4.5	6.8	6.7
44	Mikhail Youzhny	ATP	9.4	9.5	8.6	6.1	3.8	3.8	5.1	6.6
45	Thomas Johansson	ATP	6.0	4.2	4.0	5.9	6.4	7.7	11.2	6.5
46	David Martin	ATP	0.9	0.7	0.7	6.1	11.3	12.0	13.2	6.4
47	NICOLE VAIDISOVA	WTA	4.3	9.2	13.8	8.4	2.9	2.6	3.0	6.3
48	Paul-Henri Mathieu	ATP	8.8	7.9	7.8	7.8	4.1	2.4	5.0	6.2
49	Gael Monfils	ATP	6.1	9.7	8.3	9.3	4.8	2.7	2.5	6.2
50	Michael Russell	ATP	0.9	5.8	5.8	4.7	7.9	8.1	9.1	6.1

Table 8A.1   (continued)

Ranking	Joint media value 2007		April	May	June	July	Aug.	Sept.	Oct.	2007 average
51	Radek Stepanek	ATP	7.4	6.8	4.8	6.2	7.5	4.1	5.1	6.0
52	LINDSAY DAVENPORT	WTA	4.7	4.6	5.1	5.7	4.1	7.2	9.3	5.8
53	TATIANA GOLOVIN	WTA	5.2	3.8	4.0	7.0	4.9	5.0	10.2	5.7
54	DINARA SAFINA	WTA	7.0	8.0	6.9	2.9	4.8	4.5	5.2	5.6
55	Nicolas Almagro	ATP	10.1	9.5	3.9	5.2	4.8	3.0	1.6	5.4
56	Gaston Gaudio	ATP	10.9	9.5	6.3	3.5	2.3	2.0	2.2	5.3
57	kournikova	WTA					3.6	5.4	6.0	5.0
58	SANIA MIRZA	WTA	3.6	3.9	4.1	6.9	6.6	4.3	4.8	4.9
59	Fernando Verdasco	ATP	4.2	4.2	5.9	5.3	5.0	4.0	5.5	4.9
60	Nicolas Massu	ATP	9.0	8.4	4.6	3.3	2.3	2.4	3.1	4.7
61	Martin Lee	ATP	0.3	0.2	0.2	4.6	8.5	9.0	9.9	4.7
62	Arnaud Clement	ATP	6.4	5.9	7.2	4.4	3.7	2.4	2.8	4.7
63	Andre Sa	ATP	0.4	0.4	0.4	4.7	8.1	8.9	9.7	4.7
64	Benjamin Becker	ATP	6.4	4.9	4.8	3.7	3.7	3.5	5.2	4.6
65	Gilles Simon	ATP	6.4	5.1	3.4	5.4	4.5	3.6	3.4	4.6
66	SHAHAR PEER	WTA	5.2	5.1	4.2	3.2	5.4	4.7	3.9	4.5
67	Brian Wilson	ATP	2.3	1.7	1.6	4.5	6.6	7.0	7.9	4.5
68	MARY PIERCE	WTA					3.6	5.0	4.9	4.5
69	Matthew Smith	ATP	0.2	0.2	0.2	3.9	8.2	8.8	10.0	4.5
70	Mardy Fish	ATP	4.3	5.1	4.0	5.1	5.4	4.3	2.9	4.5
71	David Novak	ATP	0.0	0.0	0.0	2.0	8.0	12.7	8.4	4.4
72	Nicolas Kiefer	ATP	3.0	3.3	4.1	6.6	4.6	4.2	5.0	4.4
73	Donald Young	ATP	0.5	0.4	0.4	3.9	8.9	8.8	7.8	4.4
74	Agustin Calleri	ATP	8.8	6.8	3.6	3.4	4.1	2.4	1.5	4.4
75	Jarkko Nieminen	ATP	8.4	6.5	5.0	2.2	2.8	2.4	3.2	4.4

76	Simon Rea	ATP	0.1	0.0	0.0	4.0	8.0	8.6	9.0	4.3
77	Sebastien Grosjean	ATP	7.5	5.9	4.6	2.7	3.0	2.6	3.2	4.2
78	Olivier Rochus	ATP	6.1	5.8	4.7	2.6	1.9	3.1	5.3	4.2
79	Stanislas Wawrinka	ATP	3.7	3.4	2.0	4.1	5.4	4.6	6.1	4.2
80	Ivo Karlovic	ATP	1.8	2.3	4.8	4.1	4.4	3.3	8.6	4.2
81	FRANCESCA SCHIAVONE	WTA	3.3	3.6	3.7	5.1	3.8	4.6	5.2	4.2
82	Lee Childs	ATP	0.1	0.1	0.3	3.8	7.3	8.3	9.4	4.2
83	Jonas Bjorkman	ATP	2.0	4.3	7.7	4.0	2.0	4.1	5.0	4.2
84	Feliciano Lopez	ATP	2.8	2.3	3.1	5.3	5.3	5.1	4.8	4.1
85	Dmitry Tursunov	ATP	3.3	2.7	3.8	4.4	3.6	4.2	6.6	4.1
86	Phillip King	ATP	0.1	0.1	0.1	3.7	7.3	8.0	8.7	4.0
87	Fabrice Santoro	ATP	2.7	3.9	5.1	5.6	3.1	3.5	3.9	4.0
88	Kevin Anderson	ATP	0.9	1.0	0.7	3.4	6.4	7.2	7.9	3.9
89	Marc Lopez	ATP	0.3	0.3	0.2	3.5	7.2	8.0	8.1	3.9
90	Albert Costa	ATP	1.4	1.3	1.4	3.5	6.1	6.8	6.5	3.9
91	MARA SANTANGELO	WTA	4.8	5.2	5.9	3.8	1.7	2.7	2.8	3.9
92	Oscar Hernandez	ATP	7.8	6.0	3.4	2.1	2.4	2.5	2.4	3.8
93	Kevin Kim	ATP	0.5	0.5	0.7	4.2	6.5	6.9	7.2	3.8
94	Greg Jones	ATP	0.3	0.2	0.5	3.6	6.6	7.2	8.1	3.8
95	Potito Starace	ATP	6.7	5.9	3.9	3.1	2.3	1.7	3.0	3.8
96	ANABEL MEDINA	WTA	5.2	6.9	4.8	2.1	2.2	2.5	2.2	3.7
97	SYBILLE BAMMER	WTA	3.6	4.5	5.4	2.8	3.7	3.0	2.8	3.7
98	Kristof Vliegen	ATP	5.7	5.5	4.8	2.8	1.7	1.9	3.1	3.7
99	Jordane Doble	ATP	0.0	0.0	0.0	3.1	6.8	7.4	8.1	3.6
100	Florian Mayer	ATP	4.3	5.8	5.1	2.8	2.8	2.1	2.1	3.6
101	Alberto Martin	ATP	2.8	2.3	1.5	3.0	4.6	5.0	5.5	3.5
102	Juan Martin Del Potro	ATP	1.9	4.2	6.3	3.1	3.4	2.9	2.2	3.4
103	NATHALIE DECHY	WTA	5.3	4.2	4.2	3.2	2.6	2.3	2.0	3.4

Table 8A.1 (continued)

Ranking	Joint media value 2007		April	May	June	July	Aug.	Sept.	Oct.	2007 average
104	Julien Benneteau	ATP	5.7	5.5	4.2	2.1	2.4	1.6	2.3	3.4
105	Robin Soderling	ATP	6.8	4.3	3.5	6.2	1.2	0.9	1.0	3.4
106	Jose Acasuso	ATP	5.6	5.0	2.6	2.9	3.8	2.3	1.5	3.4
107	Marcos Daniel	ATP	0.6	1.2	0.9	3.6	6.0	6.6	4.3	3.3
108	Martin Fischer	ATP	0.1	0.1	0.1	3.1	6.3	6.7	6.7	3.3
109	FLAVIA PENNETTA	WTA	3.6	2.3	2.4	2.3	1.6	3.0	7.7	3.3
110	MARIA KIRILENKO	WTA	2.5	2.1	2.3	2.4	3.1	3.8	6.1	3.2
111	Daniel Brands	ATP	1.2	0.5	0.1	2.8	5.5	5.9	6.1	3.2
112	Nicolas Mahut	ATP	1.7	2.1	5.9	4.6	1.6	2.2	3.9	3.1
113	KATARINA SREBOTNIK	WTA	3.5	3.6	4.1	3.2	2.7	2.2	2.8	3.1
114	Michael Berrer	ATP	0.3	0.2	1.0	3.5	4.4	4.9	7.2	3.1
115	MICHAELLA KRAJICEK	WTA	3.2	4.2	4.5	4.1	2.2	1.4	2.1	3.1
116	GISELA DULKO	WTA	5.5	3.9	2.7	1.9	2.4	2.2	2.9	3.1
117	LUCIE SAFAROVA	WTA	3.8	4.7	5.1	2.3	2.2	1.7	1.5	3.0
118	VIRGINIE RAZZANO	WTA	2.5	1.8	2.2	1.3	2.9	2.9	7.0	3.0
119	EMILIE LOIT	WTA	3.0	4.8	3.9	2.8	2.3	1.5	2.1	2.9
120	Janko Tipsarevic	ATP	1.3	3.1	4.3	3.1	1.8	2.4	4.2	2.9
121	MARY PIERCE	WTA	3.1	3.6	4.2	3.5	2.6	1.5	1.6	2.9
122	Alexander Waske	ATP	6.1	4.4	1.8	1.6	1.2	2.2	2.8	2.9
123	Albert Montanes	ATP	3.9	4.8	3.5	2.6	2.3	1.3	1.5	2.8
124	JULIA VAKULENKO	WTA	7.9	4.8	1.3	0.6	2.0	1.9	1.3	2.8
125	ALONA BONDARENKO	WTA	5.8	5.2	2.6	1.4	1.6	1.4	1.6	2.8
126	AGNES SZAVAY	WTA	1.0	0.7	0.7	1.3	5.3	7.3	3.2	2.8
127	Gustavo Kuerten	ATP	3.1	3.3	4.0	1.9	1.4	2.3	3.4	2.8
128	Robby Ginepri	ATP	2.5	3.2	4.1	2.1	3.2	2.5	1.8	2.8

#	Name	Tour							
129	Guillermo Coria	ATP	4.0	3.8	3.9	2.3	1.7	1.8	1.7	2.7
130	Jurgen Melzer	ATP	3.7	4.0	2.8	1.0	1.8	2.4	3.5	2.7
131	Andrei Pavel	ATP	3.4	2.0	2.5	3.5	2.7	2.4	2.6	2.7
132	AKIKO MORIGAMI	WTA	4.3	2.3	1.8	6.0	1.5	1.2	1.8	2.7
133	AI SUGIYAMA	WTA	3.7	2.6	3.2	3.2	2.6	1.7	1.7	2.7
134	Max Mirnyi	ATP	3.6	2.8	4.0	2.0	2.4	2.3	1.4	2.6
135	TAMIRA PASZEK	WTA	2.5	3.0	4.0	2.7	1.8	2.4	1.8	2.6
136	Mario Ancic	ATP	3.1	2.8	2.5	2.1	2.3	2.2	3.0	2.6
137	SAMANTHA STOSUR	WTA	4.4	4.8	3.7	1.7	1.3	1.1	0.8	2.6
138	TATHIANA GARBIN	WTA	4.7	3.8	3.6	2.7	1.4	0.8	0.6	2.5
139	Hyung-Taik Lee	ATP	1.4	1.5	1.5	3.7	3.7	3.1	2.8	2.5
140	Stefan Koubek	ATP	1.1	1.9	1.5	3.1	2.5	2.6	5.0	2.5
141	Juan Antonio Marin	ATP	0.4	0.2	0.2	2.3	4.6	5.1	4.7	2.5
142	Florent Serra	ATP	3.3	3.1	2.7	3.7	1.6	0.9	2.0	2.5
143	Luis Horna	ATP	1.7	3.7	2.5	2.9	2.0	2.1	2.1	2.4
144	AGNIESZKA RADWANSKA	WTA	1.1	2.3	2.2	1.9	3.7	3.2	2.6	2.4
145	CAMILLE PIN	WTA	3.1	2.7	2.1	2.3	2.3	1.5	2.9	2.4
146	ELENA VESNINA	WTA	1.7	3.3	2.6	3.2	1.5	1.7	2.7	2.4
147	MEGHANN SHAUGHNESSY	WTA	2.6	3.6	3.5	1.7	2.1	1.8	1.3	2.4
148	VICTORIA AZARENKA	WTA	3.5	2.0	0.8	1.3	2.7	2.6	3.8	2.4
149	VERA ZVONAREVA	WTA	2.2	2.2	2.1	1.4	1.7	2.6	4.3	2.4
150	ANASTASIA MYSKINA	WTA	2.7	3.9	4.2	1.9	1.2	1.2	1.3	2.3
151	Andreas Seppi	ATP	2.2	1.5	1.4	4.2	2.1	1.3	3.7	2.3
152	Marc Gicquel	ATP	3.5	2.6	3.1	2.8	1.5	1.4	1.6	2.3
153	Diego Cristin	ATP	0.0	0.0	0.0	2.1	4.3	5.0	4.9	2.3
154	Pablo Gonzalez	ATP	0.3	0.2	0.1	2.3	4.0	4.4	4.9	2.3
155	NA LI	WTA	2.3	2.5	1.8	4.8	3.7	0.4	0.4	2.3
156	Dominik Hrbaty	ATP	4.4	3.1	2.0	1.6	2.2	1.4	1.1	2.3

Table 8A.1 (continued)

Ranking	Joint media value 2007		April	May	June	July	Aug.	Sept.	Oct.	2007 average
157	Rainer Schuettler	ATP	4.6	2.9	1.1	0.7	0.7	2.0	3.5	2.2
158	KAIA KANEPI	WTA	3.2	3.4	3.3	2.2	1.4	1.0	0.9	2.2
159	Dick Norman	ATP	0.5	0.5	0.5	3.1	3.5	3.7	3.5	2.2
160	ALICIA MOLIK	WTA	1.7	2.0	3.0	2.9	1.3	1.5	2.7	2.2
161	Frank Dancevic	ATP	0.4	0.4	0.9	4.6	4.8	1.5	2.4	2.1
162	VANIA KING	WTA	3.1	2.0	1.5	2.5	1.3	1.4	3.0	2.1
163	Daniel Yoo	ATP	0.0	0.0	0.0	1.8	3.8	4.4	4.5	2.1
164	Olivier Patience	ATP	2.1	3.3	3.6	1.5	1.7	1.3	1.2	2.1
165	Fernando Vicente	ATP	0.7	2.3	1.9	1.8	2.4	2.7	2.7	2.1
166	Sergio Roitman	ATP	1.7	2.5	2.5	2.9	2.0	1.1	1.5	2.1
167	SEVERINE BREMOND	WTA	3.6	2.9	2.0	2.7	1.3	0.8	1.0	2.0
168	ALIZE CORNET	WTA	1.4	3.4	4.2	0.7	1.4	1.8	1.4	2.0
169	Nicolas Lapentti	ATP	0.9	2.7	2.8	2.7	1.7	1.2	1.9	2.0
170	Alberto Francis	ATP	0.0	0.0	0.0	1.9	3.7	4.1	4.0	2.0
171	ELENI DANIILIDOU	WTA	2.3	1.5	1.4	1.2	1.7	2.5	3.1	2.0
172	LISA RAYMOND	WTA	2.6	1.5	1.6	3.8	2.1	1.1	0.9	1.9
173	Santiago Gonzalez	ATP	0.3	0.4	0.3	2.2	3.3	3.3	3.7	1.9
174	Morgan Phillips	ATP	0.0	0.0	0.0	1.7	3.7	4.1	3.9	1.9
175	Michael Llodra	ATP	1.2	2.2	2.7	2.2	1.4	1.4	2.4	1.9
176	Sam Querrey	ATP	1.8	1.8	1.8	2.2	2.8	1.7	1.3	1.9
177	James Pade	ATP	0.0	0.0	0.0	1.9	3.7	4.0	3.7	1.9
178	Jonathan Marray	ATP	0.1	0.1	0.3	1.3	3.3	4.0	4.2	1.9
179	Paul Capdeville	ATP	1.1	1.9	1.7	2.1	2.1	2.2	2.0	1.9
180	Mariano Zabaleta	ATP	1.5	2.3	2.3	2.6	2.0	1.3	1.0	1.8
181	Christopher Lam	ATP	0.0	0.0	0.0	1.6	3.4	3.9	3.4	1.8

182	Carlos Berlocq	ATP	0.9	2.3	2.3	2.2	1.4	1.4	1.8	1.8
183	Albert Portas	ATP	0.6	0.5	0.4	1.5	2.9	3.3	3.0	1.8
184	Mark Philippoussis	ATP	2.4	2.2	2.3	2.1	1.3	1.0	1.0	1.8
185	ROBERTA VINCI	WTA	1.9	1.4	1.1	2.6	2.3	2.0	1.1	1.8
186	JAMEA JACKSON	WTA	0.6	0.9	1.5	4.6	3.5	0.6	0.5	1.8
187	Jo-Wilfried Tsonga	ATP	0.6	0.3	2.6	1.9	2.3	2.2	2.2	1.7
188	Diego Hartfield	ATP	1.0	3.4	2.5	2.3	1.6	0.7	0.6	1.7
189	Lucas Engel	ATP	0.2	0.1	0.0	1.5	3.2	3.8	3.4	1.7
190	Jamie Baker	ATP	0.2	0.1	1.0	1.6	2.6	3.1	3.4	1.7
191	Amer Delic	ATP	1.9	2.7	2.1	1.1	1.7	1.4	1.0	1.7
192	Paul Goldstein	ATP	1.7	0.9	0.6	2.1	2.5	2.0	1.9	1.7
193	MILAGROS SEQUERA	WTA	1.4	3.3	2.9	2.5	1.0	0.2	0.2	1.7
194	Xavier Malisse	ATP	2.9	2.2	1.6	1.1	1.1	1.3	1.4	1.7
195	Ricardo Mello	ATP	1.1	0.9	0.7	1.9	2.0	2.1	2.8	1.6
196	Miles Armstrong	ATP	0.0	0.0	0.0	1.4	2.9	3.6	3.4	1.6
197	CATALINA CASTANO	WTA	1.6	2.7	2.0	1.1	1.1	1.2	1.6	1.6
198	Martin Vassallo Arguello	ATP	0.7	0.7	0.5	2.6	2.8	1.3	2.6	1.6
199	Tyler Cleveland	ATP	0.0	0.0	0.0	1.3	3.2	3.7	3.1	1.6
200	Greg Rusedski	ATP	2.2	1.8	2.0	1.8	1.1	1.1	1.3	1.6

9. Career duration in capital-intensive individualistic sports: evidence from ski jumping, golf and auto racing

Bernd Frick, Brad R. Humphreys and Friedrich Scheel

1 INTRODUCTION

In this chapter we analyze the determinants of career duration in three individual sports: professional golf, professional automobile racing, and professional ski jumping. In general, the careers of professional athletes appear skewed towards early exit (Witnauer et al., 2007). While a number of studies of career length in professional sport exist, these three sports have not been analyzed and most of the existing research has focused on career length in team sports. In addition, all three of these sports require relatively large quantities of specialized capital, unlike sports such as tennis, running, soccer, or basketball.

Research on career length in individual professional sport is currently in its infancy. Only a few papers have analyzed career length of athletes in individual sports. In this chapter we identify some basic patterns in career length in these three individual sports in order to provide context for additional research in this area. These three sports all require significant equipment, in the form of skis, clubs, cars, and capital, in the form of ski jump facilities, golf courses, and race tracks that are both specialized and expensive to build and maintain. Our results suggest that professional golfers have the longest careers and professional ski jumpers the shortest; both absolute and relative performance affect career length in all three sports.

In general, career duration in professional sport can be analyzed from several theoretical perspectives. Participating in professional sport over a period of time can be viewed as a labor supply decision, and analyzed in the context of standard dynamic lifecycle labor supply decisions (Mitchell and Fields, 1984). In this context, the end of the athlete's playing career represents a decision to retire from the sport. Retirement is typically a voluntary decision made by employees based on their current and expected earnings and other factors like the value of leisure time and life expectancy. The annual earnings of professional athletes can be large, and some participants in professional sport may view their employment as a way to earn large sums in a short period of time in order to retire early.

Alternatively, the end of an athlete's career can be viewed as a dismissal from the sport. In dynamic models of employee dismissal, inefficient employees are systematically eliminated from employment (Flinn, 1997). This approach to employee dismissals is related to labor market search models and employee–firm matching (Mortensen, 1978). The end of a career is involuntary in this case, and represents a profit maximizing decision on the part of the employer based on the contribution of the employee and the availability of alternative employees. A spell of employment ending with a dismissal can also be interpreted as an outcome of a promotion tournament (Syzmanski, 2003). The organizers of professional sports contests want to attract the most talented athletes in order to maximize profits; when an athlete becomes less productive due to age or injury, contest organizers will replace that athlete with a more productive competitor, leading to an end to the spell of employment.

A spell of employment in a professional sport can also be viewed from the perspective of occupational tenure (Klee, 2013). This approach emphasizes the idea that a career in professional sports is one of several occupations that professional athletes might pursue, and focuses on matching between employer and employee and the role played by occupation-specific human capital. The end of a professional sports career may or may not be voluntary in this context, but the occupational tenure approach emphasizes the importance of other related occupations, such as coaching, scouting, or providing media commentary on events, when an athlete's human capital might be useful, as well as the earnings in these related, and perhaps other unrelated occupations.

All these models imply that current performance, expected future performance, the presence of other employees that can perform the same job, and the value of leisure time affect the exit from employment. These models differ in whether or not the quit is voluntary, or forced on the employee by the employer. In practice, econometricians have limited information about why a professional athlete's career comes to an end. It could be voluntary, as explained by lifecycle labor supply models, or involuntary, as explained by models of employee dismissal and tournament theory models. Models of occupational tenure can include both voluntary and involuntary career terminations. In addition, athletes may experience career-ending injuries that may or may not be observable to the econometrician. These factors make a complete understanding of the reason for the end of the employment spell difficult to determine, and also make it difficult to determine which model to apply to career duration in professional sport.

2   EXISTING LITERATURE

Much of the existing literature on career length in professional sports focuses on team sports. Atkinson and Tschirhart (1986) analyzed career-length data on 260 National Football League (NFL) players active from 1971 to 1980 using hazard models. The average career length in this population was 4.5 seasons. First-year NFL players experienced increasing hazard early in their career but players who survived this early career 'shakeout' experienced a falling hazard rate for the remainder of their careers. Team and individual performance had a positive effect on career length.

Ohkusa (2001) analyzed career-length data for 595 batters and 350 pitchers in Japanese professional baseball over the 1977 to 1990 seasons. Average career length was seven seasons for both pitchers and hitters in this population. Higher salaries were associated with a lower exit probability for both batters and pitchers, but higher productivity was associated with lower exit probability for batters only, and was associated with higher exit probabilities for pitchers. This result was attributed the idea that the learning curve for productivity is a decreasing function of experience for pitchers, but an increasing function of experience for batters.

Staw and Hoang (1995) analyzed career length-data for NBA players picked in the first two rounds of the drafts held from 1980 to 1986. From this population, 275 players played at least one season in the NBA, and 184 exited by the 1990–91 season. The average career length was just under eight seasons in this population. Results suggested that scoring performance and the total number of rebounds and blocks were associated with longer career lengths, and draft position and the number of times a player was traded were associated with shorter career lengths.

Frick et al. (2007, 2009) analyzed career-length data for 4116 players who appeared in at least one match in the top league of professional soccer in Germany, the Bundesliga, over the 1963–64 to 2002–03 seasons. The average career length was four seasons in this population. Results suggested that defenders, midfielders and forwards had shorter careers and goalkeepers longer careers. The total number of games played and goals scored per season were associated with longer careers and yellow and red cards per season had no impact on career length.

Boyden and Carey (2010) analyzed career length data for 1100 players, including 1166 spells of employment and 3435 player-year-observations, in Major League Soccer over the period 1996 to 2007. The average career length was 2.4 seasons in this population. Player performance, in terms of games played per season, minutes played per season, and assists per season, were associated with longer career lengths.

Three studies have analyzed career length in individual professional sports. Most of these studies focused on professional tennis. Coate and Robbins (2001) analyzed career-length data for 236 male and 216 female tennis players who were ranked in the world top 50 in singles at least once between 1979 and 1994. The average career length was about nine seasons in this population. The results suggest that there was no difference between the career length of males and females, despite significantly lower prizes for women. No performance measure was included in the empirical models.

Geyer (2010) analyzed career-length data for 614 male professional tennis players who participated in Grand Slam tournaments, Association of Tennis Professionals (ATP) tournaments, and International Series tournaments over the 1985 to 2007 seasons. The average career length in this population was six seasons. Player performance, in terms of tournaments won and percentage of games won, were associated with longer career lengths, while lower world ranking was associated with shorter careers.

Frick and Scheel (2013) analyzed career-length data for 698 male professional ski jumpers competing in 766 different tournaments over the 1979–80 to 2010–11 seasons. The average career length in this population was four seasons. Athlete performance, in terms of World Cup points accumulated over a season and winning World Championships, was strongly associated with longer career lengths.

The research summarized above analyzes career length in both team and individual sports. There may be important differences in the factors affecting career length in these different types of sport. In a team sport context, player performance depends both on the individual player's ability and the ability of that player to cooperate with teammates in both strategic and tactical margins. In a team sport, players are expected to actively participate in all contests unless they are physically unable to play or are not performing at a high enough level to be put on the field or pitch by the team manager. Also, in team sports, decisions about the continuing employment of players rests primarily with the coaches and management of the team, although players also have control over the duration of employment spells, since a player can choose to retire at any point, even if the team would like to continue employing that player.

In individual sport, the athlete has more control over career duration, conditional on physical health and level of performance. Individual athletes do not have to cooperate with teammates, obey the instructions of coaches or team captains, or perform any specific action not determined by the individual athlete. Individual athletes do not have to participate in every competition held in their sport in a given season. Top-ranked professional golfers and tennis players often participate in a relatively small number of events in each season compared with the total number of events that take place on the PGA or ATP tours.

3   SETTING: SPORTS ANALYZED

We analyze career length in three different individual professional sports: ski jumping, golf, and automobile racing. We selected these sports because of the relative ease of collecting data on career length, and because differences in the nature of the competitions provides an interesting setting for comparing career lengths in these three sports.

The data on ski jumping come from 31 seasons of competition in the International Ski Federation (FIS) Ski Jumping World Cup. The FIS Ski Jumping World Cup is an annual tournament that has been held since 1979. Each season contains about 30 competitions, usually two competitions on the same hill over the course of a weekend; competitions take place primarily in Europe, but events are also held regularly in Japan and occasionally in North America. From 1979 through the early 1990s, the FIS World Cup consisted of about 22–23 events.

The sport of ski jumping was devised by Norwegian soldiers more than 200 years ago, and it has been an Olympic event since the inaugural Winter Olympic Games in Chamonix in 1924. In addition to the Olympic competition, and an annual World Championship, held since 1924, the sport features a well-established and televised professional circuit; the most prominent event is the '4-hills-tournament' which takes place around the turn of the year. Since 1979, all major events have offered prize money to a limited number of participants finishing at the top of the standings in each competition.

Ski-jumping competitions have a complicated organization that includes knock-out qualification rounds that lower-ranked skiers participate in and a main round that includes both qualifying skiers and competitors ranked among the top ten in the world at the time of the competition. Since we do not analyze the outcomes of individual competitions, the details of the structure of these competitions is not important for our analysis.

The data on golf come from 33 seasons of play in the United States Professional Golfers Association (PGA) tour, a professional golf tournament competition held in the United States and Canada. The PGA Tour began in 1929. The PGA Tour currently consists of 38 official tournaments that are played over a 40-week period. Fewer events were held earlier in the sample.

The data on automobile racing come from 35 seasons of competition in National Association for Stock Car Auto Racing (NASCAR) races, the largest sanctioning body for stock-car racing in the United States. 'Stock car' refers to an automobile that has not been modified from its original factory condition and is used to differentiate the type of cars used in NASCAR from open-wheel cars used in Formula automobile racing.

All three sports limit the number of participants in each competition; Szymanski (2003) develops a tournament theory model that predicts sporting event organizers limit the number of participants in contests to maximize effort supplied by participants. All three sports require participants to qualify to participate in a competition using preliminary events or heats. FIS ski jumping selects participants into its events by a complex procedure that limits the number of participants by country of origin and requires specific performance in preliminary rounds. Frick and Scheel (2013) provide details. The NASCAR holds qualifying events prior to each race; some entrants qualify for each race based on past performance, while others qualify by recording the fastest speeds during short races held with no other cars on the track.

The PGA limits competitions to golfers with a PGA Tour 'card' that must be earned by finishing at the top of a qualifying tournament, or according to previous season or career prize money won in PGA Tour events. The PGA also sponsors a limited number of 'Open' tournaments that any golfer, professional or amateur, can participate in by winning a series of qualifying tournaments held in the weeks prior to the competition.

All three sports offer prizes to competitors in individual events based on rank order of finish as well as prizes based on the final standings at the end of the season. The payoff structure for these prizes are typically non-linear, with larger prizes going to the winners of tournaments, as predicted by tournament theory (see Syzmanski, 2003 for details).

One key feature that distinguishes these three sports from other individual sports, such as running, race walking, swimming, or tennis, is that these sports require highly specialized equipment and capital in order to participate. Ski jumping requires specialized skis and large and expensive venues with jumps built to exact specifications. Ski-jump facilities can cost millions of dollars to build and also require extensive maintenance. Golf requires clubs and balls, and, most importantly, golf courses to practice and play on. Golf courses require large tracts of land that may be difficult to acquire or keep in densely populated urban areas; golf courses also require significant, constant maintenance to maintain ideal playing conditions.

The NASCAR requires specialized and expensive equipment in the form of cars. Despite the 'stock car' name, the cars raced in NASCAR events can cost hundreds of thousands of dollars. They also require dedicated mechanics to keep them running. National Association for Stock Car Auto Racing competitions have aspects of team sports, since the car must be serviced with fuel, fluids, tires, and other parts during the competition. A 'pit crew' or team performs this service during races; the pit crew requires specialized labor since time spent performing this service affects race time. Media reports suggest that the cost of maintaining a NASCAR racing team with drivers, multiple cars, mechanics, and a pit crew may cost as much as $400 000 per week during the season. National Association for Stock Car Auto Racing races are also held on large (2–4 mile) banked tracks that require significant resources to build and maintain.

Since athlete-supplied labor and specialized and costly capital are complementary in the production of individual and season-long contests in these sports, the large capital requirements may have an effect on the career length of the athletes participating in these competitions.

4 DATA AND EMPIRICAL ANALYSIS

We collected data on the career length and performance of male professional golfers from the PGA Tour, male professional ski jumpers from the FIS World Cup, and professional automobile racers from the NASCAR. The data on professional golfers cover the 1980–81 to 2012–13 seasons; the data on professional ski jumpers cover the 1979–80 to 2010–11 seasons; the data on professional automobile racers covers the 1975 to 2010 seasons. The PGA Tour data come from http://espn.go.com/golf/moneylist. The FIS ski jump data come from the website www.fisskijumping.com. The NASCAR data come from the website www.nascar.com. (All three websites were last accessed on 27 February 2014.)

Our data set contained 1639 golfers who played on the PGA Tour for at least one season (1381 of these golfers had exited the tour by the 2012–13 season), 696 professional ski jumpers who competed in the FIS Ski Jumping World Cup for at least one season (611 of these ski jumpers had exited the competition by the 2010–11 season), and 740 professional stock car drivers who competed in the NASCAR Cup for at least one season (689 of these drivers had exited the circuit by the 2010 season). Table 9.1 summarizes the career lengths for each sample.

From Table 9.1, professional golfers had the longest careers, and professional ski jumpers the shortest. Career length in all three sports had a very long right tail; while the mean and median career lengths were quite short,

Table 9.1   Summary statistics, career length

Sport	Career length			
	Athletes	Mean	Median	Maximum
PGA golf	1639	5.95	3	32
FIS ski jumping	696	3.79	2	20
NASCAR	740	4.71	2	35

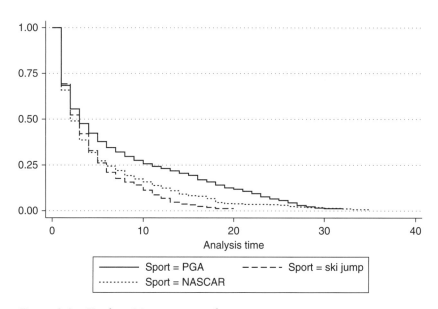

Figure 9.1   Kaplan–Meier survivor function estimates

a few athletes had very long career lengths, skewing the average above the median.

The distribution of career lengths can also be described by Kaplan–Meier survivor functions. This non-parametric estimate of the survivor function shows the probability of an individual having a career of at least t seasons. Figure 9.1 shows the Kaplan–Meier survivor function estimates for athletes in all three sports.

Note that the distribution of the survivor functions in all three sports is similar in the first years of these athletes' careers. Roughly 30 percent of the athletes in each sport have a career of only one season, shown as the first step down at the left side of Figure 9.1. After the first season, the career lengths begin to differ. Golfers are more likely to remain in the PGA Tour compared with ski jumpers and NASCAR drivers, since the survivor function for golfers lies above that for skiers and NASCAR drivers. The likelihood of exiting the sport is similar for skiers and NASCAR drivers until about season 5 of their respective careers, at which point only 25 percent of the athletes are still competing. Beyond season 5, NASCAR drivers are more likely to remain active in the sport than are ski jumpers.

While this unconditional, non-parametric analysis of career length uncovers some interesting patterns, most research on career length performs conditional, parametric or semi-parametric analysis of performance of athletes to better understand the determinants of career length. Parametric and semi-parametric methods can condition observed career length on other observable factors, such as performance, that are known to affect career length systematically in other settings.

In this conditional analysis of career length, we pool data from all three sports and assume that the baseline hazard function varies systematically across sports; this is equivalent to estimating a sport-specific effect on career length. We also explain observed career length using covariates that reflect absolute and relative performance of the athletes. In the previous literature on career length in sport surveyed above, both absolute and relative performance has been linked to career length theoretically and empirically.

The absolute performance measure is based on annual prize earnings for golf and NASCAR, and on total World Cup points for ski jumpers. For absolute performance measure x for athlete i in season j, the normalized performance measure is

$$\mathrm{NP}_{ij} = [x_{ij} - (\Sigma x_i) / \mathrm{N}] / \sigma_{xj} \qquad (9.1)$$

where σ_{xj} is the standard deviation of the performance measures in that season. This normalized performance measure is the athletes' deviation from average performance in the current season normalized by the standard deviation of performance in that season. This normalization allows us to compare absolute performance across sports and seasons.

The relative performance measure is each athlete's rank in the sport in that season. The higher the rank, the better that athlete performed relative to his competitors in that season.

The Cox proportional hazard model is the standard econometric method used to analyze duration data containing right-censored and time-dependent observations. This semi-parametric model has two advantages over other proportional hazard models: the Cox model can be applied to right-censored data, which is important here since many of the skiers, golfers, and car racers analyzed are still active at the end of the sample period. For these competitors, their exit from the competition has not yet occurred, leading to right-censored observations. Second, the Cox model makes no assumptions about the underlying survival distribution and can incorporate time-dependent variables and also deal with left-truncation. Left truncation occurs when athletes in the sample have careers that began before the start of the sample period.

In addition to a Cox hazard model, we estimate a parametric hazard model. Parametric hazard models exploit the information about career length differently than Cox hazard models, and can be interpreted as regression models (Cleves et al., 2008). The specific form of parametric hazard models depends on the distribution of the dependent variable, career length. In this setting, the Akaike Information Criterion (Akaike 1974) indicates that a log-normal parametric model where the log of career length is assumed to follow a normal distribution, is preferable to other parametric models like the log-logistic or Weibull models.

Table 9.2 contains estimates from the Cox and log-normal hazard models, in the form of both hazard ratios and regression parameters. These parameter estimates must be interpreted differently. Hazard ratios from a Cox model reflect an individual competitor's probability of exiting the competition during a specific time period, conditional on having been in the competition as of the beginning of that period. A hazard ratio estimate between 0 and 1 on a covariate reflects a reduction in the exit probability associated with that covariate. Hazard ratios closer to zero reflect a less likely exit associated with that covariate. Estimated hazard ratios larger than one indicate a reduction in the probability that a participant continues to compete in the sport.

Parameter estimates from lognormal models can be interpreted like the coefficient estimates from standard regression models like ordinary least

Table 9.2   Survival model estimates

Variable	Cox hazard model		Log-normal model	
	Param. est.	z-stat	Param. est.	z-stat
Normalized performance	0.350	−12.60	0.693	10.61
Rank	1.011	29.41	−0.011	−32.19
FIS skiing	7.250	21.51	−1.919	−23.96
NASCAR	7.042	26.03	−1.787	−28.33
Athletes				3075
Quits				2681
Time-at-risk (N)				15888

squares (OLS). Positive parameter estimates indicate that changes in that covariate are associated with longer career length and negative parameter estimates indicate that changes in that covariate are associated with shorter career length, other things equal.

All the parameter estimates are significantly different from zero at conventional significance levels. The results from the Cox and log-normal parametric models are qualitatively similar, so we discuss only the results from the log-normal model.

The omitted sport is golf, so all the fixed effects are relative to that sport. Clearly, the regression results show that NASCAR careers are shorter than careers on the PGA Tour, and ski-jumping careers are shorter than NASCAR careers, holding the effects of absolute and relative performance constant. This probably reflects the more physical nature of ski jumping, and the relatively higher injury risk in this sport, relative to automobile racing and golfing. It also reflects the greater competition for sports in each ski-jumping competition documented by Frick and Scheel (2013).

The distinguishing characteristic of these sports is the importance of specialized and expensive equipment and capital by participants. The importance of equipment and capital is likely to affect the average career length of athletes in these sports, relative to other less capital-intensive sports. Recall from above that the average career length in other sports analyzed in the literature included 9 seasons in women's professional tennis, 8 seasons in the NBA, 7 seasons in Japanese baseball, 6 seasons in men's tennis, 4.5 seasons in the NFL and 4 seasons in German football. Recall from Table 9.1 that the average career lengths in our sample are 6 seasons in golf, 4.7 seasons in NASCAR and 3.8 seasons in ski jumping. The average career lengths in these three sports are shorter than in many of the other sports analyzed in the literature, despite the fact that golf and NASCAR are significantly less physically demanding than most of these other sports. Thus the shorter careers in these sports may be attributable to the capital and equipment required to participate in these sports. Practice and competition time on ski-jump hills is limited by the number of facilities in existence and the need for cold weather to produce snow. National Association for Stock Car Auto Racing teams are extremely costly to operate because of the cost of the cars and parts (the engine for a NASCAR car can cost $100 000 and may need to be replaced repeatedly over the course of a season). These capital and equipment requirements appear to shorten the careers of athletes in these sports considerably, compared to more physical sports such as American football and basketball. Only professional golfers enjoy careers as long as athletes in the other sports surveyed.

The parameter estimates on the absolute and relative performance variables are as expected, and consistent with other estimates found in the literature. The better the absolute performance of an athlete in a season, the more likely the athlete's career will continue; the lower the relative performance of an athlete, as reflected in his or her ranking, the less likely the athlete's career will continue beyond this season, holding other factors constant. Relative and absolute performance affect career length in golf, NASCAR, and ski jumping in the same way as in other sports.

5 CONCLUSIONS

We analyze the determinants of career length in three sports that make extensive use of specialized equipment and capital. Career length in these three sports has not been studied much in the sports economics literature. We find that average career lengths in these three sports are relatively shorter than those reported in other sports that place equal or greater physical demands on participants, and have higher injury risk. These shorter careers may be related to the capital and equipment requirements in these sports. The relationship between absolute and relative performance and career length in these three sports is the same as found in other settings: better absolute and relative performance is associated with longer careers, other things equal.

Research on career length in sport is in its infancy. Only a handful of these studies have been done, and many of them have focused on team sports or on tennis. Our results suggest that career lengths in these three sports differ from others reported in the literature, suggesting quite a bit of heterogeneity in career length across sports. Expanding this research to still more sports may provide new insights into labor market outcomes.

This analysis of career length in sports requiring specialized capital can help economists better understand labor market outcomes in settings outside sport. We find that the presence of expensive and specialized capital and equipment may reduce career lengths. Other non-sport occupations also require specialized capital. Surgeons require hospitals and specialized surgical theaters; truck drivers require costly vehicles with sizable maintenance costs; airline pilots require extremely costly jet aircraft; farmers require large tracts of land. If these occupations are similar to the sports analyzed here, then career lengths in these occupations may be shorter than in occupations that do not require costly and specialized capital and equipment. This would have important effects on the cost of production in these settings.

We have not examined a number of other industry-specific and athlete-specific factors that might affect career length here. We have not examined the effects of age, experience or education on career lengths. All these factors have been shown to affect career length in other settings. We have also not examined the effects of nonlinearities in performance measures on career length. All of these topics deserve additional attention.

REFERENCES

Akaike, H. (1974), 'A new look at the statistical model identification', *IEEE Transactions on Automatic Control*, **19** (6), 716–23.

Atkinson, S.E and Tschirhart, J. (1986), 'Flexible modelling of time to failure in risky careers', *Review of Economics and Statistics*, **68** (4), 558–66.

Boyden, N.B and Carey, J.R. (2010), 'From one-and-done to seasoned veterans: a demographic analysis of individual career length in Major League Soccer', *Journal of Quantitative Analysis in Sports*, **6** (4), 1–17.

Cleves, M.A., Gould, W.W. and Gutierrez, R.G. (2008), *An Introduction to Survival Analysis Using Stata*, College Station, TX: Stata Press.

Coate, D. and Robbins, D. (2001), 'The tournament careers of top-ranked men and women tennis professionals: are the gentlemen more committed than the ladies?', *Journal of Labor Research*, **22** (1), 185–93.

Flinn, C. (1997), 'Equilibrium wage and dismissal processes', *Journal of Business & Economic Statistics*, **15** (2), 221–36.

Frick, B. and Scheel, F. (2013), 'Fly like an eagle: career duration in the FIS Ski Jumping World Cup', *Journal of Sports Economics*, 2 September, doi:10.1177/1527002514548723, available at: http://jse.sagepub.com/content/early/2014/09/02/1527002514548723.full.pdf+html (accessed 18 December 2014).

Frick, B., Pietzner, G. and Prinz, J. (2007), 'Career duration in a competitive environment: the labor market for soccer players in Germany', *Eastern Economic Journal*, **33** (3), 429–42.

Frick, B., Pietzner, G. and Prinz, J. (2009), 'Team performance and individual career duration: evidence from the German "Bundesliga"', in P. Andersson, P. Ayton and C. Schmidt (eds), *Myths and Facts about Football: The Economics and Psychology of the World's Greatest Sport*, Cambridge: Cambridge Scholars Press, pp. 327–48.

Geyer, H. (2010), 'Quit behavior of professional tennis players', *Journal of Sports Economics*, **11** (1), 89–99.

Klee, M.A. (2013), 'Estimating the duration dependence of occupational spells with unobserved heterogeneity', SEHSD Working Paper No. 2013-29, United States Census Bureau.

Mitchell, O.S. and Fields, G.S. (1984), 'The economics of retirement behavior', *Journal of Labor Economics*, **2** (1), 84–105.

Mortensen, D.T. (1978), 'Specific capital and labor turnover', *Bell Journal of Economics*, **9** (2), 572–86.

Ohkusa, Y. (2001), 'An empirical examination of the quit behavior of professional baseball players in Japan', *Journal of Sports Economics*, **2** (1), 80–88.

Staw, B.M. and Hoang, H. (1995), 'Sunk costs in the NBA: why draft order affects playing time and survival in professional basketball', *Administrative Science Quarterly*, **40** (3), 474–94.

Szymanski, S. (2003), 'The economic design of sporting contests', *Journal of Economic Literature*, **41** (4), 1137–87.

Witnauer, W., Rogers, R. and Saint Onge, J. (2007), 'Major League Baseball career length in the 20th century', *Population Research and Policy Review*, **26** (4), 371–86.

10. Determinants of national medals totals at the summer Olympic Games: an analysis disaggregated by sport

David Forrest, Ian G. McHale, Ismael Sanz and J.D. Tena

1 INTRODUCTION

It appears that many people are made happier when their country wins medals at the Olympic Games. In a BBC Global Poll, issued on 1 January 2012 (www.bbc.co.uk), a majority of respondents was found, in 18 of 21 countries surveyed, to agree that they felt proud if one of their national representatives achieved a medal. The most positive response (90 per cent agreeing) was in Kenya, a relatively poor country, but with a distinguished Olympic record in track and distance running.

Kenya is, in fact, unusual among developing countries in having achieved any significant success in Olympic competition. The medals table in the summer Games is dominated by relatively rich countries and only the most populous in the developing world appear to have much chance of winning any medals at all. In fact, some 80 of the countries expected to participate in the next Games have never claimed a medal of any colour. Even among those that have, their tallies tend to be disproportionately low relative to their population sizes. India provides a striking (if outlying) illustration. Its population is more than four times as great as that of the United States but it won only three medals in the Beijing Games of 2008, compared with the United States' 110. For India, this was actually an improvement relative to the preceding Games, Athens, 2004.

Published statistical analysis confirms that the level of gross domestic product (GDP) is indeed a highly significant and effective predictor of the shares of medals won by countries at an Olympic Games. The happiness or pride associated with Olympic success is therefore distributed similarly unevenly as world income, and this inequality will be viewed by many as a cause for concern that deserves a policy response (Groot, 2008).

The evidence on the overwhelming importance of GDP comes from an academic literature that goes as far back as Grimes et al. (1974), but the most influential paper has been that by Bernard and Busse (2004) who modelled medal shares of countries at Olympic Games between 1960 and 1996. Applying a random effects tobit regression model, they related the share of medals won by a country at a Games to the log of its per capita GDP and the log of its population (additional variables to capture superior performances by hosts and by communist states were also included). Estimated coefficients on the log values of per capita GDP and population were positive and strongly significant, but insignificantly different from each other. The implication was that it was sheer weight of GDP which drove the shape of the final medals tables (and it did not matter on the margin whether additional GDP came from higher population or from higher per capita income). The finding was consistent with a model in which the number of medals won depends on the amount of talent available which, in turn, depends on the resources available in the country in the form of the size of the population from which athletes may be drawn and the income required to allow their potential to be fulfilled.

When their model was supplemented by including a lagged dependent variable, Bernard and Busse (2004) were able to report that it was an effective tool for out-of-sample forecasting (of the Sydney Games, 2000) and authors attempting similar exercises with similar models have enjoyed similar success in anticipating changes in the medals table at subsequent Games (see, for example, Andreff et al., 2008; Forrest et al., 2010). The most striking changes recently include the rapid emergence of China as an Olympic power and this, of course, is unsurprising in the context of the model, given China's rapid and sustained growth in GDP since the time of the Bernard–Busse analysis.

Unfortunately, utility in forecasting does not necessarily make the statistical model practically useful. If medal success depends on GDP, this offers no insight into the formulation of sports policy by a country looking for a way to win more medals or for the International Olympic Committee if it seeks ways of making the distribution of medals more equitable across countries. Gross domestic product is not an instrument open for manipulation by mere sports policy makers!

The novelty of this chapter is to take a model similar to that in Bernard and Busse (2004) and to apply it sport by sport rather than to the aggregated medals table. Our hope is that this will be suggestive of ways in which individual countries can give themselves more chance of medals, given their economic status, and ways in which Olympics organizers might be able to modify the Games programme to promote greater equity. For example, we will show that medal chances in some sports are linked to GDP in a much steeper relationship than for other sports. It is in the latter group where it is more realistic for low- and middle-income countries to hope to improve national medals performance by focusing extra investment. For Games organizers, a shift in the balance of medals awarded away from the more, and towards the less, elite sports offers a possibility of reducing to some extent the dominance of the richest countries in terms of the proportions of all medals won.

Like Bernard and Busse (2004), we also include variables representing hosts and countries with a communist system of government. Comparing the strength of hosting effects across sports may offer insights into the source of the aggregate home advantage identified in Bernard and Busse. Comparing the strength of the political variables may reveal that communist over-performance in past medals tables was based on a rather specialized selection of sports. Because we include six Games before, and five Games after, the dissolution of the Soviet Union, we are also able to model and report on the rate of decay in the Soviet bloc effect as time passed and countries moved more and more towards western styles of organizing their economies and societies.

Forecasters of the final medals table always have a choice, of forecasting it on the basis of summing predictions made sport by sport or forecasting it directly using aggregated medals data from previous Games. They (at least those applying statistical models in the academic literature) appear consistently to adopt the second of the two approaches. This is perhaps a sensible choice to the extent that pooling of the data across sports should lead to random errors in each sport cancelling each other out and, consequently, to narrower confidence intervals on final estimates of medals won. However, our purpose is not to forecast the medals table but rather to add to understanding of why it takes the shape it does and the implications for sports policy at national and international levels. We expect to be able to show that disaggregation prevents valuable information from being lost and consequently yields additional and different insights from those offered by the standard approach of forecasting the aggregated medals table. Potentially it also offers a more useful tool for benchmarking national medals performances because it will identify the particular sporting disciplines in which a country's athletes may be exceeding or falling short of the level of achievement to be expected given a country's population and economic resources.

2 DATA AND MODEL SPECIFICATION

We model performance employing data from the same starting point as in Bernard and Busse (2004), namely, the 1960 Rome Games, but up to the 2008 Games of Beijing. In two editions of the Games, either the United States, and many of its allies, or the Soviet Union, and the many countries then within its sphere of influence, refused to take part. This distorted competition to the extent that, in most sports, the events could not truly be considered as world championships. Consequently we exclude from estimation of the model data relating to these 'boycott Games', held in Moscow in 1980 and Los Angeles in 1984. This left data for 11 Games over the period of study.

It was not realistically possible to estimate a meaningful model for some sports because too few medals were awarded. This led us to exclude team sports such as baseball, basketball and soccer from the analysis. We decided to apply a cut-off point whereby we modelled medal outcomes only where more than 200 medals had been awarded over the whole data period. The cut-off point was chosen for a level which was not closely approached by any of the sports so excluded.

We were left with 14 sports, namely athletics, boxing, canoe and kayak, cycling, equestrian, fencing, gymnastics, judo, rowing, sailing, shooting, swimming, weightlifting and wrestling. Collectively these disciplines will have been highly influential in determining positions in the overall medals table as they accounted for 86.6 per cent of summer Olympics medals won over the whole data period.

For each sport, we estimated a random effects tobit model. Employment of random effects was in recognition of the panel nature of the data set. Fixed effects estimation was impossible because some (indeed many) countries recorded zero medals at every observation and the country fixed effect for each of them would therefore have been estimated as minus infinity (Lui and Suen, 2008; fortunately, Lui and Suen, working with a similar panel data-set, but for the pan-American Games, where every country had won a medal at some observation, reported that there was little difference in findings between fixed- and random-effects models). Use of tobit was appropriate because there is a large mass point at medals $= 0$, that is, at any Games, most countries win no medals. The dependent variable was *medal share*, the number of medals won by country i in discipline j at Games t as a proportion of the total number of medals awarded in discipline j at Games t.

Medal share was specified to depend on *gdp share* and *population share*. Here, shares were calculated relative to the total GDP (in US dollars), or the total population, of all countries participating in the particular Games, not just those represented in the particular discipline. The implicit assumption is that countries which did not field a competitor in a given sport would not have won a medal in that sport had they done so. Specification in terms of shares (rather than size) of GDP and population allows similar variables to be included as in Bernard and Busse (2004) but without the necessity then to add year dummies to take account of increases in world GDP and population over time.

In Bernard and Busse (2004), the key explanatory variables were log per capita GDP and log population. The proposition that it was log GDP that drove medal share was derived from a failure to reject the null hypothesis that the coefficients on the two variables included were equal to each other. The conclusion was drawn that, on the margin, the impact on medal share of an increase in GDP was the same whether that increase derived from a change in per capita income or from a change in population size. In our specification, the equivalent test is whether the coefficient estimate on *population share* is significantly different from zero. If it proved not to be different from zero, then it could be concluded that what matters for medal performance is simply size of GDP (relative to other countries), as in Bernard and Busse.

Again similarly as in Bernard and Busse (2004), we include additional variables to account for hosting effects (the self-explanatory dummy variable, *host*) and for the historic tendency of communist states to win more medals than might have been expected from their levels of national income and population (*soviet bloc* and *planned*). However, the geo-political landscape has changed considerably since the period from which Bernard and Busse drew their data (which ended in 1996, before the disintegration of the Soviet bloc) and this made some changes in their definitions appropriate. In our analysis, *soviet bloc* was set equal to one if, at the time of the Games, the country was the Soviet Union itself or one of the Central or Eastern European nations within its sphere of influence. The list of countries defined as *soviet bloc* includes all those which were members of the Warsaw Pact but also, in addition, Yugoslavia. Bernard and Busse allocated Yugoslavia to the planned rather than to the Soviet bloc group; but events subsequent to the break-up of the Soviet empire, specifically the balkanization of Yugoslavia itself, persuade us that its history 'belongs' with that of Eastern Europe rather than with that of the other, mostly non-European, planned economies (Albania, China, Cuba, North Korea and Vietnam).

It also has to be taken into account whether a country at the time of a Games was a former member of the Soviet bloc. The culture and infrastructure of sport associated with communism will not have disappeared overnight and some residual 'over-performance' in terms of medals won may have persisted, perhaps indeed up to the present. We defined a variable *ex-soviet effect* for all countries which had been members of the Soviet bloc in the past (including Russia and other republics in Europe and Asia which had been within the old Soviet Union, countries which had been in, or a part of a country in, the Warsaw Pact, and countries which had been part of Yugoslavia). Our variable *ex-soviet effect* is set equal to the reciprocal of the square root of the number of Games since the country left the Soviet bloc (thus, for the relevant countries, the value is 1 for 1992). This specification (combined with the inclusion of a *new country* dummy variable, for any country appearing in its first Games) was designed to capture a residual effect from communism but one that would fade over time, for example because participation in sport fell rapidly in former communist states (Poupaux, 2006). We experimented with several other specifications of *ex-soviet effect*, but using the reciprocal of the square root of the number of Games since the country ceased to be a member of the Soviet bloc provided the greatest improvement in model fit, according to the Akaike Information Criterion. *ex-soviet effect* proved to track well the rate of decay of the influence of communism on medal shares.

The history of Germany made coding of the political variables somewhat tricky in its case. At the first two post-World War II Olympic Games at which German participation was permitted, the International Olympic Committee insisted on a unified team. Subsequently, there were separate West and East German teams until reunification; then, from 1992, there was again only one German team. For the two periods when there was one German team, we set, *soviet bloc* (or *former soviet bloc*, used in the calculation of *ex-soviet effect*) equal to the proportion of the total population of Germany accounted for by the East at the time of the particular Games.

Our specification was therefore:

$$\textit{medal share}_{ijt} = \text{f}(\textit{gdp share}_{ijt}, \textit{population share}_{ijt}, \textit{host}_{it}, \textit{soviet bloc}_{it}, \textit{planned}_{it}, \textit{ex-soviet effect}_{it}, \textit{new country}_{it})$$

3 RESULTS

Table 10.1 displays estimation results for each of the 14 disciplines covered by our analysis. First though, we comment on the results from applying the model to 'all sports'. The penultimate column relates to proportions of all medals won at a given Games and the final column to all medals awarded in our subset of 14 sports.

The strong significance of ρ, the proportionate contribution to the total variance by the panel-level variance component ($= \sigma_v/(\sigma_v^2 + \sigma_e^2)$), here

Table 10.1 *Estimated parameters for random effects tobit model with medal share as dependent variable (z-value in parentheses)*

Coefficient (z value)	Athletics	Boxing	Cycling	Canoe/kayak	Equestrian	Fencing	Gymnastics	Judo
GDP	0.6552 (7.74)	0.5768 (4.1)	1.2512 (3.49)	1.0656 (3.69)	1.5136 (2.74)	1.2071 (3.33)	0.1592 (0.41)	0.6671 (3.79)
Population	0.6087 (3.12)	0.5994 (2.71)	0.4952 (0.75)	0.3545 (0.69)	1.7425 (1.36)	1.0817 (1.74)	2.2525 (3.17)	0.7514 (2.7)
Host	0.0209 (3)	0.0742 (4.73)	0.0872 (2.63)	0.0602 (2.33)	0.1198 (2.52)	0.0366 (1.03)	0.1095 (3.24)	0.061 (3.69)
Soviet bloc	0.0452 (5.66)	0.1115 (6.96)	0.256 (4.61)	0.1214 (4.4)	0.0082 (0.07)	0.1706 (4.68)	0.1456 (3.45)	0.0935 (4.51)
1/Olympics since Soviet bloc	0.0444 (4.72)	0.0957 (5.04)	0.1345 (2.35)	0.1149 (3.1)	−2.9888 (0)	0.1792 (3.79)	0.2493 (4.85)	0.1116 (4.85)
Planned	−0.1229 (−2.32)	−0.0608 (−2.14)	−0.128 (−1.01)	−0.1055 (−1.08)	−1.593 (0)	−0.1241 (−0.99)	−0.2575 (−1.53)	−0.07 (−2.03)
New country	−0.027 (−4.23)	−0.0275 (−1.89)	−0.0347 (−0.97)	−0.0145 (−0.65)	0.039 (0.59)	−0.0446 (−1.14)	−0.0407 (−1.14)	−0.0684 (−3.72)
Constant	−0.0497 (−11.71)	−0.1042 (−11.21)	−0.29 (−10.36)	−0.2085 (−11.62)	−0.3985 (−8.74)	−0.3232 (−11.18)	−0.3227 (−10.42)	−0.1289 (−10.62)
σ_u	0.0403 (10.45)	0.0525 (8.07)	0.1453 (8.01)	0.1119 (8.29)	0.1938 (7)	0.1463 (8.8)	0.1477 (6.79)	0.0685 (8.45)
σ_e	0.021 (22.8)	0.0454 (17.14)	0.0851 (14.33)	0.0623 (14.43)	0.1047 (10.38)	0.075 (11.7)	0.088 (11.67)	0.0433 (14.25)
ρ	0.7864 (22.776)	0.5719 (9.394)	0.7448 (15.611)	0.7633 (16.321)	0.7739 (15.031)	0.7919 (19.03)	0.7381 (11.322)	0.7144 (14.104)
Medal share	0.170	0.062	0.042	0.051	0.025	0.037	0.064	0.047

Coefficient (z value)	Rowing	Sailing	Shooting	Swimming	Weightlifting	Wrestling	All	All (14)
GDP	0.8876 (3.22)	1.5728 (5.75)	1.0555 (6.14)	1.4692 (8.2)	0.7055 (3.11)	0.0873 (0.56)	0.3779 (9.1)	0.3263 (7.43)
Population	0.7377 (1.3)	0.4095 (0.8)	0.9164 (3.41)	0.7778 (2.19)	1.5912 (4.26)	0.3084 (0.95)	0.2562 (3.57)	0.3026 (3.76)
Host	0.0519 (2.22)	0.0644 (2.64)	0.0462 (2.08)	0.0485 (2.54)	0.0901 (3.05)	0.0416 (3.15)	0.025 (7.59)	0.0228 (6.88)
Soviet bloc	0.0549 (2.25)	0.0636 (1.62)	0.134 (6.6)	0.0647 (2.91)	0.2064 (7.44)	0.0943 (6.15)	0.037 (10.57)	0.0328 (9.06)
1/(Olympics since Soviet bloc)	0.0924 (2.98)	0.0829 (2.09)	0.1794 (7.33)	0.1225 (4.75)	0.2305 (6.82)	0.0634 (3.46)	0.0285 (7.4)	0.0252 (6.28)
Planned	−0.1023 (−0.81)	−0.0797 (−0.79)	−0.102 (−2.34)	−0.1312 (−1.68)	−0.1435 (−2.28)	0.0467 (1.52)	−0.0034 (−0.54)	−0.0033 (−0.5)
New country	−0.0214 (−0.99)	−0.0044 (−0.17)	−0.0226 (−1.29)	−0.0455 (−2.06)	−0.087 (−2.92)	−0.0073 (−0.68)	−0.0091 (−3.71)	−0.0088 (−3.55)
Constant	−0.2018 (−14.48)	−0.214 (−10.81)	−0.1539 (−11.55)	−0.1533 (−10.9)	−0.2124 (−10.64)	−0.1437 (−18.58)	−0.0158 (−8.34)	−0.0178 (−8.37)
σ_u	0.1182 (9.48)	0.1107 (8.31)	0.0639 (7.8)	0.0691 (7.38)	0.0827 (7.12)	0.0977 (10.13)	0.0218 (12.73)	0.025 (12.66)
σ_e	0.0545 (15.73)	0.0643 (15)	0.0585 (15.83)	0.0534 (16.4)	0.077 (13.8)	0.034 (17.18)	0.0103 (31.88)	0.0103 (30.56)
ρ	0.8249 (24.24)	0.7479 (16.494)	0.5435 (8.502)	0.6259 (9.827)	0.5355 (7.679)	0.8918 (39.376)	0.8181 (32.627)	0.8545 (40.126)
Medal share	0.048	0.033	0.047	0.118	0.043	0.078		

Note: σ_v is the standard deviation of the country-level random effects; σ_e is the standard deviation of the pure error term; and ρ is the proportionate contribution to the total variance by the panel-level variance component.

as in the equation for each sport, validates the employment of a random effects estimator. Unambiguously, treating the data as panel, rather than simply pooling the observations, is the preferred approach.

Prior to discussion of the findings, it should be recalled that the results throughout Table 10.1 are from a tobit estimator and so coefficient estimates show impacts on the expected medal share conditional on the probability of a positive medal share being equal to 1. Most countries are not predicted to (and do not in fact) win medals and it is therefore equally interesting to consider marginal effects, which provide unconditional estimates of impact on expected medal share that also take into account changes in the probability of winning any medal at all. Marginal effects are the subject of the following section.

As anticipated, the coefficient estimate on *gdp share* is positive and strongly significant. It is worth thinking about what the coefficient estimate predicts. Suppose a country like Spain, which always wins medals and which has a large economy contributing approximately 2 per cent of the total GDP of all competing countries, were to increase its share by about one-tenth, to 2.2 per cent. Given a coefficient estimate on *gdp share* of approximately 0.4, this would raise expected *medal share* by about 0.008, which amounts to less than one medal, given the number of medals awarded at Beijing, 2008. Thus, while GDP is important, economic growth evidently moves expected medals totals only slowly.

The coefficient estimate on *population share* is also positive and strongly significant (and indeed similar in magnitude to that on *gdp share*). This time the finding contradicts the conclusion in Bernard and Busse (2004), that size of population is irrelevant once total GDP has been taken into account. According to our results, a country with a given size of economy typically benefits from having a larger population pool to supply elite athletes, even though this implies lower per capita income to sustain participation and success in sport. Of course, our data embrace three more Olympiads than Bernard and Busse and we note that Andreff (2001) quantified an important role for population size (holding GDP constant) in a study of the distribution of medals at the 1996 and 2000 Games.

Estimated hosting effects are very close to those from Bernard and Busse (2004). The positive impact of *soviet bloc* is rather less than in Bernard and Busse though still positive and highly significant. The (albeit slow) erosion of the legacy of communism is clearly evident from the coefficient estimate on *ex-soviet effect*: more than one-third of the 'over-performance' attributed to communism had been lost by the Games of 2004. Probably little can be inferred from the result on *planned* (the coefficient estimate on which proves insignificant) since the countries in question are small in number and certainly heterogeneous.

Our main interest is in the results for individual sports. Here, the importance of GDP in the aggregate results is reflected in those for individual disciplines and the coefficient estimate is positive and statistically significant in 12 of the 14 cases. However, where they are significant, the magnitudes of the point estimates show substantial variation. Thus, the steepest relationships between *medal share* and *gdp share* emerge for equestrian, sailing and swimming (for all of which the coefficient estimates are a little above or below 1.5) and cycling (where it is close to 1.25). By contrast, the slope is below 0.6 for boxing and is insignificantly different from zero for gymnastics and wrestling. Relatively wide confidence intervals suggest caution in generalizing from limited evidence. Nevertheless, it is clear that some sports are, to a greater extent than others, the preserve of rich countries. The four sports which are the most 'elitist' (and which accounted for more than one-fifth of all medals awarded in the data period) have in common a requirement for expensive and specific capital inputs. It is obvious that equestrian and sailing require heavy investment in bloodstock and yachts, and all their associated facilities, and that the necessary resources will be available to only minute proportions of the populations of poorer countries. Also, while it is true that swimming and cycling can be practised in rivers and on roads, their emergence as competitive sports requires cycle tracks and swimming pools, networks of which, again, are unlikely to be available in the developing world. Strikingly, Andreff (2006) noted that Ethiopia had just one swimming pool per 6.2m population. By contrast, boxing, gymnastics and wrestling (which collectively awarded a similar number of medals as the four 'elite' sports) can all take place in relatively cheap multi-sports facilities, with relatively low need for investment in discipline-specific assets. Barriers to the achievement of medals by poor countries appear to be relatively low in these areas, consistent with Lens's (2011) emphasis on the importance of asset specificity. A policy implication is, for example, that the aid provided to poor countries by Olympic Solidarity might be concentrated on training athletes in disciplines where the general sports infrastructure is already adequate for allowing some potentially competitive players to emerge.

Population appears to matter for half of the sports, with by far the largest effects from *population share* seen in the cases of gymnastics and weightlifting, perhaps both sports where uncommon physical attributes are a prerequisite to performance at a high level. Candidates for success will be found only in the extremity of the distribution of these attributes, making it more likely that large countries will provide the winners.

Hosting effects are important according to all studies which model aggregate medals across all sports. Some of the effect will certainly be general because host nations appear to value success highly given that it is 'their' Games and will therefore typically invest more in preparing its competitors. On the other hand, the 'usual' causes of home advantage in sports – familiarity with the venue, freedom from travel fatigue, effects of crowd support on athletes and judges – will also apply and the importance of these will vary across disciplines. Hence, we would expect to find a positive effect from the dummy variable *host*, but with variation in its estimated size across our 14 sports. This is in fact what we found. The coefficient estimate on *host* was positive and significant for each of the 14 sports except fencing. But its magnitude ranged from more than 0.10 for equestrian and gymnastics to only 0.02 for athletics.

Balmer et al. (2003) examined results from all Games between 1896 and 1996 and noted a tendency for home advantage to be particularly high in sports where outcomes depend strongly on subjective judging. Gymnastics certainly falls within this category and we also found a larger than average home advantage for boxing. On the other hand, Balmer et al. found no home advantage in weightlifting, a sport with little scope for influence by officials, and thought that this provided further illustration of the importance of the behaviour of judges in accounting for hosting effects at the Olympics. But we in fact identified weightlifting as associated with one of the larger host effects (0.09) and so the evidence from our results is inconclusive. Patterns may be hard to discern because the influence of differential degrees of additional investment to improve home performance may be dominant. For example, hosts may put extra resources into 'cheaper' sports and these may not be the sports where traditional sources of home advantage are strongest.

Equestrian has the largest host effect. Here, the trauma of travel, including quarantine, for horses rather than riders, may be important. Further, jumping courses differ greatly across the world and home competitors are likely to have much more experience of the particular venue than those from other countries since it is likely to have been used for domestic championships.

Over-performance by members of the *soviet bloc* is evident across all sports except equestrian and sailing. But the size of the effect is very variable and is relatively modest (about 0.05) for the two highest profile sports at the Olympics, athletics and swimming. By contrast, the effect exceeds 0.20 for cycling and weightlifting and is around 0.15 for fencing and gymnastics. Although the success in cycling appears anomalous, there may be a loose pattern here indicating strategic specialization in those sports with the weakest relationship with GDP, and a corresponding lack of attention to those sports where GDP appears a strong constraint on winning medals (according to the results in Table 10.1). Further discussion of medal performances in communist countries is provided below when we focus particularly on the case of East Germany.

4 MARGINAL EFFECTS

Table 10.1 presented the coefficient estimates from a tobit model and these are conditional marginal effects, conditional on the probability of a medal share greater than 0 being equal to 1. For large, affluent countries, this is not too wildly unrealistic a condition. But where we are concerned with small or poor countries, they are predicted as unlikely to win any medals and the policy interest is in unconditional marginal effects, the predicted changes in expected medal share from variations in the explanatory variables.

To illustrate, Table 10.2 presents unconditional marginal effects, for three sports, athletics, boxing and swimming, for five countries: Bahamas, Brazil, China, Russia and the United States. For the continuous variables *gdp share* and *population share*, the marginal effect is the derivative of expected medal share with respect to the relevant variable. For the dummy variable, *host*, it is the change in expected medal share when the value changes from zero to one (that is, if the country becomes the host). Note that, for the United States, the marginal effect in the case of athletics appears the same as the coefficient estimate in Table 10.1. This is because the probability that the United States will win a positive share of medals is extremely close to 1. For boxing, however, GDP is less important in determining performance and the probability that the United States will win a positive share of medals is a little below 1. Accordingly, the computed marginal effect is this time lower than the coefficient estimate. For the Bahamas, marginal effects are always extremely low because the country is so small in GDP and population that it has a very low probability indeed of winning a medal in any named sport. Low marginal effects indicate little prospect of gaining medals from plausible rates of growth of GDP or population.

The implications of the values shown for marginal effects may become clearer with a concrete example. Let us consider the effect of growing an economy much faster than the rest of the world on expected medal share in athletics.

The United States is the world's largest economy and accounted for 0.273 of the total GDP of countries competing in the 2008 Beijing Games. Suppose the United States increased its share of this measure of world GDP by 10 per cent of itself, such that *gdp share* took on the value 0.3003. What would be the pay-off in terms of expected athletics medals? In 2008, the model predicts a medal share for the United States of 0.158 (the observed value was 0.165). With *gdp share* at 0.3003, predicted medal share increases by 0.018 to 0.176. Such a gain equates to about three extra medals in athletics.

Table 10.2 *Marginal effects for GDP share, population share and host for Bahamas, Brazil, China, Russia and USA for three sports: athletics, boxing and swimming*

	Athletics					Boxing					Swimming				
	Bahamas	USA	Russia	China	Brazil	Bahamas	USA	Russia	China	Brazil	Bahamas	USA	Russia	China	Brazil
δE{y}/δGDP	0.090	0.655	0.290	0.470	0.029	0.039	0.507	0.154	0.534	0.082	0.059	1.468	0.357	1.059	0.188
δE{y}/δ Population	0.084	0.609	0.269	0.437	0.068	0.040	0.527	0.160	0.555	0.085	0.031	0.777	0.189	0.561	0.099
δE{y}/δHost	0.003	0.021	0.009	0.015	0.002	0.005	0.065	0.020	0.069	0.011	0.002	0.049	0.012	0.035	0.006

Consider now the same 10 per cent increase in *gdp share* for Brazil, which accounted for 0.021 of the total GDP of countries represented in Beijing. What would be the effect on expected medal share in athletics if *gdp share* for Brazil were 0.0231 (10 per cent higher)? For 2008, the model at actual GDP predicts a value of zero (though the country did win one medal, for an observed value of 0.007). With 10 per cent growth in *gdp share*, the prediction remains zero. In fact, *gdp share* would have to grow by 230 per cent, to 0.049, before the probability of winning a positive medal share became greater than 0.5. In the last decade, Brazil's economic growth has been among the world's fastest but, even for it, any improvement in medal performance as a result will be slow coming. For economies in, for example, Africa, the slow rate of development is likely to leave countries with poor prospects for medals unless there is proactive policy by the world of sports to change the relationship between medal performance and GDP by, for example, sports aid.

Finally, it is interesting to note that, according to the marginal effect on *host*, Brazil is unlikely to benefit from its hosting of the Games in 2016 to the extent that other recent hosts have. Athletics has lower home advantage than nearly all other sports, according to our results. On the other hand, it awards a large number of medals and the computed marginal effect suggests that China won two extra athletics medals in 2008 as a result of being on home soil. For Brazil, the computed marginal effect is equivalent to one-quarter of a medal and thus no extra medals are likely to follow from hosting. Estimated hosting effects probably owe much to the impact of extra investment put into sport by past hosts. Thus, Brazil would probably have to invest even more than countries have in the past to raise performance levels at its own Games.

5 THE CASE OF EAST GERMANY

For the sake of garnering historical insights, we now return to the over-performance, relative to their income and population levels, of *soviet bloc* countries during the communist era. Tcha (2004) noted that this was based to a large extent on specialization in certain sports. Our results (Table 10.1) supported his contention: for example, over-performance was particularly marked in cycling, fencing and weightlifting, whereas it was not evident at all for equestrian and sailing and of decidedly modest magnitude in athletics and swimming.

We were mindful that East Germany claimed some 200 medals at the athletics stadium and in the swimming pool during the five Games at which it was represented independently, a seemingly remarkable performance for a small country. We therefore re-estimated our tobit equations, with a dummy variable for East Germany added to the regressors. Table 10.3 displays the results, which are little altered in terms of the coefficient estimates on the existing variables but which show a significantly positive East German effect, in addition to the Soviet bloc effect, for eight of the sports (ten if the required significance level is extended from 5 per cent to 10 per cent). This out-performance of the rest of the Soviet bloc proves to have been very large for some sports including athletics, sailing, swimming and gymnastics. Given that three of these four were disciplines in which the coefficient estimate on *soviet bloc* had been small or zero, and given that there was no (significant) extra level of performance by East Germany in the sports where the communist states most excelled (cycling, fencing and weightlifting), it could be concluded that East Germany was the most successful of them in producing medals because it achieved across a broader range of events. These achievements extended to substantial medal hauls in the two areas, athletics and swimming, which appear to attract most prestige.

Tcha (2004) argued that the Soviet bloc 'chose' to win more medals than democratic countries with similar GDPs because the decision-takers were unaccountable and valued medals more than democratic electorates would have, that is, they valued prestige highly. Moreover, medals could be 'produced' more cheaply given the state's command over resources (including, we would add, through the military, which provided competitors in many sports). Did East Germany value medals yet more highly and was it able to produce medals yet more cheaply than the rest of Eastern Europe? Certainly its leaders were in a closer competition for prestige with the West because of rivalry with West Germany, and East Germany is credited with having applied science to sport in path-breaking ways which will have lowered the marginal cost of success in sport. Its critics suggested that the application of science may sometimes have been illicit because rumours of doping abounded. However, the pattern of sports where East Germany outperformed the Soviet bloc as a whole does not obviously point to its dominance depending on sports where doping effects are thought to be largest.

6   CLOSING REMARKS

There is a significant prior literature on the structural determinants of medals totals at the summer Olympic Games. The novelty of this chapter is to have adapted the standard approach to examining the distribution of medals for individual sports. The results show that the same variables

Table 10.3 Estimated parameters for random effects tobit model with medal share as dependent variable and including East German indicator variable (z-value in parentheses)

Coefficient (z value)	Athletics	Boxing	Cycling	Canoe\kayak	Equestrian	Fencing	Gymnastics	Judo
GDP	0.6665 (8.46)	0.5759 (4.09)	1.2511 (3.52)	1.055 (3.71)	1.5181 (2.75)	1.206 (3.31)	0.1863 (0.49)	0.665 (3.78)
Population	0.5605 (3.15)	0.6028 (2.72)	0.5083 (0.77)	0.371 (0.73)	1.7028 (1.33)	1.0844 (1.74)	2.2659 (3.27)	0.756 (2.71)
Host	0.021 (3.07)	0.0742 (4.73)	0.0873 (2.64)	0.06 (2.34)	0.12 (2.52)	0.0366 (1.02)	0.1103 (3.27)	0.061 (3.69)
Soviet bloc	0.0416 (5.43)	0.1094 (6.66)	0.2351 (4.12)	0.1126 (4.12)	0.0246 (0.2)	0.1663 (4.48)	0.1326 (3.2)	0.0888 (4.17)
1/Olympics since Soviet bloc	0.0426 (4.73)	0.0945 (4.94)	0.1276 (2.25)	0.1078 (2.93)	−2.2095 (−0.01)	0.1755 (3.68)	0.2415 (4.76)	0.1091 (4.72)
Planned	−0.1143 (−2.37)	−0.0603 (−2.12)	−0.122 (−0.97)	−0.1014 (−1.04)	−1.2884 (−0.01)	−0.1212 (−0.97)	−0.255 (−1.53)	−0.0688 (−1.99)
New country	−0.0268 (−4.26)	−0.0276 (−1.9)	−0.0342 (−0.96)	−0.0143 (−0.64)	0.0408 (0.61)	−0.0444 (−1.13)	−0.0418 (−1.16)	−0.0682 (−3.71)
East Germany	0.1749 (4.7)	0.033 (0.55)	0.174 (1.1)	0.2428 (2.06)	−0.9899 (0)	0.0948 (0.59)	0.3295 (2.09)	0.067 (0.88)
Constant	−0.0464 (−11.59)	−0.1044 (−11.19)	−0.2878 (−10.2)	−0.2072 (−11.56)	−0.3982 (−8.75)	−0.3246 (−10.99)	−0.3215 (−10.03)	−0.1291 (−10.62)
σ_u	0.0347 (10.23)	0.0526 (8.06)	0.1429 (7.87)	0.1094 (8.32)	0.1936 (7)	0.1471 (8.76)	0.1438 (6.65)	0.0686 (8.45)
σ_e	0.0208 (23.12)	0.0454 (17.14)	0.0851 (14.33)	0.062 (14.51)	0.1047 (10.38)	0.0749 (11.67)	0.088 (11.77)	0.0432 (14.25)
ρ	0.736 (18.519)	0.5731 (9.41)	0.7384 (15.062)	0.7569 (16.069)	0.7736 (14.994)	0.7938 (19.245)	0.7278 (10.929)	0.7155 (14.154)
Medal share	0.170	0.062	0.042	0.051	0.025	0.037	0.064	0.047

Table 10.3 (continued)

Coefficient (z value)	Rowing	Sailing	Shooting	Swimming	Weightlifting	Wrestling	All	All (14)
GDP	0.8831 (3.58)	1.5629 (5.79)	1.0515 (6.17)	1.4911 (9.28)	0.705 (3.11)	0.0835 (0.54)	0.386 (9.49)	0.3435 (8.05)
Population	0.7148 (1.5)	0.4375 (0.87)	0.915 (3.44)	0.6895 (2.21)	1.596 (4.25)	0.3082 (0.95)	0.2583 (3.78)	0.2926 (3.97)
Host	0.0515 (2.25)	0.0645 (2.65)	0.0462 (2.09)	0.049 (2.62)	0.0902 (3.05)	0.0416 (3.14)	0.0251 (7.65)	0.023 (6.96)
Soviet bloc	0.0489 (2.11)	0.038 (0.9)	0.1259 (6.14)	0.0426 (1.99)	0.2012 (7.07)	0.0927 (6.03)	0.0357 (10.29)	0.0316 (8.89)
1/Olympics since Soviet bloc	0.0907 (3.08)	0.0732 (1.85)	0.1752 (7.19)	0.1079 (4.47)	0.2277 (6.7)	0.0621 (3.39)	0.0279 (7.34)	0.0247 (6.3)
Planned	−0.1033 (−0.97)	−0.0758 (−0.75)	−0.0992 (−2.29)	−0.1137 (−1.66)	−0.1417 (−2.24)	0.0472 (1.53)	−0.0041 (−0.66)	−0.0045 (−0.71)
New country	−0.0228 (−1.07)	−0.004 (−0.15)	−0.0227 (−1.3)	−0.0467 (−2.13)	−0.087 (−2.92)	−0.0072 (−0.68)	−0.0091 (−3.72)	−0.0088 (−3.57)
East Germany	0.3911 (3.69)	0.2292 (1.9)	0.1246 (1.72)	0.2736 (4.02)	0.0748 (0.77)	0.0791 (0.78)	0.0789 (3.69)	0.1122 (4.84)
Constant	−0.1834 (−11.8)	−0.2125 (−10.88)	−0.1532 (−11.55)	−0.1425 (−10.92)	−0.2129 (−10.61)	−0.145 (−18.7)	−0.0156 (−8.58)	−0.0169 (−8.6)
σ_u	0.0991 (8.41)	0.1083 (8.33)	0.063 (7.81)	0.0585 (7.12)	0.083 (7.11)	0.0986 (10.2)	0.0204 (12.72)	0.0223 (12.5)
σ_e	0.0539 (15.85)	0.0643 (15.04)	0.0583 (15.87)	0.0526 (16.68)	0.077 (13.79)	0.034 (17.19)	0.0102 (32.02)	0.0103 (30.78)
ρ	0.7716 (17.783)	0.7396 (15.942)	0.5391 (8.463)	0.5534 (8.163)	0.5374 (7.707)	0.8935 (40.317)	0.7993 (29.676)	0.8238 (32.996)
Medal share	0.048	0.033	0.047	0.118	0.043	0.078		

are relevant as in 'aggregated' studies but that their relative importance is different across disciplines. In the particular case of GDP, some sports present a much steeper relationship between medals and income levels than is the case for others. Sports where income matters most tend to be those requiring costly and specific assets, whereas those in which poorer countries are less disadvantaged are those which typically employ multi-sports facilities.

Where asset specificity is the issue, the problem is not so much lack of training facilities for elite athletes, because training abroad is a viable and relatively cheap option. Rather the barrier to success is likely to be the lack of resources necessary to the development of a base of recreational players from whom international competitors could emerge. Study of marginal effects does not encourage us to believe that even impressive rates of economic growth in poor countries would enable these barriers to be overcome in the future.

Thus proactive policy is likely to be required if the pride associated with Olympic success is to be distributed less unevenly between rich and poor countries. It might be considered whether the balance between numbers of medals in different areas might be altered. For example, swimming appears one of the most exclusive sports and it awards the second highest number of medals of any sport at the Games. That distinctions between different swimming events may be unusually fine is supported by the number of individual multi-medal winners that emerge, more than in other sports.

The best prospects for increased medal wins in low- and middle-income countries appear to be in disciplines practised typically in sports halls rather than in specialized facilities specific to one sport. If the international Olympic community were to favour increased sports aid (perhaps through providing a mechanism for trading rights to send competitors to the Games, as proposed by Groot, 2008), improving provision of multi-sports facilities would appear to be an appropriate priority for sports policy in low- and middle-income countries.

REFERENCES

Andreff, W. (2001), 'The correlation between economic underdevelopment and sport', *European Sport Management Quarterly*, **1** (4), 251–79.
Andreff, W. (2006), 'Sport in developing countries', in W. Andreff. and S. Szymanski (eds), *Handbook on the Economics of Sport*, Cheltenham, UK and Northampton, MA, USA: Edward Elgar, pp. 308–15.
Andreff, M., Andreff, W. and Poupaux, S. (2008), 'Les determinants économiques de la performance olympique: Prévision de médailles qui seront gagnées aux Jeux de Pékin', *Revue d'Economie Politique*, **118** (2), 135–69.

Balmer, N.J., Nevill, A.M. and Williams, A.M. (2003), 'Modelling home advantage in the Summer Olympic Games', *Journal of Sports Sciences*, **21** (6), 469–78.
Bernard, A.B. and Busse, M.R. (2004), 'Who wins the Olympics: economic resources and medal totals', *Review of Economics and Statistics*, **86** (1), 413–17.
Forrest, D., Sanz, I. and Tena, J.D. (2010), 'Forecasting national team medal totals at the Summer Olympic Games', *International Journal of Forecasting*, **26** (3), 576–88.
Grimes, A.R., Kelly, W.J. and Rubin, P.H. (1974), 'A socioeconomic model of national Olympic performance', *Social Science Quarterly*, **55** (3), 777–82.
Groot, L. (2008), 'The contest for Olympic success as a public good', Working Paper No. 08-34, Utrecht School of Economics, Netherlands.
Lens, F. (2011), 'Asset specificity in the promotion of élite sport', paper presented to the International Association of Sports Economists Conference, Prague, May.
Lui, H.-K, and Suen, W. (2008), 'Men, money and medals', *Pacific Economic Review*, **13** (1), 1–16.
Poupaux, S. (2006), 'Soviet and post-soviet sport', in W. Andreff. and S. Szymanski (eds), *Handbook on the Economics of Sport*, Cheltenham, UK and Northampton, MA, USA: Edward Elgar, pp. 316–24.
Tcha, M. (2004), 'The color of medals: an economic analysis of the Eastern and Western blocs' performance in the Olympics', *Journal of Sports Economics*, **5** (4), 311–28.

11. Economic prediction of sport performances from the Beijing Olympics to the 2010 FIFA World Cup in South Africa: the notion of surprising sporting outcomes

Wladimir Andreff and Madeleine Andreff

1 INTRODUCTION

The distribution of medal wins across nations at the Summer Olympics is extremely uneven between developed and developing countries: the former – about 40 nations – concentrate from two-thirds to three-quarters of medal wins while the latter – about 160 nations – obtain from one-quarter to one-third of medals total. This observation suggests a likely relationship between a nation's Olympic sport performance and its level of economic development. Indeed, it has been empirically verified that the number of medals a country wins at the Summer Olympics significantly depends on its population and gross domestic product (GDP) per inhabitant (Andreff, 2001). Thus, in a sense, the number of medal wins at the Olympics can be regarded as an additional index of economic development, as are the literacy rate, the percentage of children attending primary school, health expenditures per inhabitant, and mortality or morbidity rates. On the other hand, the level of economic development and population could be used as realistic predictors of Olympic performances.

The only sport mega-event which can compare to Summer Olympics in terms of fan attendance, television viewing and economic impact is the International Federation of Association Football's (FIFA's) soccer World Cup. Nobody knows if a nation's level of economic development impacts on its sport performance at a soccer World Cup since this issue has been neglected in the literature so far, whether one refers to sports economics or development economics. One motive for this chapter is to provide a first insight into this issue and, the other way round, check whether a nation's performance at soccer World Cup may have any sense in reflecting its economic development. Econometric estimations of how significant are the economic determinants of medal wins by each participating nation is now quite usual. Our core research question is: 'Would a model based on population and GDP per capita as determinants perform as well in explaining soccer World Cup outcomes as it is used to perform with Olympic medal wins? Since the estimated model has provided a good prediction of medal wins at the next Olympics, would it be able to predict FIFA World Cup outcomes with a similar success?

After a brief look at modelling and predicting Summer Olympics medal distribution (section 2), a slightly improved model is estimated and then implemented to predict how many medals each nation would have obtained at the 2008 Olympics (section 3). The prediction is compared to actual outcomes observed in Beijing (section 4). A next step is to understand why a similar prediction model has not yet emerged with regards to FIFA World Cup: a major reason is that the soccer World Cup outcome is rather unpredictable due to a number of 'surprises' – surprising outcomes – during its final tournament (section 5). Thus, adapting the model of Olympic medals prediction to FIFA World Cup requires that some football-specific or 'footballistic' variables be introduced alongside with economic variables (section 6). Such emended model is estimated on the basis of past FIFA World Cup results (section 7), and then used to predict the semi-finalists at the 2010 World Cup in South Africa (section 8). Since the predictions regarding the last soccer World Cup do not exhibit good results, performance in the latter is meaningless as an index of economic development. Moreover, this opens an avenue for further research about the notion of surprising sporting outcome and its metrics (section 9). The conclusion emphasizes that economic prediction of sport performances is to be taken with a pinch of salt.

2   ECONOMIC DETERMINANTS OF OLYMPIC MEDALS

More than 30 studies have looked for the determinants of Olympic performances since 1956 combining socio-economic variables with weather, nutrition, mortality in the athlete's home nation, protein consumption, religion, colonial past, newspapers supply, urban population, life expectancy, geographical surface area, military expenditures, judicial system and those sport disciplines taught at school. A widespread assumption among sports economists who have participated in these studies is that a nation's Olympic performance must be determined by its endowment in, and level of development of, economic and human resources captured through

GDP per capita and population. Notice that an increase in the number of medal wins by one country logically is an equivalent decrease in medals won by all other participating nations. Therefore, if you want to explain the Olympic performance of a specific nation, you have to take into account all other participating nations within the overall constraint of the distributed medals total.

During the cold war period, another significant variable emerged: a nation's political regime. The first Western work attempting to explain medal wins by nations' political regime (Ball, 1972) triggered a Soviet rejoinder (Novikov and Maximenko, 1972), both differentiating capitalist from communist regimes. The first two econometric analyses of Olympic Games (Grimes et al., 1974; Levine, 1974) exhibited that, when regressing medal wins on GDP per capita and population, communist countries were outliers; they were winning more medals than their level of economic development and population were likely to predict. A final variable has been introduced, by Clarke (2000), which is the influence on medal wins of being the Olympics hosting country, that is, a sort of home advantage. The host gains more medals than it would otherwise, owing to big crowds of national fans, stronger national athletes' motivation when competing on their home ground, being adapted to local weather, and not being tired by a long pre-Games travel.

Econometric methodology has developed in more recent studies, such as an ordered logit model (Andreff, 2001), a probit model (Nevill et al., 2002) or an ordered probit model (Johnson and Ali, 2004) in which a quadratic specification in GDP per capita is employed to capture a postulated inverted U-shaped relationship, meaning that higher levels of GDP per capita have a positive impact on medal wins though decreasing after some threshold. The most quoted reference is Bernard and Busse (2004) whose model has been widely used in further studies. In this Tobit model implemented for estimating and predicting Olympic performances, the two major independent variables – GDP per capita and population – are taken on board with three dummies that capture a host country effect, the influence of belonging to Soviet-type and other communist (and post-Soviet and post-communist after 1990) countries as against being a capitalist market economy.

3   PREDICTING OLYMPIC MEDALS DISTRIBUTION IN BEIJING 2008

Starting from Bernard and Busse, after a few emendations, a more specified model has been elaborated on (Andreff et al., 2008). The dependent variable is each nation's number of medal wins:[1] $M_{i,t}$. The first two independent variables are GDP per capita and population. Contrary to Bernard and Busse, it is not assumed here that preparing an Olympic team is timeless and, then, independent variables are four years lagged: GDP per inhabitant $(Y/N)_{i,t-4}$ in 1995 purchasing power parity dollars and population $N_{i,t-4}$ (World Bank data). The assumption is that four years are required to build up, train, prepare and make an Olympic team the most competitive in due time. A *Host* dummy is used to capture a home advantage.

Bernard and Busse divide the world into communist regimes and capitalist market economies which obviously fits with the cold war period. Since then, this is too crude with regards to post-communist transition economies: the sports economy sector has differentiated a lot across former socialist countries during their institutional transformation process (Poupaux and Andreff, 2007). Such differentiation has translated into a scattered efficiency in winning Olympic medals after 1991 (Rathke and Woitek, 2008). A first emendation to Bernard and Busse's model is introduced here with a classification that distinguishes Central Eastern European countries (CEEC) which have left a Soviet-type planned economy in 1989 or 1990, and transformed into a democratic political regime running a market economy: Bulgaria, the Czech Republic, Estonia, Hungary, Latvia, Lithuania, Poland, Romania, Slovakia (and Czechoslovakia until the 1993 split), Slovenia, and the German Democratic Republic (GDR; until German reunification in 1990). Another commonality to this group is that these countries have joined the European Union.

A second country group (TRANS) gathers new independent states (former Soviet republics) and some former Council for Mutual Economic Assistance (CMEA) member states which have started up a similar process of transition but are lagging behind the CEECs in terms of transformation into a democratic regime and are stalling on the path towards a market economy: Armenia, Azerbaijan, Belarus, Georgia, Kazakhstan, Kyrgyzstan, Moldova, Mongolia, Russia, Tajikistan, Turkmenistan, Ukraine, Uzbekistan and Vietnam. None of these has joined the EU so far or has an option to do so. The next two groups have not been Soviet regimes properly speaking in the past, although they have been both communist regimes and planned economies. In the first (NSCOM), we sample those countries which have started up a transition process in the 1990s: Albania, Bosnia-Herzegovina, China, Croatia, Laos, Macedonia, Montenegro and Serbia (and the former FSR Yugoslavia before the 1991 break-up). Two countries have not yet engaged in a democratic transformation and a market economy: Cuba and North Korea. They must be considered as still communist regimes (COM). All other countries are regarded as capitalist market economies

(CAPME), the reference group in our estimations. Table 11.1 exhibits uneven medal distribution by political regime.

Beyond Bernard and Busse, a variable supposed to capture the influence on Olympic performance of a specific sporting culture in a region is introduced. For example, Afghan (and other Middle East) women do not participate much in sports or attend sports events, even less be enrolled in an Olympic team. Resulting from these cultural disparities, some nations are more specialized in one specific sport discipline such as weight-lifting in Bulgaria, Turkey, Armenia, and the Balkans, marathon and long distance run in Ethiopia and Kenya, cycling in Belgium and the Netherlands, table tennis, judo and martial arts in various Asian countries, sprinting in Caribbean islands and the USA, and so on. It is not easy to design a variable that would exactly capture such regional sporting culture differences,[2] but it is assumed that regional dummies may reflect them. The world is divided into nine sporting culture regions: AFS, sub-Sahara African countries; AFN: North African countries; NAM, North America; LSA, Latin and South America; EAST, Eastern Europe; WEU, Western Europe (taken as the reference region in our estimation); OCE, Oceania; MNE, Middle East; and ASI, (other) Asian countries.

A first specification is simply *à la* Bernard and Busse, but with a differently defined political regime variable, with a censored Tobit model since a non-negligible number of countries that participate in the Olympics do not win any medal. Therefore, a zero value of the $M_{i,t}$ dependent variable does not mean that a country has not participated and we work out a simple Tobit, not a Tobit 2 (with a two-stage Heckman procedure).[3] Dummies test whether the Olympic year is significant, taking 2004 as the reference. These dummies turn out to be non-significant. In a second specification, a data panel Tobit is adopted, in order to take into account unobserved heterogeneity, whose test is significant,[4] and thus we opt for estimation with random effects. Data[5] encompass all Summer Olympics from 1976 to 2004, except 1980 and 1984 which are omitted owing to boycotts which have distorted the medal distribution per country. Therefore a first specification (11.1) is:

$$M_{i,t}^* = c + \alpha \ln N_{i,t-4} + \beta \ln\left(\frac{Y}{N}\right)_{i,t-4} + \gamma \, Host_{i,t}$$

$$+ \sum_p \delta_p \, Political \; Regime_{p,i} + \sum_q \kappa_q \, Year_{q,i} + \varepsilon_{i,t} \qquad (11.1)$$

where $\varepsilon_{i,t} \sim N(0, \sigma^2)$.

$M_{i,t}$ observation is defined by:

$$M_{i,t} = \begin{cases} M_{i,t}^* & \text{if } M_{i,t}^* > 0 \\ 0 & \text{if } M_{i,t}^* \leq 0 \end{cases}.$$

Table 11.1 Uneven medal distribution by political regime

	1976	1988	1992	1996	2000	2004
CAPME						
Number of medals	268	323	498	543	577	590
Mean (variation coefficient)	3.3 (3.5)	2.2 (4.2)	3.3 (3.7)	3.3 (3.4)	3.5 (3.2)	3.5 (3.2)
Number of countries	81	146	151	164	166	168
Countries with M ≥ 1	35.8%	22.6%	32.5%	33.5%	26.5%	30.4%
NSCOM						
Number of medals	8	40	57	56	59	70
Mean (variation coefficient)	8.0 (0)	13.3 (1.1)	14.3 (1.9)	8.0 (2.3)	8.4 (2.6)	10 (2.3)
Number of countries	1	3	4	7	7	7
Countries with M ≥ 1	100.0%	66.7%	50.0%	42.9%	14.3%	42.9%
COM						
Number of medals	15	0	40	30	29	32
Mean (variation coefficient)	7.5 (1.0)	0.0 (0)	20.0 (0.8)	15.0 (0.9)	14.5 (1.4)	16.0 (1.0)
Number of countries	2	1	2	2	2	2
Countries with M ≥ 1	100.0%	0.0%	100.0%	100.0%	50.0%	100.0%
CEEC						
Number of medals	195	208	99	91	93	86
Mean (variation coefficient)	32.5 (0.9)	34.7 (1.0)	11.0 (0.9)	9.1 (0.9)	9.3 (0.8)	8.6 (0.7)
Number of countries	6	6	9	10	10	10
Countries with M ≥ 1	100.0%	100.0%	100.0%	90.0%	90.0%	100.0%
TRANS						
Number of medals	126	132	114	121	143	153
Mean (variation coefficient)	63.0 (1.4)	44.0 (1.7)	38.0 (1.7)	8.6 (2.0)	10.2 (2.3)	10.9 (2.2)
Number of countries	2	3	3	14	14	14
Countries with M ≥ 1	100.0%	33.3%	66.7%	71.4%	50.0%	57.1%

A second specification (11.2) adds the above described dummy standing for sporting culture regions ($Region_{r,i}$):

$$M^*_{i,t} = c + \alpha \ln N_{i,t-4} + \beta \ln\left(\frac{Y}{N}\right)_{i,t-4} + \gamma\, Host_{i,t} + \sum_p \delta_p\, Political\, Regime_{p,i}$$

$$+ \sum_r \rho_r\, Regions_{r,i} + u_i + \varepsilon_{i,t} \tag{11.2}$$

where $\varepsilon_{i,t} \sim N(0, \sigma^2_\varepsilon)$ and $u_i \sim N(0, \sigma^2_u)$.
$M_{i,t}$ observation is defined by:

$$M_{i,t} = \begin{cases} M^*_{i,t} & \text{if } M^*_{i,t} > 0 \\ 0 & \text{if } M^*_{i,t} \leq 0 \end{cases}.$$

A third specification (11.3) contains an additional variable, $M_{i,t-4}$, on the right-hand side as in Bernard and Busse, who do not comment why they proceed in such a way. The interpretation here is that winning medals at previous Olympics matters for an Olympic national team which usually expects and attempts to achieve at least as well as four years ago. Such inertial effect is all the more relevant for those nations eager to win as many medals as possible, that is, for most nations winning more than zero medals.

The third specification (11.3) is used to predict the medal distribution at Beijing Olympics:

$$M^*_{i,t} = c + \alpha \ln N_{i,t-4} + \beta \ln\left(\frac{Y}{N}\right)_{i,t-4} + \gamma\, Host_{i,t}$$

$$+ \sum_p \delta_p\, Political\, Regime_{p,i} + \sum_r \rho_r\, Regions_{r,i} + \theta\, M_{i,t-4} + \varepsilon_{i,t} \tag{11.3}$$

where $\varepsilon_{i,t} \sim N(0, \sigma^2)$.
$M_{i,t}$ observation is defined by:

$$M_{i,t} = \begin{cases} M^*_{i,t} & \text{if } M^*_{i,t} > 0 \\ 0 & \text{if } M^*_{i,t} \leq 0 \end{cases}.$$

All estimations deliver significant results (Table 11.3). In the first one, all coefficients are positive and significant at a 1 per cent threshold, except for year dummies. It is confirmed once again that medal wins are determined by GDP per capita, population and a host country effect. Political regime is also an explanatory variable. The second estimation overall exhibits the same results. The coefficients of regional sporting culture are significant except for Latin America, an area where the North American sporting culture may have permeated, through Caribbean countries and Mexico (classified in NAM).

Table 11.2   Uneven medal distribution by sporting culture region of the world

	1976	1988	1992	1996	2000	2004
NAM						
Number of medals	122	106	163	156	155	153
Mean (variation coefficient)	12.2 (2.4)	11.8 (2.6)	16.3 (2.1)	15.6 (2.0)	15.5 (1.9)	15.3 (2.1)
Number of countries	10	9	10	10	10	10
Countries with M ≥ 1	50.0%	30.0%	60.0%	60.0%	60.0%	70.0%
AFN						
Number of medals	0	0	5	6	12	8
Mean (variation coefficient)	0 (0)	0(0)	1 (1.4)	1.2 (1.1)	2.4 (1.0)	1.6 (1.4)
Number of countries	3	5	5	5	5	5
Countries with M ≥ 1	0.0%	0.0%	40.0%	60.0%	60.0%	40.0%
AFS						
Number of medals	0	10	16	29	42	29
Mean (variation coefficient)	0(0)	0.3 (5.6)	0.4 (2.4)	0.6 (2.6)	0.9 (2.2)	0.6 (3.0)
Number of countries	3	39	39	45	47	47
Countries with M ≥ 1	0.0%	5.1%	17.9%	22.2%	21.3%	14.9%
LSA						
Number of medals	5	13	8	23	26	25
Mean (variation coefficient)	0.2 (2.4)	0.5 (2.5)	0.3 (2.4)	0.7 (3.7)	0.8 (3.3)	0.8 (2.7)
Number of countries	23	27	29	32	32	32
Countries with M ≥ 1	17.4%	25.9%	20.7%	18.8%	12.5%	21.9%
EAST						
Number of medals	328	352	214	217	233	245
Mean (variation coefficient)	41.0 (1.0)	44.0 (1.1)	17.8 (1.7)	8.0(1.7)	8.6 (2.0)	9.1 (2.0)

Number of countries	8	8	12	27	27	27
Countries with M ≥ 1	100.0%	100.0%	91.7%	74.1%	55.6%	70.4%
WEU						
Number of medals	110	129	227	243	246	242
Mean (variation coefficient)	5.0 (1.7)	5.4 (1.8)	9.5 (1.9)	10.5 (1.5)	10.3 (1.5)	10.1 (1.4)
Number of countries	22	24	24	24	24	24
Countries with M ≥ 1	63.6%	58.3%	62.5%	66.7%	58.3%	62.5%
OCE						
Number of medals	9	14	37	47	62	54
Mean (variation coefficient)	2.3 (1.2)	1.3 (3.3)	3.1 (2.6)	3.9 (3.0)	4.8 (3.4)	3.9 (3.4)
Number of countries	4	11	12	12	13	14
Countries with M ≥ 1	50.0%	9.1%	16.7%	16.7%	15.4%	14.3%
MNE						
Number of medals	2	1	12	11	11	20
Mean (variation coefficient)	0.3 (2.4)	0.1 (3.6)	0.9 (2.0)	0.7 (2.3)	0.7 (2.2)	1.3 (2.2)
Number of countries	6	13	14	15	15	15
Countries with M ≥ 1	16.7%	7.7%	28.6%	26.7%	20.0%	33.3%
ASI						
Number of medals	36	78	126	109	114	155
Mean (variation coefficient)	2.8 (2.5)	0.4 (2.7)	5.3 (2.4)	4.0 (2.7)	4.4 (2.9)	5.7 (2.5)
Number of countries	13	23	24	27	26	28
Countries with M ≥ 1	46.2%	26.1%	45.9%	44.4%	19.2%	37.0%

The economics of competitive sports

Table 11.3   Tobit estimation of medal wins at the Olympics

Independent variables	Tobit Model 1	Tobit (panel) Model 2	Tobit Model 3 with lagged M
Log population $(t - 4)$	9.14***	4.15***	2.15***
Log GDP per capita $(t - 4)$	12.42***	5.44***	2.73***
Host	24.37***	10.40***	10.04***
Political regime (ref. CAPME)			
COM	24.34***	11.18***	5.76**
TRANS	23.24***	20.97***	8.15***
CEEC	21.43***	17.94***	6.71**
NSCOM	11.98***	8.06***	5.22*
Region (ref. WEU)			
AFN		−4.45*	−1.81
AFS		3.67*	0.75
NAM		7.93***	0.076
LSA		0.57	−1.08
ASI		−4.34***	−2.58*
EAST		−5.53*	−3.5
MNE		−5.00***	−2.47*
OCE		6.277**	1.3
Year dummy (ref. 2004)			
1976	4.63		
1988	−0.2		
1992	3.33		
1996	3.35		
2000	0.31		
Medals $(t - 4)$			0.95***
Constant	−138***	−51.30***	−31.57***
Number of observations	941	941	831
Log-likelihood value	−1646.1	−1551.5	−1224.2
Pseudo R^2	0.17	0.19	0.34

Note: *** Significant at 1 per cent threshold; ** at 5 per cent threshold; * at 10 per cent threshold.

Since Western Europe is the reference, a significant coefficient with a positive (negative) sign means that a region performs relatively better (worse) than Western Europe in terms of medal wins. Sub-Saharan Africa, North America and Oceania perform better. Although a little surprising for sub-Sahara African countries since they are among the least developed in the world (except South Africa), this is due to a few countries which are extremely specialized in one sport discipline where they are capable of a non-negligible number of medal wins, such as Ethiopia and Kenya in long distance running. With negative coefficients, North Africa, Asia, Eastern Europe and Middle East perform worse. This is not surprising for North Africa and the Middle East owing to some sports practice restrictions in the culture of various countries. In the case of Asia, only few countries are capable of a significant number of medal wins (China, North Korea, South Korea and Mongolia) given their GDP per capita. Since Eastern European countries are known as outliers, over-performers (given their GDP per capita and population), a negative coefficient results from the *Political Regime* already capturing their over-performance.

The pooling estimation[6] of Model 3 may suffer from endogeneity since the results may be biased by a correlation between the lagged endogenous variable and the error term. This issue is treated with a GMM dynamic panel (Arellano and Bond, 1991), a technique which provides estimated coefficients and predictions that are robust and close to those estimated with a Tobit model. Our predictions show up in Table 11.4 for a country sub-sample.[7]

The predicted first-rank winner is the USA, followed by Russia and China which benefits from home advantage. Most developed market economies are predicted to be among the major medal winners together with some post-communist transition countries.

4 PREDICTIONS AND ACTUAL RESULTS: MEDAL WINS ARE RATHER PREDICTABLE

Comparing predictions with the actual medal distribution that has come out of the Beijing Olympics, the model performs well. It has provided good predictions: 70 per cent of the observed results are encompassed in our predicted confidence interval (among those 189 countries for which data were available and computable). If prediction is assessed as acceptable when the error margin is not bigger than a two-medal difference between prevision and actual outcome, then the model correctly predicts 88 per cent of all Beijing results. The remaining unforeseen 12 per cent accounts for surprises – unexpected outcomes. The model correctly predicts the first ten medal winners, except Japan (instead of Ukraine), misses four out of the first 20 winners, although with a slightly different ranking. However, the most interesting is when model prediction is clearly wrong, that is, basically for 23 nations, meaning that the five variables (plus the inertial variable) have not captured some core explanation of the Olympics outcome. Fortunately, economists are not capable of predicting all Olympic results, otherwise why still convene the Games?

Table 11.4   Prediction of medal wins at Beijing Olympics

	Medals won in 2004	Medal wins predicted in 2008	Lower bound	Upper bound	Medals won in 2008
CEEC					
Bulgaria	12	12	10	13	5
Hungary	17	19	17	21	10
Poland	10	14	12	16	10
Czech Republic	8	10	8	12	6
Romania	19	21	19	23	8
TRANS					
Belarus	15	17	14	20	19
Kazakhstan	8	11	8	14	13
Russia	92	96	93	100	72
Ukraine	23	27	24	29	27
NSCOM					
China	63	80	73	86	100
Cuba	27	29	25	33	24
CAPME					
Germany	49	52	50	54	41
Australia	49	51	47	54	46
Canada	12	15	13	18	18
United States	102	106	103	110	110
France	33	36	35	38	40
Great Britain	30	33	32	35	47
Italy	32	35	34	36	28
Japan	37	39	37	41	25
Less developed countries					
Brazil	10	12	10	14	15
South Korea	30	30	27	32	31
Kenya	7	2	1	4	14
Jamaica	5	1	0	2	11
Turkey	10	9	7	11	8

The major surprise in the actual outcomes, compared with model predictions, is the bigger than expected medal wins by the Chinese team – all published predictions have been wrong in this respect. The host-country effect in China has been underestimated. Possibly, Chinese performance has also been boosted by some undetected doping.[8] A second surprise is the underperformance of the Russian Olympic team, the worst since the cold war. Vladimir Putin convened the highest decision-makers of Russian sport to command a new Olympic policy likely to avoid a repeated disaster at the

2012 London Olympics. In the same vein, other transition countries, such as Romania, have won fewer medals than predicted in Beijing. The current state of restructuring the whole sport sector in these countries has not been sufficiently captured by our refined political regime variable.

The last three significant surprises are Great Britain, Jamaica and Kenya, the latter being the only two developing countries among the first 20 medal winners. Early preparation of a super-competitive team for the 2012 London Olympics may have been the cause for higher than predicted outcomes of the British team, as suggested by Maennig and Wellebrock (2008) who have introduced a 'next Olympics host country' variable in their prediction. Great Britain's medals concentration in cycling (12 medals) may trace back again to undetected doping and/or deep specialization of a nation in one sport discipline. The latter is the most likely explanation for Jamaican medals[9] concentrated in sprinting and Kenyan medals in long distance running. Although we have taken into account such specialization through our lagged $M_{i,t-4}$ variable – Kenya had won seven medals and Jamaica five in the same disciplines at the Athens Olympics – the inertia captured with this variable is revealed to be insufficient.

5   PREDICTION OF FIFA WORLD CUP SEMI-FINALISTS: WHY IS IT SO HARD?

The economics of FIFA World Cup outcome is much less developed than the economic approach to Olympic medal wins. There are two ways of explaining international soccer successes in the literature. The most common method is to explain FIFA points and ranking (the FIFA/Coca Cola World Ranking for all national football teams) at one point in time (Hoffmann et al., 2002b; Houston and Wilson, 2002; Macmillan and Smith, 2007; Leeds and Marikova Leeds, 2009; Yamamura, 2009). The second method consists in explaining a nation's success in FIFA World Cup over time. To the best of our knowledge, at the time of writing, economic determinants of the soccer World Cup outcome have only been covered three times in the literature. From the three papers, it appears that surprising outcomes are the most common occurrence.

Torgler (2004) attempts explaining the determinants of the 2002 soccer World Cup outcome. The dependent variable is a dummy that measures whether a team wins a game or not in the World Cup final tournament. Explanatory variables are not economic. A variable captures the strength of a team through its FIFA ranking, and the positive influence on success of being the hosting team. A second set of variables is introduced regarding the performance of a team during a game: shots on goal, fouls, corner kicks, free kicks, off-sides, cautions, expulsions, and actual playing time (based on ball possession). The main result is that higher FIFA ranking leads to higher probability of winning a game: a one place improvement in world ranking increases a team's probability of winning by approximately 1 per cent, but this result is not always significant. Higher number of shots on goal drives higher probability of winning; having a referee from the same region has a positive impact on the probability of winning a game, but this effect is not statistically significant.[10]

A prediction model of FIFA World Cup outcome is offered by Paul and Mitra (2008). This model is not based on economic variables either. The authors remind that in the past four FIFA World Cup tournaments, 1994 to 2006, the top team in FIFA ranking has not won, except Brazil in 1994. However, they test the relevance of the last FIFA ranking published before the World Cup final tournament as a benchmark to evaluate teams' performance. In a probit model, the dependent variable is a dummy that measures whether a team wins a game or not (1 = win, 0 otherwise). The main explanatory variable is FIFA ranking, controlling for the number of goals scored by each team, and the number of yellow and red cards. A second ordinary least squares (OLS) test considers the scored goal difference as the dependent variable and FIFA rank difference is the main independent variable, controlling for goals scored, the number of yellow and red cards, the number of corner kicks, the number of fouls, the percentage of ball possession, and match attendance. Higher FIFA ranking is significantly associated with higher probability of winning a game. Higher-ranked teams score more goals. A more surprising result is that, although a higher number of yellow or red cards are less likely to win a game, in 2002 and 2006 teams with more yellow cards were more likely to win a game (as were teams with more red cards in the 1998 World Cup). Other surprises are that more corner kicks and more ball possession are associated with losing a game. Overall higher-ranked favourites have the winning trend in their favour, but there are a number of unexpected match outcomes. This is why it is so hard to estimate determinants and make predictions.

Monks and Husch (2009) test whether the FIFA World Cup format may lead to a slightly rigged contest or, at least, whether it may favour certain teams, in particular the host country. During the tournament's history, only seven teams have ever won the World Cup (Brazil five times, Italy four, Germany three, Argentina and Uruguay two, England and France one). Of the 18 tournaments held to date, the host has won six times. The authors test the impact of seeding, home continent and hosting on FIFA World Cup outcomes from 1982 to 2006. The dependent variable is a national team's World Cup final standing (from the winner down to

the team ranked 32 among those qualified according to their performance during the final tournament), and it is regressed on a team's FIFA
rank before the World Cup, a dummy variable for being top seeded, a host
country dummy, and a dummy variable if the World Cup is being played
on a team's own continent. *Ex ante* rank is positive and significant in
determining a team's final standing. Being top seeded results in an increase
in final standing of approximately five places and the home continent
advantage is approximately 2.8 places (but not significant). Both effects
probably overlap with the host country variable (the host country is top
seeded by definition) which provides three places better than the expected
final standing, but the result is not significant. Rank, being the host
country and playing on one's home continent[11] determine advancement in
the tournament to either the quarter-finals or semi-finals.

6 ADAPTING THE OLYMPICS MEDAL MODEL TO THE FIFA WORLD CUP OUTCOME

From the above mentioned studies it is clear that explaining the FIFA
World Cup outcome is much harder than finding in socio-economic
variables the determinants of Olympics medal wins, for different reasons.
Soccer is a sport which is more widespread in some countries (for instance
Latin American countries) than others, whatever their level of economic
development, the size of their population and their democratic or auto-
cratic regime. Such specificity requires the introduction of some 'footballistic' variables in the estimation. However, the Olympics cover so many
sports that overall economic development of a nation affects overall
nation's sporting outcome, beyond disparities in performance across different sports – thus GDP and population are germane to stand for a significant share of the determinants. The number of surprising outcomes is also
much higher with the soccer World Cup than with the Olympics because
in one case the surprises pertain to just one sport discipline whereas with
the Olympics there are unexpected (surprising) medal wins in some sports
that may, on average, compensate surprising medal 'losses' in other sports
for the Olympic teams from big (population) and rich (GDP per capita)
nations.

Moreover, the two contests have different formats. In most Olympic disciplines,[12] after a preliminary knock-out selection, eight athletes remain in
contention for the finals and the first three are rewarded with (gold, silver
and bronze) medals during the finals. Thus it is not difficult to build up an
estimation of the determinants of medal wins – the first three ranked athletes (nations). It is more complex with FIFA World Cup final tournament

since this contest combines a round-robin first stage before the 1/8th finals (the finals immediately prior to the quarter-finals) and, then, a knock-out second stage from the 1/8th finals on. The uncertainty of outcome markedly increases from the first to the second stage (Monks and Husch, 2009) and, thus, the impact of economic variables might well dilute in the course of some knock-out games (thus the surprising outcome). This prepares the ground for the choice of dependent variable to be as comparable as possible with medal wins: it is chosen as the four nations making it to the semi-finals (*Semifin*) of a soccer World Cup final tournament. The determinants of being one of the four highest-ranked teams in the final tournament are looked for – and this facilitates using the same estimation model as the one explaining Olympics medal wins. The four highest-ranked are the winner, the finalist and two losing semi-finalists which play a ranking game the day before the final. Given the dependent variable (making the semi-finals = 1; otherwise 0), a probit model is estimated.

All national teams which have participated in the semi-finals are exhibited in Appendix Table 11A.1 with their cumulative participation from the first 1930 World Cup up to 2006. Retaining the semi-finalists as the dependent variable also makes sense when referring to FIFA economic incentives. Given FIFA distribution rules, each team entering the World Cup final tournament earns a €3.79 million bonus (in 2006). The next step – reaching the 1/8th finals – increases this amount by an extra €1.59 million, followed by an additional €1.90 million bonus when making it to the quarter-finals. Then, qualifying for the semi-finals, there is a huge jump to €6.33 million, followed by only €630000 extra to make it to the final, and winning the finals adds another €1.27 million (Coupé, 2007). In economic terms, it is rather significant to qualify for the semi-finals.

Independent variables are selected with a double purpose in mind: (1) comparing whether the same socio-economic variables play a role in determining FIFA World Cup outcome as with Summer Olympics medal wins; and (2) finding a sample of socio-economic and 'footballistic' variables that explain the soccer World Cup outcome in the long run, in order to come up with an *ex post* benchmark model that can be used further in *ex ante* predicting the semi-finalists of the 2010 World Cup. Owing to data availability, the retained observation period runs from the 1962 soccer World Cup up to 2006, which includes 12 final tournaments. Data cover all national teams which have participated to soccer World Cup final tournaments since 1962 – that is 16 from 1962 to 1978, 24 teams from 1982 to 1994, and then 32 teams from 1998 on, that is, 272 observations in an obviously unbalanced panel.

Population (*Pop*) and GDP per 1000 inhabitants (*GDP/cap*) are the first two independent variables considered just like in the Olympics medal model (World Bank data). Squares are added for both variables (Pop^2 and GDP/cap^2), in tune with Houston et al. (2002) and Macmillan and Smith (2007), in order to control for possible decreasing returns of population and GDP per capita in terms of soccer World Cup performance. The expectation is that population would have a positive effect on reaching the semi-finals while the specificity of soccer may lead to either a significant or a non-significant effect of GDP per capita. These variables are introduced in the model with a two-year time lag under a similar assumption as with the Olympics: the economic size and level of development of a nation two years ago is the context in which the preparation and training of a national soccer team starts up. In the two years after a FIFA World Cup, national teams are used to participate in a regional international contest such as Union of European Football Associations (UEFA) European Championship (EURO) or the African Cup of Nations. Preparing the World Cup really starts after the end of such contests (which means in $t - 2$) when countries start playing the preliminary World Cup qualification stage at a regional level.[13]

In previous studies, it has appeared that a nation's history in the football domain, such as World Cup appearances and the length of FIFA membership, matters when explaining its international soccer performance. Given our objective of explaining semi-finals participation, a specific semi-final history variable (*SFstory*) is derived from the data in Appendix Table 11A.1. It is calculated by dividing all the figures in Appendix Table 11A.1 by the number of FIFA World Cup final tournaments from 1930 up to the year appearing in a column of Appendix Table 11A.1 (for instance, in the 2006 column, all figures are divided by 18, in 2002 by 17, and so on). This variable describes the uneven long-term capacity of a national team to make it for the semi-finals in a historical perspective and ranks nations according to this capacity. When one talks about 'footballistic' nations or football-involved countries, Germany, Brazil, or Italy are often mentioned; indeed, they have been the most frequent semi-finalists at FIFA World Cups. As in previous studies, *FIFA rank* is tested as one explanatory variable, taking FIFA ranking one month before the beginning of the final tournament, and a dummy (*Host*) for being the hosting country.

A regional variable (*Reg*) is different from the one used in the Olympics medal model. The latter's purpose was to capture a regional sport culture effect, while in the case of the FIFA World Cup it must measure the relative strength and density of elite football in six different geographical zones into which FIFA is divided, that is: AFC for Asia, CAF for Africa, CONMEBOL for South America, OFC for Oceania, UEFA for Europe, and CONCACAF for North America, Central America and the Caribbean. Seeding of the final tournament round-robin stage varies across years but is based on teams' successes from each region in previous World Cups and organized in such a way as to assure that top-seeded teams will not have to play each other until the second phase (1/8th finals) of the final tournament (Monks and Husch, 2009).

A last assumption to be tested is whether a soccer-orientated nation, that is, a nation in which the number of players is relatively high compared with overall population, is successful in international soccer. The argument goes alongside a pyramidal explanation of elite sport stating that the larger the mass of sport participants at the pyramid base, the better the elite top. Thus, most football-orientated nations should have the highest probability of qualifying for FIFA World Cup semi-finals. The number of (registered) soccer players (*Players*) divided by population can capture such possible effect.

Estimating the determinants of FIFA World Cup semi-finalists relies on a probit model:

$$
\begin{aligned}
\Pr\left(Semifin^*_{i,t} = 1\right) = \; &\Phi\left[a + b\,SFstory_{i,t-4} + c\,N_{i,t-2} + d\,N^2_{i,t-2}\right.\\
&+ e\left(\frac{Y}{N}\right)_{i,t-2} + f\left(\frac{Y}{N}\right)^2_{i,t-2} + g\,Host_{i,t} + h\,FIFArank_{i,t}\\
&\left.+ \sum_r \rho_r D_r Reg_i + k\,Players_{i,t}\right]
\end{aligned}
\tag{11.4}
$$

where Φ is the cumulative normal distribution.

The paucity of available data for *FIFArank* and *Players* has led to estimate three different specifications. The FIFA ranking has only been available since 1993, when FIFA started publishing it, whereas the number of registered soccer players in all national federations has been published only in 2000 and 2006 (FIFA Big Count, 2000 and 2006), which markedly reduces the size of the data sample. Thus in a first M1 specification, these two variables are not taken on board. In a second M2 specification, FIFA ranking is introduced but the sample is reduced to four World Cup final tournaments (1994 to 2006). Since FIFA ranking does not show up as statistically significant with M2, it is excluded in a third M3 specification whereas the proportion of registered players in the population is taken on board, assuming that the data for 2000 is acceptable for estimating the 2002 FIFA World Cup outcome.

With a small and unbalanced panel, probit estimation is used as a first step. Then to tackle the endogeneity of the semi-final history variable, a probit model with an endogenous regressor and instrumental variables is resorted to. Valid instruments must be exogenous sources of variation in the semi-finalists, and it is difficult to think of relevant candidate instruments to explain international soccer performance (Macmillan and Smith,

2007). Thus, those exogenous variables of the best previous estimated model are retained as instruments.

7 SOCIO-ECONOMIC AND 'FOOTBALLISTIC' DETERMINANTS OF FIFA WORLD CUP SEMI-FINALISTS

Before estimating M1, a preliminary testing has shown that adding year dummies to M1 comes out with none of these year dummies being significant. Therefore we do not proceed with panel data estimation.

The estimation of M1 shows that population and population squared is significant at a 1 per cent threshold; the size of a nation matters with decreasing returns. Hosting the World Cup is also a significant determinant of making it to the semi-finals. The host country has often muddled through the first round-robin phase of the tournament to qualify for the semi-finals. The impact of belonging to each of the six regions on qualifying for the semi-finals is not significant for four regions out of six. Taking

Table 11.5 Estimation of the determinants of the soccer World Cup semi-finalists

Independent variable	Variable name	M1 model	M2 model	M3 model
Semi-final participation history	*SFstory* $(t-4)$	1.185*	2.880*	4.399**
Population	$Nt-2$	0.019***	0.004	0.037**
Population squared	$(Nt-2)^2$	−0.001***	−0.00002	−0.0002*
GDP per capita (1000 inhabitants)	$(Y/N\ t-2)$	0.004	0.012	0.361*
GDP per capita squared	$[(Y/N\ t-2)]^2$	−0.0003	−0.001	−0.010*
Hosting country	*Host* (t)	1.958***	7.089	
Europe region	*DEurope*	2.233***	5.717***	0.750
South America region	*DAmSud*	1.941***	4.614***	−0.313
FIFA ranking one month before	*FIFA rank* (t)		−0.013	
Proportion (%) of soccer players	*Players* (t)			−0.049
Constant		−3.649***	−6.175	−5.575***
Number of observations		272	120	64
Pseudo R^2		0.284***	0.361***	0.409***

Note: *** Significant at a 1 per cent threshold; ** at 5 per cent threshold; * at 10 per cent threshold.

these four regions as the reference, Europe and South America show up as significant variables at a 1 per cent threshold. Being a European or South American team significantly increases the probability of being a semi-finalist. Most semi-finalists have been either European or South American teams so far. A last significant variable, although only at 10 per cent, is the semi-final history variable. Having participated in past semi-finals has a positive effect on the probability of reaching this stage again. Gross domestic product per capita and its square are not significant. This makes a major difference between FIFA World Cup based on a single sport discipline and the multi-sport Olympics. The latter's outcome is determined by the level of economic development in participating countries whereas the former is not.

With M2, tested from 1994 to 2006, the introduction of FIFA ranking as an independent variable has a devastating effect. Most variables, namely, population, population squared and hosting the World Cup, become nonsignificant. The FIFA rank itself is not significant either. The problem with this variable is endogeneity, since its calculation includes each team performance (namely, qualifying for the semi-finals) in the past three World Cups[14] and thus the FIFA ranking interferes with the semi-final history. The host country effect fades away from the determinants of qualifying for the semi-finals, against the frequent host nation expectation that its team has a home advantage to qualify. Overall, M2 is the most difficult specification to interpret even though it maintains the European and South American regions as significant determinants of making it to the semi-finals. The semi-final history remains significant at 10 per cent and prevails over the FIFA ranking as the relevant 'footballistic' variable.

The number of soccer players per inhabitant in each participating nation is introduced in M3 instead of the FIFA rank. The estimation is run for the last two World Cups, which is in itself a limitation to M3. Then, the host variable is automatically dropped because there are only two observations. The number of players is not significant which may be interpreted as follows: soccer mass participation is not a determinant of a nation's participation in the semi-finals of the World Cup final tournament. This invalidates for soccer the pyramidal view of sport where the larger the pyramid base of mass participation, the higher performance in international contests. On the other hand, population is significant, the semi-final history variable is even more significant (at 5 per cent) than in previous specifications, while GDP per capita and squared become significant at 10 per cent. However, regional variables, Europe and South America, are not significant because only two World Cups are kept in: in 2006, no South American team reached the semi-finals, whereas in 2002 one semi-finalist was neither European nor South American (South Korea).

Finally, a control for endogeneity between the dependent variable and one explanatory variable, the semi-final history, is required. The latter is influenced by the results from each new World Cup, although in the long run these results have a decreasing marginal effect on our cumulative variable. Thus, the semi-final history is used as an endogenous regressor and all other variables are taken on board in M1 as instruments. First, the semi-final history variable is regressed on population, population squared, GDP per capita and squared, hosting the World Cup and regional variables, and then the relationship between the dependent variable (making it to the semi-finals) and the endogenous 'semi-final history' regressor is studied.

Table 11.6 shows that all the instrumental variables are explanatory of the semi-final history except the host dummy. It is logical since the semi-final history variable is a cumulative percentage over 18 World Cups whereas a country has been hosting the World Cup only once or twice.[15] Now the model is consistent and close to the Olympics medal model since not only population and regional variables but also GDP per capita are significant determinants of the FIFA World Cup outcome. A clear specificity is that hosting the soccer World Cup is not a comparable advantage to that

Table 11.6   Instrumental variables explaining the semi-final history variable

Semi-final participation history	$SFstory\,(t-4)$	Coef.	$P > |t|$
Population	$Nt-6$	0.001	0.001***
Population squared	$(Nt-6)^2$	−7.98e-07	0.001***
GDP per capita (1000 inhabitants)	$(Y/N\,t-6)$	0.005	0.005***
GDP per capita squared	$[(Y/N\,t-6)]^2$	0.0001	0.024**
Hosting country	$Host\,(t)$	0.079	0.144
Europe region	$Europe$	0.147	0.000***
South America region	$AmSud$	0.234	0.000***
Constant		−0.828	0.000***
Number of observations		256	
Wald Chi 2		27.77***	

The relationship between qualifying for the semi-finals and the semi-final history:

Qualifying to the semi-finals		Coef.	$P > |t|$
Semi-final participation history	$SFstory\,(t-4)$	5.536	0.000***
Constant		−1.611	0.000***

Note: *** Significant at a 1 per cent threshold; ** at 5 per cent.

of hosting Summer Olympics. However, such reality has been blurred for a long time by the World Cup having been located always either in Europe or South America, until 1990. Since then, the number of exceptions has increased with one location each in North America (1994), Asia (2002) and Africa (2010).

8   THE PREDICTION FOR THE 2010 FIFA WORLD CUP IN SOUTH AFRICA: STILL SO HARD!

The model estimated with instrumental variables as well as M1 specification are now used to forecast the 2010 FIFA World Cup semi-finalists, taking into account the data for population and GDP in 2008, and the cumulative semi-final history variable up to 2006. The prediction is exhibited in Table 11.7.

The four teams with the highest probability of making it to the semifinals in South Africa are the same with both M1 and the model with instrumental variables. If you interpret the two highest ranks (probabilities) as the most probable finalists, the former predicts Germany playing Italy in the final while the latter forecasts Germany playing Brazil. France is ranked fourth in both cases. Compared with FIFA rankings published in May 2010, these results are strikingly different: the first four FIFA-ranked teams are Brazil and Spain (potential finalists), then Portugal and the Netherlands. Brazil is the most widely admitted semi-finalist whatever the methodology used for prediction. If one goes so far as to interpret these rankings as a probability to participate in the 1/8th finals, there is a good chance that Argentina, Brazil, Chile, England, France, Germany, Greece, Italy, the Netherlands, Portugal, Serbia, Spain and Uruguay would qualify for the second stage of the 2010 soccer World Cup final tournament. Since the two models encompass a host country effect, both predict South Africa to qualify for the second stage of the final tournament contrary to this nation's FIFA ranking (ranked 83 in May 2010). Of course, those 14 teams[16] which are not mentioned in Table 11.7 would be big surprises if they qualified for the semi-finals. None of them made it!

Actually, the four semi-finalists for the 2010 World Cup have been: (1) Spain, (2) the Netherlands, (3) Germany, and (4) Uruguay. Thus our model did not perform with the soccer World Cup as well as it did with Olympic medals since it correctly predicted only one semi-finalist (Germany). Nobody (see below) expected Uruguay to qualify for the semifinals while it is the fifth best probability (behind France) to qualify in our model prediction.

The banking business has started to use predictions of the soccer

Table 11.7   Prediction of the four semi-finalists at the 2010 FIFA World Cup

Model with instrumental variables			M1 model			FIFA rank
Teams	Rank	Proba*	Teams	Rank	Proba*	May 2010
Germany	1	96.2%	Germany	1	55.6%	1. Brazil
Brazil	2	92.9%	Italy	2	42.2%	2. Spain
Italy	3	80.2%	Brazil	3	41.4%	3. Portugal
France	4	47.1%	France	4	35.7%	4. Netherlands
Most probable quarterfinalists						
Uruguay	5	35.2%	England	5	22.1%	5. Italy
Argentina	5	35.2%	Argentina	6	21.2%	6. Germany
Netherlands	7	24.6%	Spain	7	18.7%	7. Argentina
England	8	16.0%	South Africa	8	17.5%	8. England
Most probable 8th finalists						
Serbia	8	16.0%	Serbia	9	13.8%	9. France
Portugal	8	16.0%	Portugal	10	12.6%	10. Croatia
Spain	11	9.6%	Netherlands	11	10.7%	11. Russia
Chile	11	9.6%	Chile	12	8.8%	12. Egypt
South Korea	11	9.6%	Slovakia	13	8.6%	13. Greece
USA	11	9.6%	Uruguay	14	8.4%	14. USA
South Africa	15	5.4%	Greece	15	8.3%	15. Serbia
Greece	15	5.4%	Slovenia	16	6.5%	16. Uruguay

Note: * Probability of participating in the semi-finals

World Cup outcome as an appealing factor to investors for integrating these predictions in the promotion of financial products. Consequently, some banks' economists have elaborated on prediction models that can be compared – including their results – with our model. Goldman Sachs, J.P. Morgan and Union des Banques Suisses (UBS) have produced a prognosis about the semi-finalists of the 2010 soccer World Cup.

Goldman Sachs (2010) has predicted the following semi-finalists, ranked according to their probability to qualify: (1) Brazil, (2) Spain, (3) Germany and (4) England – two correct out of four – with a methodology primarily based on bookmakers' odds (Ladbrokes.com) on 4 May 2010 and partly on simulating the outcome of each qualification group and then of each of the hypothetical resulting match during the knock out stage. However some guesstimates interfere: 'from Group A, France would seem the strongest, but Mexico looks dangerous, Uruguay is a bit of an unknown, and then there are the hosts, South Africa . . . This could be quite a tricky group for the ageing (and some – especially Irish observers – might say undeserving!) French. I am going to assume that Mexico wins and South Africa is runner-up' Goldman Sachs, 2010, pp. 3–7. Wrong anyway, but from a methodological point of view this sounds hardly more than a toss-up!

The study by J.P. Morgan (2010) adapts its QUANT scoring model (used to identify long/short trading opportunities in financial markets) to forecasting the soccer World Cup outcome by combining several 'footballistic variables'. This scoring model delivers the following ranking: (1) Brazil, (2) Spain, (3) England and (4) the Netherlands. Then, the calculated scores (for all teams) are used – excluding any tied game – together with a 'penalty shoot-out' metric to decide which country will win each of the 64 fixtures; the calculation comes out with an England–Spain final won by England owing to a better penalty shoot-out index. This model confines itself to FIFA World Cup variables but does not perform better, predicting only two of the actual semi-finalists.

The UBS (2010, pp. 27–31) approach states from the very beginning that 'socioeconomic factors like population size or GDP growth have no explanatory power when it comes to forecasting the performance of a specific team' and that 'at every World Cup there is at least one surprise participant in the semi-finals'. The UBS model takes on board: a team's past performance in the World Cup; whether or not a team is a host nation; an objective quantitative measure that assesses the strength of each team three months before the start of the World Cup. The last variable is calculated by using the Elo rating system, developed to measure and rank the strength of chess players; it is assumed to be better than FIFA ranking because it takes into account not only the number of a team's wins, losses and draws, but also the specific circumstances under which those events occurred. Brazil is predicted to have the highest probability of winning the 2010 World Cup (Spain has only the seventh best probability). The best probabilities to make for the semi-finals are: (1) Brazil, (2) Germany, (3) the Netherlands and (4) Italy. Still 50 per cent correct predictions are found – which also means 50 per cent wrong.

9   SPORTS' SURPRISING OUTCOMES AND THEIR METRICS: AN AVENUE FOR FURTHER RESEARCH

Unexpected or surprising outcomes of a game or sport contest have not really been analysed so far. The first point to clarify is the difference between the concept of outcome uncertainty and a surprising outcome. On the one hand, the uncertainty of outcome basically is an *ex ante* concept – it results from the equality or closeness of sporting forces which are going to be opposed in a game or a sport contest – while a surprising outcome is necessarily an *ex post* notion: the actual outcome has appeared surprising compared to some *ex ante* expectation or prediction or standing. A surprising outcome is, to some extent, the opposite of outcome uncertainty which is deeply rooted in outcome unpredictability. The latter is very high when two teams are so close in terms of sporting forces that it is impossible to predict the game outcome (or all teams are so close that the league's final ranking cannot be predicted). A surprising outcome is quite the opposite in so far as it occurs when a sporting outcome is predictable but happens to be different from the prediction. This happens when opponents in a game (contest) have clearly uneven sporting forces, and the underdog wins, for instance a low FIFA-ranked national team defeats a high FIFA-ranked nation. So, a surprising sport outcome may be defined as the *ex post* invalidation of an *ex ante* rather high outcome certainty (predictability), whereas outcome uncertainty is the *ex ante* unpredictability of an *ex post* actual outcome.

Many metrics may be conceived for measuring the occurrence of a surprising sporting outcome. This is an avenue for further research and as a first step macro- and micro-assessments of a surprising sporting result can be suggested.[17] With the aforementioned FIFA World Cup prediction model, a macro-surprise would occur when a team had not made it to the semi-finals while the model was predicting its qualification – and symmetrically when an unpredicted team qualified for the semi-finals. As to this model, Spain and the Netherlands qualification (and to a lesser extent Uruguay qualification) were surprising, as was Brazil, Italy and France not making it to the semi-finals. To obtain an overall metrics, suffice it to say that when a team is higher (lower) ranked by the model than the actual ranking of the final tournament, there is a surprising sport macro-outcome. The magnitude of surprise can be assessed by the rank difference between the model's prediction and the actual outcome (Table 11.8). In the same way, it would be possible to define macro-surprises comparing FIFA ranking and FIFA World Cup outcome or comparing the latter with banks' predictions.

With all predictions, three big surprises emerged: Ghana, Paraguay and Japan making it to the 1/8th finals. Uruguay also is a rather big surprise, since its qualification for the 1/8th finals and even the quarter-finals were only predicted with our model. To some extent England's ranking, owing to a severe loss (1–4) against Germany in the 1/8th finals, was also surprising. Notice that Goldman Sachs did not find any big surprise, while the

Table 11.8 Quantifying surprising sport outcomes (2010 soccer World Cup)

Achieved outcome	Predictions and difference between achieved and predicted ranking							
	Andreff model	Ranking difference	FIFA ranking	Ranking difference	Goldman Sachs	Ranking difference	J.P. Morgan model	Ranking difference
Spain 1	11	−10	2	−1	2	−1	2	−1
Netherlands 2	7	−5	4	−2	6	−4	3	−1
Germany 3	1	2	6	−3	3	0	10	−7
Uruguay 4	5	−1	16	−12	13	−9	17	−13
Ghana 5	17	−12	17	−12	17	−12	17	−12
Brazil 6	2	4	1	5	1	5	4	2
Paraguay 7	17	−10	17	−10	17	−10	17	−10
Argentina 8	5	3	7	1	5	3	5	3
Japan 9	17	−8	17	−8	17	−8	17	−8
USA 10	11	−1	14	−4	9	1	17	−7
Slovakia 11	17	−6	17	−6	17	−6	15	−4
South Korea 12	11	1	17	−5	17	−5	17	−5
Portugal 13	8	5	3	10	12	1	16	−3
Mexico 14	17	−3	17	−3	11	3	11	3
England 15	8	7	8	7	4	11	1	14
Chile 16	11	5	17	−1	17	−1	12	4
Variance predicted/achieved	609		728		634		1030	

Note: For the quarter-finals and 1/8 finals, teams are comparatively ranked according to usual criteria (win>draw>loss; goal difference; goals scored and allowed); 17 is given to those teams not predicted to make for the 1/8 finals.

210

variance between its predictions and achieved outcomes is higher than with our model. The latter detects two big surprises: Uruguay qualifying for the quarter-finals and the failure of England's team. J.P. Morgan's predictions have the highest variance with the achieved outcomes, and it is confirmed that FIFA ranking is not a good predictor either.

However, differences in the exact meaning of measured surprises must be underlined. A comparison between the actual FIFA World Cup outcome and our model's predictions exhibits sporting surprises with regard to nations' economic development and their past performances in the World Cup. With J.P. Morgan's prediction and FIFA ranking, strictly speaking 'footballistic' surprises are indicated: the actual outcome is surprising compared with exclusively 'footballistic' variables. Goldman Sachs' prediction shows how much bookmakers' odds before the World Cup were distant from the achieved outcomes. Betting, in accordance with Goldman Sachs, on Germany as the World Cup winner would have resulted in a gambler's monetary loss, while betting on Spain as one of the finalists would have yielded some return.

A micro-metrics of surprising sport outcomes may be based on a weaker team (underdog) winning against a stronger team (favourite). If one lower FIFA-ranked team beat a higher FIFA-ranked team, this would be a micro-surprise. With our model, Ghana–USA (2–1) in the 1/8th finals was surprising as well as the Netherlands–Brazil (2–1) in the quarter-finals and Spain–Germany (1–0) in the semi-finals. With FIFA ranking and Goldman Sachs' prediction, the micro-surprises were only Ghana–USA (2–1) and Netherlands–Brazil (2–1). On the other hand, J.P. Morgan's prediction was surprised by Ghana–USA (2–1) and Germany–England (4–1) in the 1/8th finals and Netherlands–Brazil (2–1) and Germany–Argentina (4–0) in the quarter-finals. J.P. Morgan's prediction definitely is the furthest from actual outcomes when looking at both micro- and macro-surprises.

The notion of surprising sporting micro-outcomes may be refined with the historical variable of our model, checking whether in the 2010 World Cup final tournament a nation which never made it to the semi-finals has been able to beat a nation which already qualified for the semi-finals at least once since 1930. With such a criterion, the following outcomes are surprising: Ghana–USA (2–1) in the 1/8th finals and during the round-robin stage Mexico–France (2–0), South Africa–France (2–1), Serbia–Germany (1–0), Slovakia–Italy (3–2), and Switzerland–Spain (1–0). Two teams did not survive their surprising losses in the qualification groups (France and Italy) whereas the two others made it to the semi-finals (Germany and Spain).

10 CONCLUSION

Since our modelled prediction had been able to correctly detect 70 per cent of actual medal winners at the Beijing Games, a nation's size (population) and level of economic development, once completed with a few dummies, are good predictors of medal wins. The latter can be taken as a relevant index for comparing economic development across nations in addition to other economic and social indexes. The same model does not perform as well with predicting the 2010 FIFA World Cup semi-finalists. Soccer World Cup outcomes are in no way an acceptable index of economic development. The host country effect (home advantage) is less significant in soccer World Cups than in Summer Olympics. However, any economic prediction of sporting performance must be viewed with some caution, owing to the number of surprising sporting outcomes. Elaborating on a metrics to quantify them should be a promising avenue for further research.

NOTES

1. Bernard and Busse use the percentage of medal wins by each country i for $M_{i,t}$ instead. Our regressions are calculated with both the absolute number of medals (Table 11.3) and the percentage of medals per country, and the results are not significantly different.
2. Hoffmann et al. (2002a) consider that an important determinant of Olympic successes lies in the degree to which sporting activities are embedded in a nation's culture. The proxy used to capture such determinant is the total number of times a country has hosted Summer Olympics from 1946 to 1998.
3. A discussant has suggested to test in a first stage a 'winning versus not winning a medal' hypothesis and then estimate, in a second stage, the number of medal wins (when > 0). Here we assume that winning zero medal or winning 1, 2, . . . , n medals results from the same procedure and must be estimated with the same explanatory variables.
4. A test of maximum likelihood shows that the rho coefficient is significant ($Pr = 0.00$).
5. Our data panel is not balanced since the number of participating countries has increased between 1976 and 2004, namely owing to the break-up of the former Soviet Union, former Yugoslavia and former Czechoslovakia ($+ 20$ countries in the world), only partly compensated by the re-unification of Germany and Yemen ($- 2$ countries).
6. A test of maximum likelihood shows that the rho coefficient is not significant ($Pr = 0.26$) which allows to opt for a pooling estimation.
7. Result for any other country is available on request addressed to the authors.
8. This issue is discussed in depth in Andreff et al. (2008) explaining why we were not able to integrate doping among independent variables despite the fact that we wished to do so.
9. Some Jamaican sprint finalists have been controlled positive in doping tests during the weeks after the Beijing Games, which may be another explanation.
10. The role of referees is neglected here for two reasons: an imperfect referee is a source of competitive unbalance as demonstrated in Groot (2008), and a corrupt referee paves the way for another kind of study about corruption in soccer. We make the (rather naive) assumption that there is no match fixing and no rigged games even though it is definitely a simplifying assumption in current international soccer (Hill, 2009).
11. All the results are obviously plagued with endogeneity since the final standing is

correlated with *ex ante* ranking and top seeding is determined by *ex ante* ranking. No methodology is implemented to clean or circumvent it.

12. Exceptions are team sports and some other sports such as tennis and table tennis.
13. Here participating countries refer to those qualified for the soccer World Cup final tournament. Our model does not attempt to estimate the determinants of this qualification.
14. The calculation formula of FIFA ranking encompasses, among other, a weighted average of the team's three previous FIFA World Cup results.
15. The FIFA World Cup final tournament has been hosted twice in France (1938 and 1998), Germany (1974 and 2006), Italy (1934 and 1990) and Mexico (1970 and 1986).
16. Algeria, Australia, Cameroon, Denmark, Ghana, Honduras, Ivory Coast, Japan, New Zealand, Mexico, Nigeria, Paraguay, RDP (North) Korea, and Switzerland.
17. Micro here means at a one-game level, and not an aggregated result as the final ranking of the World Cup final tournament – which defines a macro-surprise (coming out from 64 fixtures).

REFERENCES

Andreff, M., Andreff, W. and Poupaux, S (2008), 'Les déterminants économiques de la performance olympique: Prévision des médailles qui seront gagnées aux Jeux de Pékin', *Revue d'Economie Politique*, **118** (2), 135–69.

Andreff, W. (2001), 'The correlation between economic underdevelopment and sport', *European Sport Management Quarterly*, **1** (4), 251–79.

Arellano, M. and Bond, S. (1991), 'Some tests of specification for panel data: Monte Carlo evidence and an application to employment equations', *Review of Economic Studies*, **58** (2), 277–97.

Ball, D. (1972), 'Olympic Games competition: structural correlates of national success', *International Journal of Comparative Sociology*, **13** (3–4), 186–200.

Bernard, A.B. and Busse, M.R. (2004), 'Who wins the Olympic Games: economic resources and medal totals', *Review of Economics and Statistics*, **86** (1), 413–17.

Clarke, S.R. (2000), 'Home advantage in the Olympic Games, in G. Cohen and T. Langtry (eds)', *Proceedings of the Fifth Australian Conference on Mathematics and Computers in Sport, Conference Proceedings*, Sydney: University of Technology Sydney, pp. 43–51.

Coupé, T. (2007), 'Incentives and bonuses – the Case of the 2006 World Cup', *Kyklos*, **60** (3), 349–58.

FIFA Big Count (2000 and 2006), 'Big Count', accessed 31 December 2014 at fifa.com/worldfootball/bigcount.

Goldman Sachs (2010), 'The World Cup and economics 2010', Goldman Sachs Global Economics, Commodities and Strategy Research, May.

Grimes, A.R., Kelly, W.J. and Rubin, P.H. (1974), 'A socioeconomic model of national Olympic performance', *Social Science Quarterly*, **55** (3), 777–82.

Groot, L. (2008), *Economics, Uncertainty and European Football. Trends in Competitive Balance*, Cheltenham, UK and Northampton, MA, USA: Edward Elgar.

Hill, D. (2009), 'How gambling corruptors fix football matches', *European Sport Management Quarterly*, **9** (4), 411–32.

Hoffmann, R., Chew Ging, L. and Ramasamy, B. (2002a), 'Public policy and Olympic success', *Applied Economic Letters*, **9** (9), 545–48.

Hoffmann, R., Chew Ging, L. and Ramasamy, B. (2002b), 'The socio-economic determinants of international soccer performance', *Journal of Applied Economics*, **5** (2), 253–72.

Houston, R.G. Jr and Wilson, D.P. (2002), 'Income, leisure and proficiency: an economic study of football performance', *Applied Economic Letters*, **9** (14), 939–43.

Johnson, D. and Ali, A. (2004), 'A tale of two seasons: participation and medal counts at the Summer and Winter Olympic Games', *Social Science Quarterly*, **85** (4), 974–93.

J.P. Morgan (2010), 'England to win the World Cup! A quantitative guide to the 2010 World Cup', J.P. Morgan Europe Equity Research, May.

Leeds, M. and Marikova Leeds, E. (2009), 'International soccer success and national institutions', *Journal of Sports Economics*, **10** (4), 369–90.

Levine, N. (1974), 'Why do countries win Olympic medals? Some structural correlates of Olympic Games success: 1972', *Sociology and Social Research*, **58** (4), 353–60.

Macmillan, P. and Smith, I. (2007), 'Explaining international soccer rankings', *Journal of Sports Economics*, **8** (2), 202–13.

Maennig, W. and Wellebrock, C. (2008), 'Sozioökonomische Schätzungen olympischer Medaillen-gewinne. Analyse-, Prognose- und Benchmarkmöglichkeiten', *Sportwissenschaft*, **2**, 131–48.

Monks, J. and Husch, J. (2009), 'The impact of seeding, home continent, and hosting on FIFA World Cup results', *Journal of Sports Economics*, **10** (4), 391–408.

Nevill, A., Atkinson, G., Hughes, M. and Cooper, S. (2002), 'Statistical methods for analyzing discrete and categorial data recorded in performance analysis', *Journal of Sports Sciences*, **20** (10), 829–44.

Novikov, A.D. and Maximenko, A.M. (1972), 'The influence of selected socioeconomic factors on the levels of sports achievements in the various countries', *International Review of Sport Sociology*, **7** (1), 27–44.

Paul, S. and Mitra, R. (2008), 'How predictable are the FIFA World Cup football outcomes? An empirical analysis', *Applied Economic Letters*, **15** (15), 1171–6.

Poupaux, S. and Andreff, W. (2007), 'The institutional dimension of the sports economy in transition countries', in M.M. Parent and T. Slack (eds), *International Perspectives on the Management of Sport*, Amsterdam: Elsevier, pp. 99–124.

Rathke, A. and Woitek, U. (2008), 'Economics and the Summer Olympics: an efficiency analysis', *Journal of Sports Economics*, **9** (5), 520–37.

Torgler, B. (2004), 'The Economics of the FIFA Football World Cup', *Kyklos*, **57** (2), 287–300.

UBS (2010), 'UBS investor's guide. Special edition: 2010 World Cup in South Africa', UBS Wealth Management Research, April.

Yamamura, E. (2009), 'Technology transfer and convergence of performance: an economic study of FIFA football ranking', *Applied Economics Letters*, **16** (3), 261–6.

Table 11A.1 National teams cumulative participation to the soccer World Cup semi-finals

Teams	Until 1958	1962	1966	1970	1974	1978	1982	1986	1990	1994	1998	2002	2006
Argentina	1	1	1		1	2	2	3	4	4	4	4	4
Austria	2					2	2		2	2	2	1	
Belgium	0			0			0	1	1	1	1	1	1
Brazil	3	4	4	5	6	7	7	7	7	8	9	10	10
Bulgaria	0	0	0	0	0			0		1	1		
Chile	0	1	1		1		1				1		
Croatia	0										1	1	1
(Ex-)Czechoslovakia*	1	2	2	2			2		2				2
England	0	0	1	1			1	1	2		2	2	2
France	1		1			1	2	3			4	4	5
Germany	3	3	4	5	6	6	7	8	9	9	9	10	11
Hungary	2	2	2			2	2	2					
Italy	2	2	2	3	3	4	5	5	6	7	7	7	8
Netherlands	0				1	2			2	2	3		3
Poland	0				1	1	2	2				2	2
Portugal	0		1					1				1	2
South Korea	0							0	0	0	0	1	1
Spain	1	1	1			1	1	1	1	1	1	1	1
Sweden	3			3	3	3			3	4		4	4
Turkey	0											1	
USA	1								1	1	1	1	1
Uruguay	3	3	3	4	4			4	4			4	
(Ex-)USSR**	0	0	1	1			1	1	1	1			
(Ex-)Yugoslavia***	1	2			2		2		2		2		2

Notes:
* Czech Republic after 1992; ** Russia after 1991; *** Serbia Montenegro since 1998.
A blank means that a team has not participated to the final tournament this year.
Since 1962, a non-increasing figure means that a team has participated in the final tournament without reaching the semi-finals.

Index